Hellenic Traveller

HELLENIC TRAVELLER

A Guide to the Ancient Sites of Greece and the Aegean

GUY PENTREATH

*Honorary Secretary of the Hellenic
Travellers' Club.
One time Classical and History Scholar
of Magdalene College, Cambridge.
Canon Emeritus of
Rochester Cathedral*

FABER AND FABER

3 Queen Square

London

First published in 1964
by Faber and Faber Limited
3 Queen Square, London WC1
Second impression 1964
First published in this edition 1971
Reprinted 1974
Printed in Great Britain by
Alden & Mowbray Ltd
at the Alden Press, Oxford

ISBN 0 571 09718 9 (Faber paper covered editions)

To MY WIFE

Contents

Contents

Note: Because of the ease with which they can be directly consulted the Index does not cover any of the items of Glossary or Chronological Table.

Illustrations

9

Illustrations

Preface

So many people, most of them unconsciously, have helped me to write this book, that not all can be thanked by name. But in any case at the outset, where I could wish to give my earliest and warmest thanks, I am forbidden to name my ingenious friend and benefactor who, hiding his identity from me, contrived through the hands of a distant bank manager to present me with my first cruise ticket to Greece. In the course now of twenty-seven cruises to the Aegean, light from a galaxy of classical and archaeological professors in their lectures on board and on the sites has relit the Hellenic Traveller's road to keen enjoyment and some understanding of the Ancient Greeks, first illuminated for me long ago at Cambridge by Professor A. B. Cook.

Then, at their lectures in London to the Hellenic Travellers' Club, the most varied banquets of good things have been set before us by a further host of classical lecturers from many Universities.

I am much in the debt also of Sir Mortimer Wheeler, Chairman of the Company which undertakes our cruises. His frown at any archaeological statement unsupported by clear evidence is akin to a death-ray. With equal gratitude I salute Sir Maurice Bowra who on frequent cruises surveys the wide classical scene as only an Olympian can and with penetrating insight extracts, examines and elucidates the very essence of the Greek contribution in so many fields.

Nor must I omit thanks for all that I have learnt from that gay and friendly company of Greek Guide-Lecturers of whom six join us the moment we set foot in Greece—Pat, Cleo, Avra, Tony, Dimitri, Jimmy, Marie and Lolita (for in a land where one word serves for both 'stranger' and 'friend', this pleasant familiarity is freely offered to us all). They seem to know and love every stone and marble on the ancient sites, and they share their knowledge with a contagious zest and a quiet, deep pride in the Greek achievement.

Arion, in legend, had a dolphin for transport in Aegean seas, Europa a bull: we Hellenic Travellers in fact have a very broad-backed Swan. Let me add my voice to the paean from several thousand grateful philhellenes who have travelled on that broad back of Mr. R. K. Swan and been enabled to see so much of Greece and the Middle East so happily.

To absorb all this delightful experience of travel and to see and hear so much of beauty and interest seems an end in itself: to get it out again and put some of it on paper has often seemed a task without an end. Had I not been given the help of a friend (who also once sat at the feet of Professor A. B. Cook) I doubt if it would have been achieved. So I am immensely grateful to Mrs. Joan Gibbs who did the lion's share of the necessary hunting in the Hellenic Library, and added to her kindnesses convincing criticism of my more blatant omissions, obscurities and inaccuracies, and a number of valuable suggestions. Finally, from my hideous palimpsests she typed untiringly till Sisyphus himself must have felt beaten at the endless game of 'doing it over again'.

Finally a word in self-defence about the spelling of proper names. Consistency as between Greek and Latin forms will not be found. For I have tried only to give the names in their most familiar forms. An unfamiliar spelling of a well-known name is apt to annoy the reader—or so it seems to me, as Socrates might say.

Beaulieu,
Hampshire

Hellenic Traveller

CHAPTER I

Introduction to Greece

Thucydides prophetically wrote in the first book of his famous work, 'My history is a possession for all time'. The fact that the Greek achievement as a whole is for civilized men no less than that, is the compelling power which sends so many people to Greece to-day. When your hostess can say in advance something about the beautiful stranger to whom she is keen to introduce you—where she comes from, a word about her home, what she does, her children, her great interest —conversation is easy. And so with Greece and her ancient sites. When one goes to meet her, and her lovely domain, with some knowledge and understanding of her, she—and they—will speak miraculously with you. This is the message in letters of bronze on the façade of a museum in the Palais de Chaillot, in Paris:

> '*It all depends on you whether I am a tomb or a treasure-house: whether I have much to say to you, or am dumb. Do not come to me unless you are on fire to know. Yes—it all depends on you.*'

So this book is intended for those who visit Greece without a great store of previous knowledge, who go as amateurs: to help them fit the various sites into their places in history, to show their chief significance—to give the stones a chance to come alive and speak for themselves. The professed classic will find here no new and startling theories—at least the writer hopes so. And let the professor know that the book is not aimed at him.

It is a strange situation today: a widely-felt conviction in England, at least, that the classics as an educational subject are dead, and, in contrast, such swarms of enthusiastic travellers

17

coming to see the ancient sites of Greece as—literally—outnumber the invading armies of old. And the American archaeologists are at work in Athens, Corinth and Samothrace, the French at Delphi, Delos, Thasos and Mallia, the Germans at Olympia and Samos, the Italians at Phaestos, the British at Knossos, and the Greeks at numerous sites. And a wider public reads books about Greece than ever before. It is said that more copies of the *Iliad* and the *Odyssey*, translated by Rieu in the Penguin edition, have been sold than of any other book published by anyone in recent years, except only the 'New English Bible'.

There are perhaps three magnetic forces in the notion 'Greece'. The beauty of Greece itself and its islands and seas and sun: the friendliness of the modern Greeks, and the fact that fundamentally we both think on the same lines, share the same values, 'know where we are with them', in a word, like them: and, behind all this, the western world recognizes in our Hellenic inheritance one of the three main strands of its civilization and salutes it. In Greece we see achievement through precise, clear thinking: in Rome, power through law and order: in Palestine, inspiration through faith in a holy God whose love is for all and for each. These are the three strands which stretch out to us from the past, for us to lay up tight together into a single rope to pull us up the steep ascent.

But first, the land of Greece. Four-fifths of the land is mountains; even with terracing on steep hillsides only two-fifths is cultivable. As Odysseus said of his home, Ithaca, to King Alcinous, 'It's a rough land: but a good nurse of men: and I want no sweeter home.' But where the soil from the mountains still lies in the valleys, and water can be drawn up by windmills (in their hundreds in Crete and Rhodes—one for every field) or by pumping-engines as in the plain of Argos, then the crops are good. Improved agricultural methods between the wars not only doubled the area cultivated, but doubled also the yield per acre in cereal crops. Drainage schemes have turned mountain lakes and marshes into good land: improved crop rotations, seeds and manuring have increased the yields. Olive oil and wine have been important exports of Greece since ancient times; but it was a surprise to see a British ship in Katakolo, the port for Olympia, being loaded with potatoes for Liverpool. This is a new product and reflects the new efforts of Government to plough agricultural science into the soil of Greece.

Because Greece stretches from Crete in the south, with a latitude of 34° 80' (nearer to the Equator than Tunis), to northern Thrace, latitude 41° 47' (120 miles north of the entrance to the Dardanelles), it has in effect two climates, 'Balkan' in the north and 'Mediterranean' in the south. The variety therefore of the landscape and of the products of the soil is exceptionally large; and the altitude, and consequently temperature, varying so much—for the mountains are in every region—there is that additional factor making for variety in all parts of the country. Crete has its mountain-tops covered with snow while the corn is golden in the plain below and the banana trees on the northern coast are growing lush. There is cattle ranching in the uplands of Epirus and Macedonia, while in the south the peasant farmer often counts his stock on one hand, and his child takes a solitary sheep to pasture on a glorified dog-lead and sits for hours in charge of it. But the large part of his property may be up in the mountain, his flock of goats, eating the prickly, often flowering and scented scrub, with another son in charge. On the Acropolis at Mycenae one hardly needs a watch to tell that it is time to go. From the stony, almost bare mountain-sides above, the tinkle of goat bells interrupts one's reverie about Agamemnon and his murderous wife, and there, coming down the ravine, is the same black torrent of cheerful goats, a hundred of them, as on one's last visit and the time before. No tree will ever grow again there, or on a thousand other mountain sides, until the Greek goat is tethered.

The farms are mostly very small, and few walls or hedges mark the boundaries between them; and that is why grazing stock are attended, generally by a child herdsman who carries his or her responsibility with skill and spirit. A well-aimed stone, throwing up the dust, diverts the errant animal. No wonder the shepherds of Theocritus sat in the shade and played the pipe: there was so much sitting to do.

Greece in spring dress and in the brown of high summer looks quite different. Both seasons bring their varied delights. The green of spring is bright with wild flowers: the lecturer on an ancient site may have to turn on all his eloquence to hold the attention of his party, fascinated by the bee-orchids in the grass by the old grey stones. Some rain, at least in spring, is the hope of every farmer. In summer, where there is no irrigation, all but the grey olive trees and the pines, the planes and orange trees is burnt brown, and the sun blazes in a sky empty of cloud. The heat beats up from the rocky ground; but if one is properly clad, and drinks a quite remarkable quantity of the excellent water of Greece, and if sun-glasses are not forgotten, then the sun is 'glorious sun', and bathing in the blue sea the purest of joys. The Greeks and Romans diluted their wine with water. The connoisseur of wine may deplore this habit; but it was a sensible practice in the Greek summer climate at least. To cope easily with the body's loss of moisture by evaporation, one must drink a great deal more liquid than would be possible if one confined one's attention to wine.

In the country parts of Greece, many of the older houses are made of sun-baked brick, a traditional building material in Greece and the East for several thousand years. Walls of sun-baked brick need a protective covering of whitewash, or coloured lime-wash, against the rain. The whiteness reflects the sun, and makes for a cooler interior. Hence the great majority of houses are white, often with pastel-blue, or pink or light green 'facings'. Generally the wash is applied by the whole family party twice a year, once in honour of Easter, and again before the autumn rains. The result is an air of splendid cleanliness; and the favourite red for countrywomen's dresses shows up brilliantly against this background. The houses are very much alike; simple cubes of white, all with flat roofs in some villages, all with pitched tiled roofs in others. There seems to be a tacit agreement about this uniformity, but there is probably an economic cause behind it. Mykonos is all flat-roofed, except for the solitary post office, presumably designed in an office at Athens where somebody forgot the Mykonos tradition. Skiathos is all pitched roofs, Melos and Ios flat. As the ship approaches Tinos, one might suppose there were snowdrifts in the folds of the distant hills, but they turn out to be snow-white villages. To return to the paper-strewn pavements of an English town after a visit to the Greek islands is to feel a shock of shame at our messy habits.

It is claimed by some observers that Greeks are the only Westerners who can be perfectly happy without the aid of tobacco and alcohol. They grow and make large quantities of both: but it is obviously true that sobriety is a national trait, and that the chairs and tables of the innumerable tabernas and cafés are often occupied by people doing nothing else but talking —not even drinking. The political columns of a newspaper seem essential to the good life, and tearing them to pieces in a taberna the proper activity of man. Greeks excel at discussion, and a special high tone of loud, far-carrying voice, supported at the crisis by arms thrown out, palms uppermost, and head tossed back as in appeal to the high gods of Olympus, is employed to make a point, political, personal or commercial, which the uninitiated might mistake for passion. Greeks are not shy: they welcome a stranger with kindness and with interest, plying him with questions. There is a pride and self-confidence and an easy naturalness, especially noticeable in the islanders, which the traveller admires and respects. In Skiathos, an island which has only rare foreign visitors, the chief of police asked, as I was leaving, 'What do you think of our island?' I answered truthfully, 'It is one of the most beautiful places I have ever seen, and quite the cleanest, too.' His reply was, 'And I can say that it is as good as it looks. I've had no unpleasant work to do in the year that I've been here.'

Like Odysseus, Greeks love their homeland, and with pride, and even though the hardness of life sends them as emigrants to the United States, Australia or elsewhere, they keep their interest, maintain contact, send money not only to relatives but to Greek good causes, and often follow their gifts home in later life. Greeks began to leave home by sea for a better living elsewhere as early as the eighth century B.C.: and they have always been good seamen. The sea is never very far away, for the coastline in proportion to the mainland area is twelve times as long as our English coast. So, with so many arms of the sea reaching inland and offering shelter, and with the multitude of islands near at hand, the Greeks were from early times as much at home on the sea as the Dutch or British claim to be. There is constant inter-island sea traffic today, and the shapely and brightly-coloured caiques are a feature of every passage in the Aegean and of every waterfront. But the seamen and fishermen of Greece, like others, depend now on engines, some indeed of almost archaeological interest.

There is no known explanation of why this ancient people who entered the Greek peninsula with fire and sword in different waves of immigration about 2000 B.C. and then again about 1200 B.C., should have developed as they did, the best attaining to an intellectual level which, with its fruits in philosophy and religion, science, literature, art and drama, is 'a possession for all time'. But we think we can discern some natural attitudes in the Greeks behind the things they made and the thoughts they expressed. Sir John Wolfenden names four attitudes of mind which marked the Greek thinker: his mind sought clarity; possessed a sense of wonder; demanded and expected a rational explanation of things; was always seeking unity behind the appearance of the many.

We see this clarity in the very light of Greece which gives a sharp edge to mountains, buildings and all the world about. The Greeks built finely and with precision, cutting marble blocks without a flaw, arranging tackle to lower them into position with no damage to the vulnerable edges, and designing their temples with horizontal and vertical lines so that the construction was visible and the whole clear, precise and final. They enjoyed that clarity in stone. Similarly, with their sculpture. At the best period, the figure of the athlete says one thing and says it with clarity and truth: this is the athlete—the perfect human form. And in their language, above all, we can see the care taken to make a meaning clear beyond all doubt. In the speeches put into the mouths of statesmen, generals, and ambassadors by Thucydides, we marvel at the dissection of motives he lays bare, at the power of analysis and argument. These men used their minds. Logic, not flowers of oratory, thought, not windy sentimentalism, won respect, and moved to action. Again, the fact of death is faced with dignity. The sculptured tombstones of the fifth century avoid the sentimental, and show the dead one at his best, in life—the hunter with his hound, the lady with her casket of jewels.

Aristotle said, 'Wisdom is the child of wonder': wonder, opening wide the eye and leading to enquiry and ultimately to knowledge. Even in the days of decline, this characteristic of wanting to know continues. In the Acts, St. Paul is brought before the Court of Areopagus and, typically, he is asked, 'May we know what this new doctrine is that you propound? You are introducing ideas that sound strange to us and we should like to know what they mean.' And Luke, the writer of Acts, explains that 'the Athenians in general and the foreigners who lived there had no time for anything but talking and hearing about the latest new idea'. Indeed, the word used by the Greeks for a man who was only concerned with himself and took no interest in what was going on, or in the problems and decisions of public life, was *idiotes*, 'idiot'.

For everything there must be a reason: if we observe it, examine it, discuss it, compare it with others like it of which we know something, we will eventually find the truth and reason in it. So began scientific enquiry. And in their search for unity and a single principle behind all the multiplicity of phenomena and the limitless variety of things in creation, they reveal a quite astonishing intellectual insight. Most people imagine that the discovery of the atomic structure of all material things is a modern one. It is only the discovery of this truth by actual experiment which is new. Democritus and his master, Leucippus, at Abdera (460 to 370 B.C.), without any apparatus and by sheer reason, came to this conclusion. That feathers, lead, and the flesh of the body are in the last analysis made up of the same particles in space, but colliding and inter-weaving and making different things by different groupings, is an amazing conclusion. It is now known to be true. The minds of ancient Greeks achieved this truth, handed on to the Roman world later by Lucretius.

The Greeks were well aware that 'man is a political animal', and that only in a city-state, in a community, could the full life be lived. 'Politics' is a Greek word; and the gathering of people into a fortified city, with the temple of the patron god or goddess to protect it, from the many scattered settlements and villages round it, is a normal process in Greek history. The 'good life' must be lived in community. There would not only be strength in unity, but wisdom through discussion by all the citizens: man's duties and reverence to the gods could better be performed and shown in splendid festivals at the temples which would be the finest buildings in the city: and, of course, the city would provide a theatre and a gymnasium and stadium, and a picture gallery to record the great deeds done: all this would make the people one in their pride in their city. In the city there would be a large open space—the agora—where everyone could meet and talk and do business; it would be surrounded by public buildings worthy of the city and a source of pride. On big decisions, in some cities, the citizens, after hearing the various viewpoints, would give their vote, and that would decide the policy. For in those city-states where democracy had supplanted oligarchy the people were the Government.

But bold experiments in democracy did not solve the problems of living together, either in a particular city, or at peace with other cities. Much of Greek history is marred by bitter quarrels between oligarchs and democrats: many a city many a time was betrayed to outside enemies in time of war by one faction or another.

Civil strife and a dreadful capacity for cruelty are dark spots on the bright picture. And some will cry out, 'and slavery: that's a black spot too. They could not have achieved what they did without that ghastly institution.' Both statements are true. Slaves were the tools of industry, and they were personal servants. The treatment they received no doubt depended upon the attitude of master and of slave. But we are judging the Greeks by our own standards, paying an unconscious compliment to them in thus condemning their system of slavery. Such is our respect for them, we are disappointed that they kept the institution of slavery. It must be remembered that it took Wilberforce and Clarkson and the Clapham Sect years of work, study and prayer before the British Parliament paid £20,000,000 to buy up the slaves of the Empire and set them free.

The story of Hellas and her high achievement is of undying interest. Enough of her works of art, her buildings, walls, temples and theatres are there in Greece still to be seen and enjoyed and in a lovely setting of mountains and valleys, blue seas and islands, that a visit to see these records in stone and marble and to meet the friendly Greeks of today, is an experience which is also a possession for life.

CHAPTER II

Athens: the Acropolis

To ATHENS . . .
> *'where on the Aegean shore a city stands
> built nobly, pure the air and light the soil.'*
> MILTON.

All the world knows that Milton is right about the nobility of the buildings, and the clarity of the atmosphere—at times: but his geography is weak. Athens was not built on the Aegean shore, but two and a half miles away from it. The city came into existence where it did because at that point there rose out of the plain of Attica an isolated steep-sided limestone outcrop with a flat top, some three hundred feet above the plain and, moreover, provided with a spring accessible from the summit. Here, then, was a place where men with their wives and children might be safe in time of trouble, especially if they built a strong wall and a gateway they could defend. If there was not room for everyone to live there, at least there was room for the king and his captains—Cecrops, legend said, was the first king—and for the house of the divine patron: and when the alarm was raised, the people could leave the homes that clustered tightly round the base of the hill (as they still do on the eastern side) and shelter behind the walls of their fortress. The Acropolis, as we know this essential hill, became the nucleus of an organized community certainly in the Bronze Age, and parts of the Mycenaean fortification walls are still visible. Thucydides says that in his day this rock was still called 'the City', exactly as in London we call 'the City' that small area contained inside the line of the old Roman city walls.

The distance from Athens to the coast, to the long curving sweep of Phaleron Bay, was in Milton's time even greater, because the sea had receded, and so had the perimeter of Athens. The Athens of Pericles, the city which, in his words, 'cheered the heart and delighted the eye day by day' was, for those days, a great city of 250,000 people, including slaves; but, like the sensitive plant, it had recoiled and closed up at the touch of a series of intruders, till under the last and longest intrusion, that of the Turks from 1458 for nearly four hundred years, it was a poor market-town of only three hundred houses! Certainly Lear's paintings and other travellers' sketches in the early nineteenth century confirm this dreadful shrinking. So much the more splendid the faith of the Greeks, when they won their independence and in 1834 declared Athens to be the capital of their resurgent nation. Today Athens with its port Piraeus is again a city great in size with nearly 2,000,000 people in it.

As Milton wrote, the soil is light. But strangely, had it not been so, had the plain of Attica been a fertile well-watered region like the plain of Argos, on which the people could grow fat and well-content, Athens might never have grown to become the greatest city of all Greece. It was because Athens could not prosper by the cultivation of its wretched stony dusty soil and because at the same time, for reasons we cannot wholly explain, intelligence could and did flourish there incredibly, Athens turned to the sea and grew by the use of the seaways, by overseas trade and empire. Wordsworth wrote of Venice that

> *when she took unto herself a mate*
> *she did espouse the everlasting sea.*

It is equally true of Athens. Toynbee's dictum (if one may call a dictum what it took him twelve volumes and a survey of all the world to prove), that since history began, nations and civilizations have only achieved greatness by having difficulties to fight against and overcome, is beyond doubt true of Athens.

One man, a statesman of long sight, saw the necessity and the immense advantages of such a marriage between Athens and the sea, and arranged it. Themistocles. His grave is properly at Piraeus, close to the harbour mouth. For Piraeus, now one of Europe's busy harbours, is the child of Themistocles' brain and power of persuasion. In the years immediately before the Persian invasion Samos and Chios had a naval strength greater than that of Athens. Even her rival, Aegina, was too strong for Athens' comfort. Themistocles began the fortification and use of Piraeus as a harbour. Up to that time the Athenian seamen had been content with the open roadstead of Phaleron Bay, two and a half miles from the city. If weather conditions allowed, they would run their ships ashore and laboriously drag them up on rollers out of harm's way in case of an onshore blow. This was a hopeless technique for a city which was to live and expand, as Themistocles was the first to see, on imported food and overseas trade. After the naval victory of Salamis, won through Themistocles' insistence on new ships and then more ships, he persuaded the citizens that it was well worth while to double the distance of their port from Athens since the three new harbours he proposed to build in the inlets of the rocky peninsula of Piraeus would be safe in all weathers. Thucydides wrote that 'the Piraeus seemed to Themistocles of more real consequence than the upper city and he was fond of telling the people that if they were hard-pressed in war they should go down to the Piraeus and fight the world at sea'. (Jowett's translation.)

Since a city and its harbours must be a unit, and Athens and Piraeus were five miles apart, Themistocles, says Plutarch, planned to join city and port with fortification walls. This huge undertaking was to follow the fortification of the Piraeus peninsula which Themistocles achieved in monumental fashion. Thucydides made space in his history for an enthusiastic description of it. 'The wall round the Piraeus was of a width to allow two chariots to pass on the top of it. It was a solid wall, no gravel or clay filling was used, but large squared blocks of stone, clamped together with iron and lead.' But for Themistocles time ran out, and it was left to Cimon, and later to Pericles, to bring this wonderful conception of the Long Walls into existence. For, as happened too often in the fifth century when a statesman or a general was doing well and developing power, his political rivals or personal enemies played on the feeling of a democratic citizenry, and he was voted into exile. This happened to Themistocles. The process was called ostracism, from the use of pottery sherds (ostraka) as 'voting papers' in a secret ballot; on the sherd the citizen scratched the name of the man—so often a successful man, whom he wished to bring down. With 6,000

27

sherds cast and his name prominent, a man was down, and out into exile. Used sherds have been found in large numbers, and recall the fate of several valuable leaders of the fifth century, not one of whom ever looked like becoming the tyrant whom the long memory of democracy feared and guarded against.

Like most travellers in the last twenty-five centuries who have come to see Athens, let us enter by the port of Piraeus. As our ship steams into a harbour packed, probably, with as much shipping as can be seen at any one time anywhere, and we see all round the harbour the smoky evidence of a modern commercial and industrial centre, there may be some slight sinking of the expectant heart, for the 'glory that was Greece' seems for a moment to have vanished under the street-cars. But wait: Piraeus may still produce glories to surprise us. In 1959, during a sewer repair, one of the finest groups of large bronze statues ever found was dug out, only four feet below the road.

Our route to Athens takes us along the shore of Phaleron Bay, and then we turn for a straight run up a fine new boulevard to the city itself. The Acropolis soon comes into view, and the Parthenon holds every eye, serene, majestic, dominating all the tall blocks of flats and making them somehow look but a passing fashion. We pass the Arch of Hadrian and the guide tries to interest us in it: we condescend a moment's glance at the gigantic remains of the Roman-period temple of Olympian Zeus, completed by Hadrian in A.D. 131. The Roman Emperor Marcus Aurelius wrote:

'The poet says "Dear city of Cecrops" and wilt not thou say "Dear city of Zeus".'

But no, our minds are set on the Acropolis where King Cecrops had his palace. The power of the Acropolis to command and hold the heart is undiminished.

We work our hesitant way to the Acropolis through the noise and pressures of a crowded modern city, perhaps half-surprised to feel such pulsing life in a place so ancient and revered, and suddenly, from the canyons of modernity, we emerge into the open and find another world—the world we sought. We are moving uphill along the southern slopes of the towering rock. Here and over a wide arc from the north to the southwest of the Acropolis, the Government has made a green-belt or a national park, because in this area lie the chief monuments of antiquity. These are cared for with respect, with skill and with sensitive feeling, and the whole district is a preserve of open space, of trees and flowering shrubs. The modest public notices are couched in a delightful imperative: 'Agapate ta dendra'—'Love and care for the welfare of the trees'. More civilized than our own 'Keep off'.

Already, at the foot of the Acropolis, we catch sight of the remains of ancient buildings, rows of arches, foundations, and white marble gleaming through the trees; but it seems sensible to go first to the summit. For when we have passed through the great Doric Propylaea or gateway to the Acropolis which the citizens so much admired, have stood to allow the Parthenon to make its powerful impact on us, and given an answering smile to the graceful, lovely Ionic Erechtheum and its porch of maiden Caryatides, we shall be much better equipped, when bare foundations or ruins lie before us, to rebuild them in our mind's eye and see them with an increasing understanding.

As we climb towards the western, and only, entrance to the Acropolis, we may stop to recover our breath and turn to enjoy the wide prospect below us. Beyond the protecting park-lands, the city and the suburbs sprawl spaciously in the usual urban way, but the horizon to the plain of Attica is a noble battlement of mountains. To the south-east, Hymettos, famous of old for its honey, and at the moment before the sun dips below the western mountains, often suffused with a violet glow that gave Athens its unusual soubriquet of 'violet-crowned'; to the north-east, Mount Pentelicon, source of that iron-hard marble which takes and keeps through the centuries a knife-edge, and develops a golden colour adding to its beauty as the iron particles in it oxidise—the marble of the best of Athens' buildings; to the north, Parnes, a redoubtable barrier against invasion on that dangerous side; to the south-west, Aegaleos and the pass to Eleusis and the rest of mainland Greece.

We resume our easy climb on the paved roadway, trodden surely by every Athenian who ever lived, to the high-point of Classical Greece. Some will think again the thoughts of Cicero expressed in his treatise 'On the Laws':

'Movemur, nescio quomodo pacto, locis ipsis in quibus eorum quos diligimus aut admiramur, adsunt vestigia, me quidem ipsae illae nostrae Athenae non tam operibus magnificis exquisitissimisque antiquorum artibus delectant quam recordatione summorum virorum ubi quisque sedere, ubi disputare sit solitus, studioseque eorum etiam sepulchra contemplor.

'We all find it strangely moving to be in a place where there are still signs and traces of those now dead whom we loved or admired. Yet in Athens with all its splendid architecture and its historic treasures of fine art, my deepest delight is to recall the great men of the past and reflect that here was the favourite haunt of one, here the scene of another's famous oratory: and I gaze even at their tombs entranced.'

There are many tombs in the lower slopes of the Acropolis, but they are not those of the great men Cicero admired, but date from a thousand years before, when Athens was a Mycenaean fortress.

We stand now in the Propylaea, begun in 437 B.C. It was good psychology on the part of Pericles to have built such a splendid entrance, unique in Greece. For it led the mind of the spectator to realize that what he would see inside must be of superlative beauty if the Propylaea was of such a standard of excellence. To build an imposing entrance to a sanctuary or to an agora (a city-centre is perhaps a better translation of 'agora' than market-place) was common practice, a development of an idea first seen in Minoan Crete; but this Propylaea far surpassed all others— and cost 400 talents (in modern terms almost £1,000,000). It was built of the finest Pentelic marble, and this in itself was far from normal practice. Mnesicles was architect: he faced an unusual problem for a builder in ancient Greece, that of designing a building to be set on a steep slope. The difficulty arises from the nature of the Doric Order of architecture. It would be out of the question for Mnesicles to use Doric columns of one height here and of another there. There were intricate relationships between the various members of the order, the columns, architrave, metopes and triglyphs, which seemed immutable. Mnesicles' solution was, however, a daring one: to use the Ionic Order as well, with its taller and more slender columns. Essentially, the building is a wall with five openings for passage through it, a shallow portico on the inner side, and another, much deeper and providing a roofed roadway bordered by columns, on the outer side. There were to have been wing-rooms to north and south, but only the northern room was built. The other would have trespassed on ground long sacred to the Goddess of Victory, and Mnesicles had to be content with mere curtain walls to provide balance in the design. The one room, the Pinakotheke, displayed paintings by Polygnotus, the first great painter of Greece (*floruit* 450 B.C.). His favourite themes were heroic episodes in Athenian history. Pericles thought as Renan did that 'a people is made into a nation by the recollection of great deeds done together, and the will to perform great deeds together in the future'.

The colonnaded platforms on either side of the Panathenaic roadway require for their coffered ceiling marble beams strengthened exceptionally with hidden iron, giving a span of eighteen feet and each weighing over eleven tons. Pausanias in his tour of Athens of course spotted these huge beams and wrote of the building, then six hundred years old, 'The propylaea has a roof of white stones, and down to the present day it is unrivalled for the beauty and size of its stones.' Such beams were new in Greek architecture. There is, of course, no mortar in the walls: their strength lies in the perfect fit of stone on stone in the Greek tradition coupled together by invisible interior clamps of bronze, lead or iron. The precision of these marble blocks, the proportion of the size of each to the whole high wall, the colour, the entire surface unimpaired by any intrusive architectural feature of decoration, all these have created beauty in a singularly pure form.

The Peloponnesian War broke out before the whole plan was completed, and building stopped. After her defeat by Sparta Athens' finest hour had passed, and the citizens never finished a building of which they had once been so proud. On the southwest walls, on the Acropolis side, the rough stone lugs which gave a hold to the ropes lowering the stones into position without damage to their sharp edges, were not even smoothed away —mute evidence of the havoc of defeat to men's spirit.

There is a terrace to the right of the Propylaea, as one approaches, and on the same level as the porches, where the little temple of Athena Nike stands on the edge of the bastion. This lovely building seems always to be described as 'a gem of Ionic architecture', and it is nothing less than that. All the way up the sloping Panathenaic Way (as the approach road was called) its white and delicate beauty held the eye. We know that its statue of Athena Nike was dedicated in 425 B.C. The temple consists of a rectangular cella for the statue, and porticoes of four Ionic columns on the front and back. A sculptured frieze ran round the building, and there is the usual base of three steps which gives a visual balance and matches the bulk of the architrave above the columns with weight below them. That's all there is—'a straight-forward, simple and minor building'. But the eye takes it all in, at once, as a unit, and delivers it so neatly to the brain that thought finds content in the 'wholeness' of it and in the propor-tions each part bears to those related to it; and pleasure, too, in the colour and quality and texture of the warm marble surfaces: and more—the brain happily consents to the idea itself of raising an unpretentious but lovely little temple to Victory on such a site, high on the edge of the bastion, so that men look up to see it. And all this varied process of the mind is completed by such a sense of total satisfaction as merits the rare word 'joy'. A sculp-tured balustrade originally marked out the limits of the precinct. The very beautiful 'Victory tying up her sandal', in the Acropolis museum, is one of thirty-two reliefs which adorned it.

Pausanias reminds us that it was from this high bastion that King Aegeus threw himself in sorrow for the presumed death of his son Theseus. For Theseus had sailed for Crete with the party of young men and maidens required, as living tribute, by the powerful King Minos of Knossos: they were to be trained for the dangerous, often lethal, sport with the 'Bull of Minos', and the ship sailed with the black sails of mourning. Theseus was deter-mined to break the Minoan hold on Athens and thus destroy this grim sport of Cretan kings. If successful in his venture, he was to announce success from afar to his watching father by setting white sails on his ship. But the wretched man who, by the aid of Ariadne, Minos' daughter, had indeed succeeded, forgot his promise to change the black sails to white.

Before we leave the Nike terrace we can see, if we turn our backs on the temple and face eastwards, a short run of the Mycenaean fortress wall dating from about 1400 B.C. This kind of wall, made of large boulders piled on each other with small stones filling up the interstices, is characteristic of the Mycenaean period of Greek history in the Bronze Age. Alone among the Mycenaean fortresses, Athens did not fall to the Dorian invaders at the end of the second millennium. Something of the colour, vitality, flow and freedom of Mycenaean art, learnt from Minoan Crete, may, I feel, despite the intervening Dark Ages, have become part of the heritage of classical Athens from the distant days when this wall ringed the first Acropolis.

The up-hill zigzag Sacred Way, leading through the Propylaea to the Parthenon on the summit, is usually packed with people of many countries and races. Their faces look less like those of tourists than of pilgrims, expectant of a great experience. For Athena's temple—the house for her gold and ivory statue—was the focus of the spirit behind the Athenian achievement: Athena was real to Athens, her protection vital, her power, they believed, at work in her citizens. She was their pride and their secret weapon. Probably no building in the western world is more familiar in outline shape than the Parthenon: its picture hangs in every school. So there is a joyful moment of recognition as one steps through the columned portico of the Propylaea on to the rock of the Acropolis itself. But wonder overwhelms this moment, and astonishment at the superb silhouette of marble gleaming gold against the sky, the only background at this point of entry. For the siting of the temple is supremely right: we are below it, and its great size and height are thereby magnified for us, and the whole sweep of the northern and western sides is visible at once, the two architraves converging at a striking angle. There is mastery, too, in the fixing of its proportions, and mastery in the working of the material, the costly, time-defying Pentelic marble. The Parthenon is a vision of an ancient people's faith and hope in their goddess, and still a tremendous reality.

The rich Greek cities of Sicily and southern Italy had built their temples of limestone or similar material. Athens, comparatively, was poor. 'We are lovers of the beautiful,' said Pericles, 'but without extravagance.' How could she afford the superlative marble buildings that Pericles raised within a few years, to the astonished admiration of most Greeks and the envy of others? There were two purposes in the minds of Pericles and the Athenians: to glorify Athena their patron goddess, and to glorify their city Athens. If we trust the opinion of Thucydides and the verdict of history as Plutarch gives it five hundred years later, we will scorn the cynic who adds 'and to glorify Pericles'.

But there is an uncomfortable ethical question in regard to the vast sums expended on the beautification of Athens. After the defeat of the Persian invasions in 479 B.C., Athens had taken the lead in forming a confederacy of Greek states for defence against renewed Persian aggression. Each state and island member contributed ships and forces, or money. Delos, Apollo's sacred island, was at first the headquarters and the treasury of this confederacy. But soon most member states found it more convenient to hand over their defence contribution in money; and in 454 B.C. the Athenians for safety moved the Treasury to the Acropolis at Athens. By 445 B.C. peace had been concluded with Persia and with Athens' enemies on the mainland of Greece, but the cash defence contributions continued to be imperiously required. Samos and Byzantium broke away from the alliance. Their suppression by force of Athenian arms proved that the true title for the Confederacy of Delos was now the Athenian Empire. Pericles considered Athens entitled to use the funds, paid over by other states for defence, to adorn the sanctuary city of Athena. Such a policy, he argued, would make Athens 'the school of Hellas', set a standard for Greeks of all cities to follow, fill her own citizens with pride, and encourage them to great deeds. Practical as he was, he added the economic argument of full employment. These public works would put money into every craftsman's pocket; every merchant's, too. All would gain from security. As for the 'subject' allies and their tribute, they had paid for safety: they had had it: they would go on paying for it and would get it from the greatness of Athens in the future, as in the past. With the problem of funds settled to the satisfaction only of Pericles and the Assembly of the people at Athens, 'works were raised', wrote Plutarch, 'of an astonishing magnitude and inimitable beauty and perfection, every architect striving to surpass the magnificence of the design with the elegance of the execution and all during the administration of one man. They were built in so short a time, and yet built for ages: for as each of them, on completion, had the venerable air of antiquity, so now they are old they have the freshness of a modern building. A bloom is diffused over them, which preserves their aspect untarnished by time, as if they were animated with a spirit of perpetual youth and unfading elegance'.

Pericles inevitably began his building programme with the

construction of the Parthenon for in the Persian capture of the Acropolis in 480 B.C. a new temple, then under construction, had been burnt and damaged. Ictinus and Callicrates were the architects for the new and still larger temple, but Pheidias the sculptor is said to have had a general supervision of the entire Periclean building scheme. A Greek temple was never intended as a place of assembly for worship, but rather as the house of the god or goddess to contain the cult statue. The ground plan of a Doric temple was simple: the main room, or cella, was rectangular and had its ceiling carried not only by the walls but on two lines of small columns, above the horizontal architraves of which ran a second tier of similar small columns. At the temple of Athena Aphaia in Aegina some columns of this double-tiered arrangement are still standing. The cult statue was placed towards the far end of the cella, facing the high doorway and the east. This doorway opened on to an open porch formed by the prolongation of the long side walls, and having its ceiling supported by two or more columns. At the west end of the temple there was a similar porch and doorway giving access to a second room, the opisthodomos or back room, used as a treasury: there was generally no access from the cella to the opisthodomos. Finally, a colonnade, or peristyle, ran round the building, the whole structure standing on a stepped platform, or stylobate, to give height to the building and, in its mass, to balance the entablature of architrave, cornice and so on above the columns.

The Parthenon followed this general Doric scheme and did so on a great scale in a beautiful material worked at the highest possible level of craftsmanship and taste, and after a quite remarkable amount of mathematical calculation in the decision of the best proportions. To give an instance: the distance between columns compared with a column's diameter was 9:4, and this proportion is the same in the length-to-width ratio of the building, and in the width of the temple compared with its height. But the mathematicians did more than fix these ratios. It had been noticed that, the human eye not being a very precise instrument, a row of columns on a horizontal platform, alternating light and dark with their shadows on the wall behind, caused the platform to seem to sag in the centre. The whole stylobate was therefore raised in a curve—along the sides and along the ends—to counteract this optical illusion. Similarly, the

sides of the columns are not straight: if they were, the eye would
see a 'waist' effect half-way up the columns; they would seem
pinched. So each column has a slight outward curve, called
entasis, and the eye is completely happy and sees them all
straight. Again, if the columns were set vertically, they would
seem to fall outwards. They are therefore inclined inwards and
in such a way that all would meet, if projected, at a single point.
These optical corrections demand extreme precision in the skill
of the mason, as well as implying the mind of the mathematician.
The result of all this thought and skill devoted to the Parthenon
is the impression it makes—beyond that of other Doric temples
—of serene, untroubled grandeur: of a building in repose,
content to be at one for ever with the rock which it
crowns.

The temple was opened in 438 B.C., with the cult statue by
Pheidias in its place. Some details of it are known. Athena was a
standing, helmeted figure nearly forty feet in height. She held a
winged Victory in her right hand and in her left a spear. By her
side a round shield, with a serpent coiled in its hollow, stood on
its edge, balanced by her touch. The goddess' face, arms and feet
were of ivory, and so to prevent cracking through the dryness of
the air, a shallow pool of water was arranged before the statue to
add humidity. Her helmet and her long garment, the chiton,
were made up of gold plates (detachable in case of a financial
crisis in the State). The value of the statue was a thousand
talents: most of this obviously lay in the gold plates. This way of
storing gold reserves is more picturesque than burying them in
concrete vaults. Pausanias, regrettably, when he visited the Parthenon, seems to have been interested only in detail, such as the
figures carved in relief on the edges of the goddess' sandals. No
word from him about the impact the statue made on mind and
soul. Was this blindness in Pausanias, or a failure in the sculptor's skill? We can hardly make an excuse for Pausanias on the
ground that the small and late 'copy' of the statue in the National
Museum, known as the Varvakeion Athena, is unspeakably
unconvincing—in fact, stone dead; for we know from many
references in classical literature that the power of Pheidias'
chryselephantine Zeus at Olympia to move men's hearts and
bring new hope to human life was immense: it was, indeed, the
statue's spiritual quality which made it one of the Seven

Wonders. It is unlikely that Pheidias failed to rise to his great challenge at Athens.

To cope with the very large amount of sculpture needed to fill the pediments, the ninety-two metopes above the architrave, and the continuous frieze, 172 yards long, which ran high up round the outside of the cella wall (a new idea in a temple of the Doric Order), Pheidias of course employed a large group of sculptors. Whether he designed the whole seems uncertain, for there is a marked variation in the standard of design as well as of execution. Some of the metopes are positively ungainly: whereas all of the frieze, though variable in execution, is of uniformly fine design.

To fit sculptured human figures into the triangular shape of a pediment, with no alteration in scale, was always a problem. Fortunately, there were divine figures of superhuman stature to fill the centre of the composition and the apex of the triangle. In the east pediment of the Parthenon the theme was the birth of Athena from the head of Zeus. Fully grown, clothed and armed, in her sudden appearance at the will of Zeus the goddess, patron of Athens, represents the emergence, under heaven's decree, of Athens as a great power in the Greek world, endowed with all her qualities of intellect and artistic skill and craftsmanship. In the west pediment Athena and Poseidon contested together for the possession of Attica. We must rely on drawings by Carrey made in 1674 to show the composition of the pedimental sculpture of which little now survives. The Three Fates from the east pediment are in the British Museum, with a reclining Theseus and a horse's head. Reproductions in concrete of the two latter figures have been placed in the pediment.

The subject of the ninety-two metopes is the familiar one of combat between Greeks and Amazons, gods and giants, Lapiths and Centaurs, all symbolizing the victory of civilization, law and order over chaos and barbarism—an implied reference to the victorious struggle against Persia.

As all the world knows, the greater part of the frieze of the Parthenon was brought to England for safety's sake by Lord Elgin in the early nineteenth century and is now among the chief treasures of the British Museum. Its theme is the procession of the high festival of the Great Panathenaea, held every four years in Athena's honour. The procession of the officials mustered at the Dipylon Gate and, with an escort of cavalry, made its way across the Agora up the sloping way to the Acropolis. All the components of the procession are sculptured on the frieze in low relief: the magistrates, the priests and attendants and musicians, the beasts for sacrifice, the maidens carrying the sacred vessels and the young men water-pots, the escorting cavalry, and the new embroidered robe to be placed upon the prehistoric xoanon, or crude statue, of Athena, preserved in the Erechtheum. In the procession, as the central feature of the whole cavalcade, this new robe was set as a sail on the yard-arm of a ship which was dragged up the slope on a long carriage. At the east end of the temple, the frieze shows Zeus sitting on his throne, surrounded by the whole assembly of the Olympian gods, waiting to receive the procession and the worship of the Athenian people. It is typical of the meticulous care spent on all the calculations in the design of the Parthenon that, in order to counteract the steep angle of sight at which the spectator would view this frieze, set high on the wall as it was, the relief was cut deeper at the top and graded to be very slight at the bottom. A few sections of the frieze are of superlative design: a heifer stretches out its neck, lowing in alarm at all this movement and strange tumult; the manes of four spirited horses flutter in a momentary canter— and these four heads are sculptured one behind the other in receding planes only three inches deep in all. Pheidias surely did more for this panel than the design.

The Parthenon has suffered many vicissitudes. The first big change saw it converted into a Christian Church of St. Mary, complete with apse, after Theodosius the Christian Emperor in A.D. 393 had closed down the pagan sanctuaries. In the Turkish phase, it became a Moslem mosque and was inevitably provided with a minaret, of which the roughly-built lower part is still visible at the west end. Tragedy befell the Parthenon when in 1687, during a war against the Venetians, it was used by the Turks as a powder magazine, and a well-aimed but misguided Venetian cannon-ball blew out the centre of the building. Yet it is still not possible to insert a needle between the column drums on the eastern side—experto crede—with such superb precision did the Greek masons build in honour of their protecting goddess and their city of Athens.

At a short distance to the north of the grand, austere and masculine temple of Athena Parthenos is the Erechtheum in the Ionic order, smaller, more graceful, decorative and feminine, and in fact a charming foil—and also balance—to it. Each building seems to add to its own character by contrast with the other. The Erechtheum, begun in 421 B.C., was the temple of Athena and Poseidon-Erechtheus, and was sited in this position because here was holy ground—the spot where Athena and Poseidon had contested together for the lordship of Attica and its city. Were her people to live by the produce of the land, or by the sea? Athena won the contest: for an olive-tree had sprung out of the ground at the touch of her spear (since replaced by the gift of a kindly American and still struggling with the winds and rocky soil close to the west side of the temple), while Poseidon with a stroke of his trident against the rock had produced the lesser gift of a spring of salt water. The paving of the north porch has an opening in it which permits a view of Poseidon's effort on the rock. Athena and Poseidon were, historically speaking, talking economic nonsense. It was not a case of 'either . . . or'. The olive oil of Attica did indeed produce wealth and gave rise to an important pottery industry; but Poseidon's ships and sea were essential to carry this export to the many parts of the Mediterranean where it was of value. Here on this site, too, was the house of Erechtheus, the legendary and semi-divine king of Athens. And so, to incorporate all these ancestrally sacred areas in the new Erechtheum, the architect was obliged to depart from the usual temple plan. The result is a building on two levels and of a unique, unhappy shape. But again, according to the Periclean plan, the materials and workmanship are superbly good, and the beauty of the capitals and the decorative mouldings freely used and the elegance of the north doorway take the Erechtheum into an unrivalled eminence among all Ionic buildings. Osbert Lancaster, in his attractive *Classical Landscape*, scoffs at the south porch where, raised on a terrace, six strong sculptured women stand most capably supporting the heavy marble cornice on their heads. Atlas, for a short while, carried a heavier weight with no protest from anyone: these Caryatid women still carry their loads with dignity and grace, and add to that touch of femininity so pleasant in this gracious building.

The present uneven and rocky surface of the Acropolis is the result of centuries of rainfall and neglect. Clearly there must have been a more 'finished' surface of paved pathways and soil or gravel. And to see the sanctuary as it was in classical times we must imagine statues, large and small, single and in groups as Pausanias describes them, standing in what we should now regard as regrettably large numbers side by side in long rows. We set off our best buildings when we can with areas of lawn and trees and flower beds: the ancient Greeks, with statues. These, however, were not the white ghosts we see in museums; for details were picked out in colour, the hems of garments, the hair, eyes, lips and so on, and bronze and silver, even gold, were used for belting, fillets round the head, ear-rings and the like. The largest of the statues in the open area was the Athena Promachos, a colossal bronze figure by Pheidias, twenty-seven feet high, fully armed and helmeted in her role as Defender of the city.

With a fine sense of fitness, the authorities arranged that the first two statues to greet a visitor to their Acropolis were those of Pericles himself and of Athena whom he had so greatly honoured. This bronze Athena, known as Lemnia, was considered by Pausanias and by the more intelligent Lucian as Pheidias' most beautiful work. Athena, bare-headed, wears the majesty and calm of a goddess, but she does not conceal the warmth and beauty of womanhood, idealized in her by a master's hand and thought.

From the eastern edge of the Acropolis there is an excellent view. The conical hill of Lycabettus rises high to the north-east —a rock, so legend tells us, that Athena accidentally dropped on her way to help in the fortification of the Acropolis. It was outside the walls of fifth-century Athens, and does not figure in ancient history, perhaps because there was no water-supply anywhere near the top. Among the texture-pattern of tiled roof-tops spread out below, varied in several places by the little blue domes of churches, the observant eye will pick out, to the east, the fourth-century Monument of Lysicrates. This small, round building, surrounded by Corinthian half-columns and with a sculptured frieze, once supported a bronze tripod, the prize in a boys' choir contest at the Dionysiac festival. Lysicrates, at his own cost, had trained and entered a choir and, as winner, had the reward of putting up this memorial in the Street of the Tripods.

Athens: The Acropolis

Looking over the southern parapet we see the Theatre of Dionysus with its semicircle of stone seats, the front row round the orchestra provided with marble chairs, each inscribed with the name of an official of the festival of Dionysus or of the priests of the various temples. The priest of Dionysus naturally sat in the centre seat; and it is significant that on his right hand, in the next most honourable position, sat the representative of the Oracle at Delphi. It must be remembered that the dramatic performances in the theatre were part of a religious festival in honour of Dionysus. Every year three tragic poets were chosen to compete and a prize was awarded at the end of the three-day festival. Here then is the birthplace of European drama. The seats were of wood. It is the general view that there was no stage when the plays of Aeschylus, Sophocles and Euripides were performed: painted scenery, incorporating a central door of a palace or temple through which actors might appear, was set up on the far side of the orchestra in which chorus and actors performed on the same level. However, the latest research throws open a possibility that, after all, fifth-century drama was played on a raised stage. Hitherto such a stage was thought to be an expedient required later by the new 'Comedy of Manners' introduced in the fourth century, in which the great name is that of Menander. For in this new style of drama, acting, movement, expression, gesture and all the tricks of the trade were necessary to support the new plots drawn from everyday life—and often from the seamy side of it. The present marble cavea and orchestra date from 342 B.C., the time of Menander, but in Hellenistic and Roman times there were alterations and additions, particularly in the construction of the stage. Yet here it was, in this hollow of the Acropolis, that fifteen thousand Athenians sat all day watching and listening to the great trilogies—three plays at one sitting (with a satyr play to follow)— in which the pioneer dramatic poets thrashed out the old heroic stories and human problems of vendetta, of justice, first loyalty, right and wrong: and often pondered over the divine solutions put before them by the deus ex machina, the figure of a god who was made suddenly to appear (perhaps by some contrivance at a height) to give his answer to questing mortals. And, as relief, an Aristophanes comedy in turns boisterous, caustically political, lyrical and often coarse and bawdy enough to call for expurgation in many printed editions (except of course the most modern) would laugh the exhaustion out of them on the fourth day.

Adjacent to the theatre on the west are the ruins of a sanctuary of Asclepius, the healing god whose chief centre was Epidaurus in the north-east of the Peloponnese. This sanctuary is on a low terrace retained by the long colonnade of Eumenes. It ran from the theatre to the still high-standing stage building of the Odeum or music hall, given to his city by the wealthy Herodes Atticus about A.D. 160 in memory of his wife. The steep cavea of the Odeum has been restored, and festivals of Greek plays are regularly held which show that Greek drama still has the power to stir the deeps of feeling and that the movements of a well-trained chorus add immensely to that power.

The Museum is at the south-east corner of the Acropolis; and a visit to it is an essential part of the Acropolis experience for it contains some of the most beautiful and exciting Archaic sculptures which survive, as well as fifth-century work from the Parthenon frieze. An account of some of these sculptures is given in the chapter on Sculpture at the end of this book.

On the descent from the Propylaea, to the right the Areopagus rock fills the view, with the new excavations of the Agora beyond and below. In the open air on this rock, at least in the early days, an important Council and Court of Archons and ex-Archons used to sit at their business of dealing with cases of homicide, and of giving general supervision to the Constitution, and to manners and morals and religious matters. But it is known that the Areopagus Council in later times also sat in the Royal Stoa in the Agora. Whether St. Paul spoke his famous words to the men of Athens on this rock—Mars' Hill—or whether he was summoned to appear before the Court in the Royal Stoa, we do not know. Nevertheless, on this rock on St. Paul's day each year the Metropolitan of Athens, the clergy of the Orthodox Church and a great concourse of the people meet for thanksgiving to God for the life and work of the Apostle. Acts xvii, 22-end gives St. Paul's speech: it opens (in the New English Bible) like this:

'Then Paul stood up before the Court of Areopagus and said: "Men of Athens, I see that in everything that concerns religion you are uncommonly scrupulous. For as I was going round looking at the objects of your worship, I noticed among other things an altar bearing the inscription 'To an Unknown God'. What you worship but do not know—this is what I now proclaim." '

His address to the Areopagites was probably his last speech in Athens, where in the Agora, the Acts tells us, 'he disputed daily with them that met him'.

The low hill directly in front of the Propylaea is the important Pnyx, the open-air place of the Assembly of the citizens—the Ecclesia. A large semicircular area was levelled and the speakers' bema or platform was cut in the rock. Originally the speaker faced the sea to the south-west, and the citizens could therefore look north-east to the Acropolis, with the Agora laid out below them. In the black year of defeat by the Spartans in 404 B.C., the 'Thirty Tyrants' reversed the arrangement and the speaker had his back to the sea, for the diminished citizenry could no longer gaze with pride at their splendid city or at the Acropolis, then garrisoned by Spartan troops.

More to the left still is the long, high wooded Hill of the Muses on the top of which is a funeral monument of Philopappos, a Syrian prince, consul in A.D. 109, and an obvious admirer of Athens. One could wish for admiration to be shown less obtrusively than by a tall monument overlooking the Parthenon. This area within the walls of Athens was in the fifth century B.C. a slum section of the city where the homes were built into caves and holes cut out of the limestone hillside. Almost any one of these rock houses may be pointed out to innocent travellers by the taxi-driver as the prison of Socrates.

CHAPTER III

Athens: the Agora

Below the Acropolis and to the north-west is the newly excavated Agora, an area of twenty-five acres on which, in 1930, stood 350 nineteenth-century houses. The huge project of buying these properties, and of an excavation which required the removal outside the city of 300,000 tons of earth was, as one might have guessed, an American one. For this immense effort by Mr. John D. Rockefeller, Jr., and the Rockefeller Foundation, 'Marshall Aid' and the Fulbright Foundation, the American School of Classical Studies and Professor Homer Thompson, the directing archaeologist, and his team, the classical world owes deep gratitude. True, the whole place once looked like a bomb-site in the city of London: but the passing seasons are already bringing to fruition the work of the landscape gardeners, and in a few more years the Agora will be a pleasant as well as an intensely interesting site for all who want to know Athens as it was in antiquity.

The Agora is a large square of level ground, 200 yards wide, at the foot of the slopes rising to the Areopagus rock and to the Acropolis on the south. It is bounded on the west by the low flat-topped hill of Kolonos from which the Periclean marble temple of Hephaestus (erroneously named the Theseum) looks out over the scene below; on the north side now runs the railway from Athens to Piraeus, and the whole of the east side of the square is bounded, as in the first century B.C., by a handsome long white marble colonnaded building. Enough of the original stoa of Attalus, king of Pergamum, was found to enable it to be said that the new building—the Museum to contain the 60,000 catalogued objects found in the Agora, including coins—is a true reproduction of the first. This Museum must be one of the best ever built anywhere in arrangement, design, and in the beauty of its materials. Its shining newness surely helps us in imagination to raise up on the dun-coloured foundations in the Agora the bright marble walls and columns, colonnades, temples and altars, and statues by the score which once brought the citizens of Athens here in their thousands for their business, governmental, judicial and commercial, and for domestic shopping, and for talk and argument and social intercourse. One cynic wrote that everything was for sale here, figs and witnesses, grapes, turnips, lawsuits, lambs and laws.

Professor Homer Thompson has given us the foundations of all the main public buildings in the Agora from the time when Solon declared this area reserved as the city's centre right down to the latest period in the fifth century A.D. when, over the ruins of an Odeum laid waste at the time of the invasion of Herulian barbarians, a university building was made. The two sculptured Giants now standing high in the centre of the Agora were part of an ornamental main entrance to the University.

A stairway led down to the Agora from the rising ground where the temple of Athena and Hephaestus stands. This temple is the best preserved of all Greek temples, and the first building of the Periclean programme after peace was signed with Persia in 449 B.C. The barrel-vaulted ceiling of the cella dates from the time of its conversion into the Christian Church of St. George in the fifth century. The arrangement of the frieze above the columns of the pronaos, or inner porch, facing the Agora and bridging the peristyle, or colonnade, of the temple on both sides, suggests that the building was sited to give what was considered its optimum view from the Agora and the monumental steps which led up to it. But the idea does not now look an effective one: indeed, the temple is strangely unimpressive to most people. Is it badly sited—its length at right-angles to the Agora so that the view for the majority of people in the Agora is chiefly of one end? Does it lack height through a rather mean podium, or base, which emphasizes the columns and the verticality too much, without the balance effect of strong horizontal base with the horizontal architrave? Let us return, perhaps a little puzzled, to the Agora.

Below us, if we look out from the temple of Hephaestus, and beginning at the railway line, is the Stoa of Zeus, the Royal Stoa. It was built in 409 B.C. in honour of, and in thanksgiving to, Zeus Eleutherios who liberated Greece from the Persian menace. One ancient writer described the Athenians as the most religious of all Greeks, and Aeschines, the fourth-century B.C. orator and a passionately proud Athenian, does not forget divine assistance when speaking of the famous war record of the Athenians in the Persian Wars: he declares, 'If you were to say that it was the Athenians who won the war, that would be true; next to the gods, it was they who repulsed the invader.' On the walls of the Stoa of Zeus the laws were written or posted for all to see. We know that Socrates liked to walk and talk in its portico. He was, possibly, tried and condemned in the room behind it. As the Areopagus Court also used this place, it may be that St. Paul spoke his famous words to the men of Athens here. The foundations of the altar of Zeus are marked by the pile of marble chips in front of the Stoa.

Next to the Stoa, to the south, are the remains of two small temples of Zeus Phratrios and Apollo Patroos: the title of Zeus indicates his care for the religious brotherhoods of which the citizens were members, and that of Apollo reminded citizens who were registered here that the god was father of their Ionian race.

Below us, close to the bank on which we stand, was the Metroon, the sanctuary of the Mother of the gods, in which the State archives were kept; and, built into the hillside, was the new Bouleuterion (or Council House) with a courtyard and a propylon. Here the great alternatives of State policy were thrashed out, for confirmation or rejection by the Ecclesia, or Assembly of the citizens, on the Pnyx.

The foundation of the circular building, the Tholos, adjacent to the courtyard of the Council House, is of interest. There the Executive of the day worked, ate and slept, ready for emergency action—a wise provision when communication of danger might be made only by a beacon fire or a breathless runner or a messenger on a galloping horse. Close to it, in the south-west corner of the Agora, was the Generals' headquarters and club-house.

Running from west to east along the south boundary of the

Agora are the heavy foundations of a series of colonnades, once thought to have provided a largely enclosed shopping area. But, out of place in such an area, in the south-west, close under the terrace wall at the foot of the slope, was one of the first of the Agora buildings, the Heliaia, the main law-court of Athens, begun in the sixth century B.C. and added to later. Recent American excavations make it seem likely that the colonnades on the south were not a shopping area but were all connected with the work of the Law Courts.

As we stand near the temple of Hephaestus on the edge of the bank, looking down on the foundations of the buildings below us, our eyes have moved from the railway all along the western side of the Agora to its south-western point, and then followed the line of the stoas along the south side to the medieval Byzantine Church of the Holy Apostles, the first of the eleventh-century churches in Athens. If we now look back again to the railway, we see a bridge and a roadway which runs diagonally across the Agora. This is the line of the old paved Panathenaic processional way, and where it rises on the slope to the Acropolis a large area of the original paving has been laid bare. There is a passage in Xenophon's *Hipparchikos* in which he suggests to the officer in charge of the cavalry escort at the Panathenaic Festival that it would please both the gods and the spectators if he ordered a salute to the gods and their statues when passing through the Agora. Perhaps he had specially in mind the peribolos, or sacred enclosure, and altar of the Twelve Gods, hard up against the railway line and only part of it visible, fifty yards in front of the Stoa of Zeus. This was a place of asylum and, as Thucydides states, was a gift by the grandson of the great Peisistratus in 521 B.C.: it is probably the Altar of Pity to which the useful Pausanias refers in his descriptive tour of the Agora. Close to this peribolos is what looks like a hard tennis court. It is, in fact, the site of the temple of Ares, designed by the same Periclean architect who planned the temple of Hephaestus. But masons' marks of the time of Augustus on its stones suggested that it had been removed from its original fifth-century site and re-erected in the Agora in Roman times. It has recently been established that the temple's first home, in the fifth century B.C., was at Acharnai, seven miles north of Athens, and that it was dismantled and rebuilt in the Agora at the time when interest

47

in Greek art and architecture of the Classical period revived. So the removal of historic buildings from the Old World to the New is after all only a development of an earlier practice. There are signs that when the temple's new foundations were being laid, the workmen's spades broke into a Mycenaean tomb, furnished with pottery as was the custom; but this was not the first time that the tomb had accidentally been disturbed in digging operations, for there were vases of the fifth century B.C. also, evidently placed there as a sign of respect for the dead, and apology for the accidental disturbance of the tomb.

Right in the centre of the Agora (where Pausanias saw them close to the temple of Ares) the Athenians set up statues of the Tyrannicides, Harmodius and Aristogeiton, who in 514 B.C. killed Hipparchus, son of the tyrant Peisistratus. The Persians carried off these statues in 479 B.C., so new ones were made and set up in their place. The bronze statues looted by the Persians were found intact at Susa among the royal treasures captured by Alexander the Great in 330 B.C.; in a gesture of conciliation to Athens, he had them sent back.

For one looking at the Agora from the temple of Hephaestus, on the right (or south) of the new Museum is the Library of Pantainus who gave it for the city about A.D. 100 with a dedication to Athena and Trajan. An inscription, evidently from the doorway, states that 'the Library will be open from the first hour to the sixth' (from daybreak to noon), and adds even less encouragingly, 'No book may be taken out.' After the raid of Herulian Gauls in A.D. 267, the ancient circuit of the city walls was considered too big to be defended and a new, contracted fortification was rapidly and ruthlessly built. Just as Themistocles, 750 years earlier, to save precious time had used for the Acropolis wall the column drums and blocks of marble ready for what was to have been a new temple of Athena (and still visible towards the top of the north side of the Acropolis), so now statues and bases, monuments, capitals and columns, masonry of all sorts from the Agora and its buildings were called into service for the defence of the city. The front of the Library was built into the wall, and so too was the front of the shops in the colonnade given by Attalus; and the Agora then outside the new walls was left a shambles. A hundred and thirty years later, however, the huge complex of the University of Athens rose in the centre of the site. Here its foundation lines are most difficult to follow, for they are superposed upon the old Odeum, given in 15 B.C. by Agrippa, son-in-law of Augustus. This Odeum in its day was an architectural phenomenon, for it seated a thousand people under a ceiling with a clear span of seventy-five feet. It was too much: the ceiling and roof lasted only 150 years and then collapsed. In the reconstruction, a cross wall reduced the seating by half. When the Herulians raided, the Odeum was burnt down; and it was left for Professor Homer Thompson to clear up the enormous debris of the fire after he had excavated the University building planted right on top of the ruins.

It would be tedious to catalogue here all the numerous other places and objects found in this remarkable Agora excavation. But a few more details will perhaps illustrate the sort of interest that lies here. Against the wall of a public building forty yards south-east of the Tholos, a tanner and cobbler had set up a probably unauthorized lean-to hut. Bronze nails and bits and pieces of the cobbler's trade were found; so, too, was a black cup with 'CIMON' scratched upon it. There was a Cimon, a tanner, who was a friend of Socrates. Was this, then, the little shop where Socrates liked to sit and relax in the rare intervals of talking? Just west of this point, sixteen yards east of the Tholos, is the stone which declares 'I am the boundary of the Agora'. Inside the official precinct of the Agora certain criminals were not allowed. Further to the east, on the same line, is an upright marble slab on which are cut the 'standard' sizes for roof-tiles.

There is a free-standing Roman statue of Hadrian which neatly puts a truth we already know, that the Emperor (A.D. 117–138) was an admirer of Athens. It stands, headless, close to the Metroon, directly to the east of the temple of Hephaestus; sculptured on the breastplate, Athena, crowned by winged Victories, stands with her foot upon the Roman wolf which suckles Romulus and Remus. The inscription reads, 'Captive Greece takes the captor captive.'

But we must try to find the vital spirit which once pervaded all this place of present ruin. In his fine survey of Greek buildings, *How the Greeks Built Cities*, Professor R. E. Wycherley opens his chapter on the Greek Agora with a quotation from Herodotus: 'Cyrus said, "I have never been afraid of the kind

of people who make a place in the middle of their city where they can all go and talk—and tell each other lies under oath." '
This shows, says Wycherley, how well Cyrus, king of Persia, knew this essential arrangement of any Greek city. But does it not also show how little Cyrus understood the will of free men to resist attack upon a city they felt to be their own—their very own and not the great domain of any tyrant lording it over them? Herodotus sees the high morale of these free democratic talkers and, in another place, he says, 'Equality is obviously a good thing, because even the Athenians when under tyrants were not a scrap more brave than anybody else: but when tyranny was overthrown, they became the bravest of all men.' The reason for the change, he says, is simply that they had nothing to lose when under tyrants: defeat by the enemy would merely be a change of masters. But once democratic freedom was theirs, they would fight to retain what was their own.

There is no equivalent in our cities to the Greek Agora. For one thing they are too big and populations too large for a single centre to be feasible. But the Agora was much more than a mere geographical centre with the chief public buildings, important temples, and places for commerce concentrated there. It was a focus point of pride and confidence in citizenship; and nowhere was this more marked than at Athens. Here, as Lycurgus notices, instead of the statues of athletic champions usual in most Greek cities, the Athenians had set up statues of successful generals and those who killed the tyrant and gave men freedom. In the Agora the Athenians had many a memorial of past achievement to inspire them to new efforts. 'Think of the Stoa Poikile,' says Aeschines of the Agora picture gallery where more of Poly-gnotus' paintings of famous battles kept pride alive, 'the memorials of all your great deeds are there. Think of the battle of Marathon . . .' This kind of appeal may leave us cold in peace, but not in time of war. Then it meets with response and a lift of the heart and hand for action. In the dark days of Dunkirk, Winston Churchill used it with supreme effect; across the Atlantic, Dorothy Thompson used it and kindled the flames of feeling that led to Lend-Lease.

There was a spiritual value, too, in the Agora, for in temples, statues and altars to their gods the Athenians expressed their faith that they were not alone. From the Agora they could lift

ZEUS HURLING HIS THUNDERBOLT: IN THE NATIONAL MUSEUM
AT ATHENS

This seven foot high bronze masterpiece seems to display the calm, the majesty and the power of a god immune from the troubles that beset mankind. It was made about 465 B.C. and was found in the sea off Cape Artemisium.

THE PARTHENON: NORTH-EAST CORNER

The slight upward curvature of the stylobate—4 $\frac{5}{16}$ inches on the sides and visibl
in the photograph on the steps running into the distance—produces from some wa
off the optical illusion that the columns stand on a horizontal base, which is th
impression desired.

their eyes to the Acropolis and the huge and splendid outline of
the Parthenon, and in the smoke of sacrifice rising from Athena's
altar see the evidence that they were doing their part and would
be assured that the protecting goddess of their city would do hers.

The Agora, moreover, was the obvious place for men to meet
together anyway: their homes, in the great days, were poor
places. Dicaearchus, writing in the fourth century B.C., com-
plains that the city was dusty and had a wretched water supply
and, because it was old, was badly laid out. It had just grown.
The houses, he says, were mostly bad. Indeed, a stranger walk-
ing about in the streets of Athens at first might doubt if it
was Athens at all. Demosthenes, about the same date, actually
rebukes rich citizens for the new fashion creeping in of building
fine private houses. 'The republic had plenty of money, but no
one raised himself above the crowd. Could we see the homes of
Themistocles, Cimon or Aristides, we should find them just
ordinary little houses. But the public buildings . . . they were
countless and of superb construction.'

So as we look upon 'the valley of dry bones' before us, perhaps
we may now answer the same question that was put to Ezekiel,
'Can these bones live?' with an emphatic 'Yes', and in our mind's
eye see the old foundations 'rise up, an exceeding great array'.

THE KERAMEIKOS—THE POTTERS' QUARTER

The Panathenaic Way which crosses the Agora on its route
to the Acropolis is a continuation of the ancient road from
Eleusis. This Sacred Way entered the city fortifications through
the Sacred Gate, only fifty yards south-west of a second entrance,
the Dipylon Gate. Outside the walls at this north-western point
of the ancient city is the Kerameikos cemetery. The preservation
of that part of the cemetery on the Academia road is due to Sulla,
the Roman general, who laid siege to Athens in 86 B.C. and, in
order to get his attacking forces literally over the fortifications,
built up a huge ramp of earth to the top level of the walls. Much
of this protecting earth over the Kerameikos remained until the
last century. It was here that the magnificent Dipylon vases were
found, placed over the tombs as markers. Many of these are in
the National Museum. They belong to the Geometric period
(900–700 B.C.), so called because the style of decoration is

at first almost entirely of geometrical patterns: meanders, chevrons, chequers, hatched lines, parallel lines, dots, lozenges and the like; later there are crude elongated human figures with narrow waists, and horses and chariots, birds and funeral scenes. Some vases are as much as four feet high. Though the style is rudimentary, the total effect of the design with its neat arrangement, the shape of the vase, and the sheen and finish on the light brown surface make the Dipylon vase a notable and splendid work of early art.

Graves of the Mycenaean, Protogeometric (tenth century B.C.) and Geometric periods, and of the sixth century have been found in and around the Agora; but evidently later burials were required to be made outside the city walls, and many were made on the Sacred Way and along other roads built off the Sacred Way for this purpose. Here are long ranges of family tomb enclosures, some with walls of brick and others of fine masonry. Among the most impressive is the monument to Dexileos, a young cavalry officer who is typically shown riding his fallen enemy into the ground at a moment of victory in life, not at the sad moment of his own death. This same idea characterizes the most beautiful of funeral stelai which originally came from the family enclosure a few yards to the west of that of Dexileos and next to the powerful bull monument on a base eleven feet high. This stele is in an honoured position in the National Museum: it is a memorial to Hegeso, daughter of Proxenos. She is sitting on a chair, at her best and loveliest, enjoying looking at a jewel she has just taken from the jewel-box held before her by her slave girl. This is the spirit typical of the fifth century. Towards the end of the fourth century, however, there is a new element of the emotional in sculpture which makes itself felt also in the grave stelai. In a memorial of this period, a slave offers a box of jewels, but her mistress looks into the distance, uninterested, full of melancholy, for she has felt Death's hand upon her.

But the use of these elaborate and often beautiful sculptured memorials came to an end in Athens in 317 B.C. when, at a time of financial crisis, Demetrius of Phaleron brought in a sumptuary regulation forbidding luxury spending of this sort. From then on for a long period, graves were marked by a small stone column of any height from one to three feet which was tapered upwards and flat-topped. The ugliness of these is a surprise for, with the exception of the harpies and other un-birdlike birds of which their sculptors were too often guilty, Greek artists and craftsmen touched nothing that they did not adorn.

· In another part of the Kerameikos lay the war cemetery described by Thucydides as the most beautiful spot outside the city walls: here the ashes of her men who had died in distant battles were brought home by ancient custom for burial and a funeral oration delivered over them at a civic ceremony. It was here that Pericles made his famous funeral speech, in which every word was given weight, every phrase emotive power to turn mourning for the dead into pride in their self-sacrifice. Here is a single paragraph from the long speech:

'I would have you day by day fix your eyes upon the greatness of Athens, until you become filled with the love of her; and when you are impressed by the spectacle of her glory, reflect that this empire had been acquired by men who knew their duty and had the courage to do it, who in the hour of conflict had the fear of dishonour always present to them, and who, if ever they failed in an enterprise, would not allow their virtues to be lost to their country, but freely gave their lives to her as the fairest offering which they could present at her feast. The sacrifice which they collectively made was individually repaid to them; for they received again each one for himself a praise which grows not old, and the noblest of all sepulchres—I speak not of that in which their remains are laid, but of that in which their glory survives. For the whole earth is the sepulchre of famous men; not only are they commemorated by columns and inscriptions in their own country, but in foreign lands there dwells also an unwritten memorial of them, graven not on stone but in the hearts of men. Make them your examples . . .'

(Translation by JOWETT.)

The German Institute of Archaeology has continued excavations on this site and there are also public works involved. For the time being the Kerameikos is not 'the most beautiful place outside the city walls'. The Kerameikos Museum, however, contains much that is beautiful, especially the vases.

CHAPTER IV

Attica: The Mysteries of Eleusis. Sunium. Brauron. Marathon

ELEUSIS

Eleusis is now an industrial town on the busy main road from Athens to the Peloponnese and to central and northern Greece. It is fourteen miles from the capital, and on the sea: for much of the distance the modern road follows the ancient Sacred Way, along which each year from Mycenaean times for about seventeen centuries a huge procession of worshippers moved to her Eleusinian sanctuary at the command, as they believed, of the goddess Demeter, to take part in mystic rites instituted by the goddess herself.

If one makes the journey to Eleusis without any prior understanding of what the Mysteries meant to the Greeks, and, in the later phases, also to the Romans, carried along only by a cheerful expectation of 'enjoying another beautiful site anyway', the expedition will be a tiring disappointment. For Eleusis is not now a beautiful site. A low but steep and rocky hill, which was once a Mycenaean fortress and settlement, and an apparent confusion of broken stones on the slope below the hill, where heavy ancient walls of varying periods make the sanctuary look like a fortification, present a somewhat dismal scene. As for the placid waters of the Bay of Salamis close by, their beauty is marred and cut by the chimneys of the soap-works and the steam-laundry and other modern essentials of the good life. It calls for some knowledge and much imagination to see these ruins as those of a sanctuary of peculiar holiness and spiritual value for the Greeks, from which, after a festival which lasted ten days, the initiated worshippers emerged deeply moved, inwardly fortified and confidently serene in the secrets they carried faithfully locked in their minds and hearts for the rest of their days.

That faithfulness is not the least of the mysteries of this extraordinary place. In the course of its long existence, from the time when the Festival of Demeter was a local Eleusinian one (before Athens, under King Erechtheus, conquered Eleusis and, a little later, absorbed it into the Athenian state under Theseus) until the sanctuary was either closed at the end of the fourth century A.D. under the orders of the Emperor Theodosius, or sacked at the time by Alaric and his barbarians, the High Priests of Demeter had exhibited 'the holy things' and spoken 'the unutterable words'—the secret proceedings of quite enormous effect upon the initiates—to literally millions of people; and no one broke the vow of secrecy enough for history to record the secret's content. Except perhaps Alcibiades, who was condemned to death (in his absence) for this sacrilege, even though he was joint commander of the vast Sicilian expedition. Aeschylus had been thought to be divulging these secrets in a play which we do not possess. He was mobbed by furious citizens in the theatre, fled for refuge to the altar of Dionysus, and escaped with his life only because the Areopagus Court decided that he did not know that the particular matter divulged was, as it were, 'classified' and on the secret list. For the rites and ceremonies of the Festival were conducted in several places and anyone could watch what was done, for instance, outside the Eleusinion at the foot of the Acropolis below the Propylaea at Athens where the procession to Eleusis formed up, or at the purificatory ceremony of a mass bathing on the beach at Phaleron Bay; or at the killing by each initiate of his small sacrificial pig on his return to Athens from the all-cleansing sea; or, again, outside the sanctuary at Eleusis where crowds would welcome the procession's arrival at the outer propylaea and the temple of Artemis outside the entrance, and see honours done at the well by which Demeter had sat and rested. It was in the sanctuary itself at Eleusis, above all in the window-less Telesterion (or Demeter's Hall of Initiation) that the proceedings were veiled and unspeakably secret: and the great walls, like fortress walls with towers and bastions, were built to keep out careless eyes and impure minds. Pausanias does not describe the buildings in the sanctuary because they were not visible to the 'outsider' (so high were the walls) and his dream had warned him not to speak or write about things which the uninitiated were prevented from seeing. But we know that all the great 'builders' who had beautified Athens each in their day added to the splendour of Demeter's sanctuary. Solon and Peisistratus before the Persian Wars; Cimon, Pericles, Ictinus, architect of the Parthenon, in the generation after them; Lycurgus and Philo in the Hellenistic period; and in Imperial Roman times the Emperors Hadrian, Antoninus Pius and Marcus Aurelius have all left their mark in the magnificent walls or buildings on this ever-growing precinct. For eventually all who could speak Greek and who were not guilty of homicide—men, women, children and even slaves—were welcomed as initiates.

Legend, tradition, the literary documents, and archaeology are at one as to the foundation and growth of the cult of Demeter at Eleusis in the Mycenaean period, in the latter half of the fifteenth century B.C.

The legend of Demeter and of her daughter Persephone, carried off by Pluto to the underworld, is one of the best known stories in the world, and has been retold by poets and painted by artists countless times. To appreciate the Mysteries, the story must be known in the form in which the late seventh-century Homeric Hymn to Demeter gives it; for the Hymn was probably composed as the official version of the foundation of the cult for the sanctuary authorities.

Persephone, daughter of Demeter and Zeus, wandering in a meadow and picking here a poppy and there an iris or narcissus, was carried off by Pluto, god of the underworld, through a chasm in the earth which opened suddenly. For nine days Demeter vainly searched for her by land and sea. Then Helios told her what had happened, and Demeter, furious with Zeus for allowing such an act of rape by Pluto, withdrew from any contact with Olympus, the seat of the gods. Tennyson writes of her wrath:

> *Then I, earth-goddess, cursed the gods of heaven,*
> *I would not mingle with their feasts: to me*
> *their nectar smack'd of hemlock on the lips,*
> *their rich ambrosia tasted aconite.*
> *The man that only lives and loves an hour*
> *seemed nobler than their hard Eternities.*

So Demeter disguised herself as an old woman, preferring the habitations of humans, and came to Eleusis and sat to rest by a well where the women were wont to dance—the Kallichoron well. Here the king's daughters found her and took her to the palace, for the queen was looking for a nurse for her young son. Demeter was unusually successful in this role, providing the babe with a diet of ambrosia by day and holding him in the fire by night to harden him for immortality. The mother was intrigued by her child's phenomenal growth-rate, but when the 'nurse' revealed the nutritional method employed and her own identity, further questions were at an end, and the goddess' command was given and obeyed.

'Build me a noble temple and an altar below it, beneath the acropolis and its steep rock, upon the hillock, and above the Kallichoron well. Then will I teach you my ceremonies. So will you win grace.'

But Demeter—for Persephone was still lost to her—decided to punish the gods by inhibiting the growth of all vegetation and thus putting an end to the first-fruit offerings the gods received from men. Tennyson speaks for Demeter:

> *My quick tears kill'd the flower, my ravings hush'd*
> *the bird, and lost in utter grief I fail'd*
> *to send my life thro' olive-yard and vine*
> *and golden grain, my gift to helpless man.*

Zeus yielded to her demand for the return of Persephone; but wily Pluto, before handing the girl over, ensured her return to him in the underworld for at least a part of every year by offering her a few pomegranate seeds to eat. She could not resist them: and Demeter, overjoyed at the return of her daughter, had to be satisfied with her child's presence for only nine months of the year. So, at Demeter's order, all the world sprang again with growth and harvest. After all, the seed buried in the dark earth through the short winter months, will burst again to life and blade and fruitfulness. Of that Man may be sure—and of more: that Man himself, when buried, dead, in the dark and cold of earth, will walk immortal the fields of asphodel below in peace and happiness. To enable him to do so, Demeter then revealed to the leaders of Eleusis—Triptolemos and Diokles and the brave Eumolpos—her famous Mysteries 'which none may disobey or ever utter, for fear of the gods'.

And that was how it all began. Awe at the wonder and the miracle of the life-giving grain growing from the dry 'dead' seed as a gift of heaven to mortal men, deepened into faith that for those who obeyed the goddess' command and were purified and initiated into her Mysteries, faithful unto death in keeping them secret, death and their dry bones beneath the earth were but the beginning of a new life and happiness in Elysium below. So Pindar can write: 'He who has seen the holy things (of Eleusis) and goes in death beneath the earth is happy: for he knows life's end and he knows too the new divine beginning.' Four hundred years later, Cicero could say with all his high appreciation of the legacy of Athens in men and monuments: 'The greatest gift of Athens to mankind and the holiest is the Eleusinian Mysteries.' The Greek scholar and archaeologist G. E. Mylonas, whose book *Eleusis and the Eleusinian Mysteries* is the latest on this subject and adds much to our knowledge through his archaeological findings, sums up the value to the ancient world of the Mysteries in these words:

'Whatever the substance and meaning of the Mysteries was, the fact remains that the cult of Eleusis satisfied the most sincere yearnings and the deepest longings of the human heart. The initiates returned from their pilgrimage to Eleusis full of joy and happiness, with the fear of death diminished and the strengthened hope of a better life in the world of shadows.'

Let us then try to untangle the complex web of fallen stones, foundations and walls which meet us on our arrival at the outer gate of the sanctuary. We come to a halt—as did the procession of worshippers from Athens long ago—on a paved courtyard outside the entrance, facing it and with the foundations of the temple of Artemis now close behind us. The Pentelic marble propylaea was the gift of Marcus Aurelius: an exact copy in plan of the central part of the propylaea on the Acropolis of Athens. What a tribute to the enduring and imposing quality of Mnesicles' work, five hundred years earlier, that Roman builders, always prone to work on the big scale and always in love with the principle of the arch, should have copied a pure Greek building in the horizontal Doric style for a new entrance presented by an Emperor—even to copying the rare use by Mnesicles of

Ionic columns adjacent to Doric to line the entrance way. On the pavement are many Christian crosses—perhaps prophylactic in intention to drive away old pagan spirits, suggests Mylonas.

We are now inside the encircling walls of Cimon who extended the area of the precinct after the Persian destruction of the sanctuary. This wall—far to our left—was rebuilt in Hellenistic and again in Roman times. But we are not yet inside the walls of Peisistratus of 550 B.C.: their foundation is close, on our right hand as we make our way to the lesser, and inner, propylaea. This also is Roman, a gift of Appius Claudius in 54 B.C., and took the place of the gateway of Peisistratus. His circuit wall foundations run from this gateway in a southerly direction for seventy-five yards, then turn at a right-angle westward, running, as we shall see, under the corner of the great Hall of Initiation which was increased in size by Pericles. Immediately on the right, as we pass through the inner entrance, is a cave in the acropolis rock where first Peisistratus and later, in 329 B.C., a second builder, set up a temple to Pluto. Here, from a hole through the rock from a further cave, it is likely that Persephone made each year a dramatic appearance up from the underworld, when, in the course of the festival, the story of Demeter and Persephone was perhaps re-enacted before the crowd of initiates.

Immediately to the south of the Plutonion Cave is a platform approached by steps: this was the site of Demeter's treasury. What may be, Mylonas suggests, the lower half of a collection-box—a hollow cut into a large stone—stands on the side furthest from the cave. In the middle of the pathway is a worked stone which stands up 'proud': proud it would be if this is indeed 'the Mirthless Stone' on which, according to the Hymn to Demeter, the goddess sat, exhausted by grief and futile searching for Persephone, on her arrival at Eleusis. Next to the treasury site and cut into the acropolis rock, on the right of the pathway, are the scanty remains of a Roman temple.

In front of us now opens up a large rectangular area where once stood a building which was probably the largest in Greece, the Telesterion, or Hall of Initiation. The Hall was square, and round the sides there were narrow, rock-cut or stone steps like the seats of a theatre, but for standing. Ictinus had designed, for Pericles, a roof to be supported by four rows of five columns; but, possibly because such exceptional spans were called for in this plan, his design was abandoned, and a scheme of six rows of seven columns took its place. Many of the bases of this thicket of columns—a serious impediment to the spectators' view of the proceedings—are visible on the site. Ancient authors refer to some form of lantern, or opaion, which admitted light, for the walls did not have windows. About 310 B.C. an immense Doric portico, 180 feet long, was completed on the east side by Philo.

The area of the Hall of Initiation is a classic site for the archaeologist, in that, as he digs down, he can find traces of the long series of buildings, constructed each over the foundations of its predecessor, and each larger, as the growing cult required, until the earliest building of all is reached and found to be of Mycenaean type. It consisted of a rectangular room with two central pillars and a pillared porch. This form was typical in Mycenaean times of the megaron of the king's palace. But we must see this Mycenaean megaron as Demeter's house—in fact, her first temple—and not the palace of the king of Eleusis, for the following reasons. This megaron is surrounded by a precinct wall: it had a small terrace for an altar to the east of it: it is precisely where Demeter in the literary tradition, ordered it, beneath the rock of the acropolis: it is on a 'hillock' (hence the need of the series of buttressed terraces on the east side which this and all the later and larger buildings on the site required): and, finally, it is above Demeter's well. That the well in the south-east corner of this levelled area was of special importance is seen in the way the Archaic wall deals with the problem that its proper line would cut right across the ancient well: the wall avoids this desecration and tightly curves round the well, forming a protecting niche. And one further point—kings' palaces are not sited outside the fortification walls of an acropolis: the king of Eleusis obviously had his palace on the once fortified summit of the rocky and precipitous hill above the sanctuary.

It is possible in the excavations to see the remains of this first sacred place, and a later Mycenaean extension of it, deep below the level of the last Telesterion. The curve of an apsidal building of the Geometric period (*c.* 700 B.C.) cuts across a Mycenaean wall; in turn, the Geometric wall is cut by one of the Archaic period (*c.* 650 B.C.); then we can see how in 550 B.C., in order to make the stone foundations for the columns of the enlarged Telesterion of Peisistratus, the builders dug through all these various layers to the solid ground beneath. Remains of the Peisistratid terrace wall and of the walls of Cimon, Pericles and Lycurgus are visible.

Though the Telesteria were built larger in each succeeding rebuilding, the sanctity of the original little sacred place, where Demeter taught her rites, was never lost. For the heart of all these later buildings was a small chamber—the anaktoron— which preserved the sacred spot. That the anaktoron was not in the actual centre of the new buildings did not matter: the preservation of the holy ground did. Only the High Priest could enter this holy of holies, and in it were kept the hiera, the sacred objects, the exhibition of which to the initiates was the crisis of the Mysteries.

SUNIUM

Pausanias opens the first chapter of his first book with a mistaken attribution to Athena of the temple on the peak of the promontory which, facing the Cyclades islands, stands out from the coast of Attica. There was indeed a temple to Athena, but not on the peak of the promontory. Poseidon, Lord of the Sea, had his white marble temple there, and Athena's temple was at a lower level on the ridge or saddle which joined the promontory to the mountain mass inland. An inscription found near the sanctuary on 'Sunium's marbled steep' set out an official decree of the third century B.C. and among its provisions was one which ordered the cutting of its clauses on marble and the placing of this marble in the precinct of Poseidon.

It was surely a seaman who first had the idea that the right place for a temple to Poseidon was on a promontory. On many a promontory stood a temple to the God of the Sea, for squalls and currents and irregular and breaking seas are often the sailor's lot off headlands and he would need Poseidon's protection. Not that Poseidon gave it, as Homer tells, to Phrontis, Menelaus' helmsman as he sailed past Sunium on the passage to Troy. His reputation as a seaman stood very high; on this day, perhaps, he was exhausted in the struggle to round the cape, for while he was taking his trick at the steering oar, he had a heart attack— 'he fell before Apollo's gentle shafts'—and died.

But Sunium was more than a cape to be rounded: for the Athenian seaman homeward bound with a cargo of wheat from

the Black Sea, the cape spelt 'home waters' as do the cliffs of
the Channel or the sight of the Lizard to the British seaman
steaming in from the Atlantic. Once round Sunium and on a clear
day, home itself was visible to the seaman in the form of a flash
of sunlight from the spear held by the colossal statue of Athena,
protectress of the city and her men, on the Acropolis at Athens.
There are mentions of this in Greek literature, in Herodotus and
in Pausanias.

As might be guessed from the modern name, Cape Colonna,
some columns of the temple are standing. The marble Doric
temple dates from the time of Pericles: it was built on the local
soft limestone, or *poros*, foundation of an earlier temple burnt by
the Persians in 480 B.C. The flutes of the columns are fewer than
was usual at the date of its building, and so the normally vulnerable sharp edges of Doric flutes are here thicker and less likely
to be damaged by salt-laden winds on the exposed headland. A
great many people have written or scratched their names on the
temple stones, fortunately a rare barbarism on an ancient Greek
site: among the names, and cut more deeply than most, is that of
Byron. Who can now say whether he, or an admirer, cut it? But
anyway his name in Greece is that of a hero in the classic sense—
almost a demi-god—and what Greek would call it sacrilege to
have that name cut deep in such a place?

The temple sanctuary included a portico for the shelter of
pilgrims and the whole was protected by a fortification wall with
towers at intervals. These walls were partly renewed in 412 B.C.,
marble blocks replacing sections of the archaic polygonal
wall.

On the eastern side at the foot of the steep cliffs there is a
narrow creek where ships could lie in safety if the winds were
strong westerlies, and await a slant for the home port of Piraeus.
Thucydides says that the fortification was rebuilt by the
Athenians during the war against Sparta to protect their ships
bringing corn to Athens.

On a later occasion, the slaves from the silver mines of neighbouring Mount Laurium broke out, killing their guards, and
seized the acropolis—which must refer to the fortified sanctuary
of Sunium. It was to prevent any such concerted slave revolt that
the Athenians adopted a mining system which must have been
economically most unsound. They subdivided their efforts into

hundreds of separate small tunnels dispersed over many square miles of metalliferous mountain-side. The mountains now are bare of trees, like so many in Greece: but in Homer's day Sunium was wooded.

The pleasure of a visit to Sunium is threefold: the coastal scenery on the way is excellent, as is the road itself; at Sunium it is not too difficult in imagination to sense the effect upon the mind of the beauty of the white marble temple high and serene above the sea in the days of its reassuring service to the seamen of Athens; and the view, out over the island-studded waters, east, south and west, is far and fine. If, at Sunium, one does not oneself recall Byron's famous lines, someone in the party is sure to try to do so. Then, for Byron's sake, let us get them right:

> *Place me on Sunium's marbled steep,*
>   *Where nothing, save the waves and I,*
> *May hear our mutual murmurs sweep;*
>   *There, swan-like, let me sing and die:*
> *A land of slaves shall ne'er be mine—*
> *Dash down yon cup of Samian wine!*

BRAURON: SANCTUARY OF ARTEMIS

At BRAURON, or Vraona in modern Greek, twenty-four miles to the east of Athens and about a mile from the sea, a sanctuary of Artemis has recently been excavated by Dr. Papadimitriou, late Director of the Greek Archaeological Service. It is of quite peculiar interest. For here, if we could penetrate clearly enough through the mists of legend and tradition, we might see the figure of the priestess of Artemis bending over the altar and touching the neck of a man gently with a dagger point to let fall one symbolic drop of blood upon it. It would be none other than Iphigeneia, daughter of King Agamemnon, settled here as priestess after desperate adventures.

The king on his way with the Achaean fleet to capture Troy was delayed somewhere in the Euboean channel by unfavourable winds. This delay was the work of Artemis to whom the king had made a sacred vow which he had not honoured. Only the sacrifice of his daughter would satisfy Artemis and thus enable the fleet to proceed. It is a ghastly predicament for the king, and we suffer with him as in the parallel and terrible story of Abraham, preparing to sacrifice his son Isaac to prove his obedience to God. In Euripides' play, *Iphigeneia in Tauris*, as in the Bible story, to our profound relief an animal substitute at the last moment is providentially provided, and Iphigeneia herself is snatched away by Artemis to the Tauric Chersonese (the Crimea), and immured there as priestess of her temple and guardian of her image which had fallen from heaven. She is, however, ineluctably involved in human sacrifice, for her duties include the sacrificial execution of strangers who set foot in that most inhospitable land. Adventure reaches a breathless peak when Orestes and Pylades arrive there in obedience to the Delphic Oracle: only if Orestes sailed to the far north and seized the wooden image of Artemis and brought it to Athens would he shake off his melancholy madness. They are caught by the Taurians and must be sacrificed. But these are the first Greeks Iphigeneia has seen since she was spirited away many years before from her native land; and she cannot refrain from asking about her home, though she does not reveal her identity. Excitement mounts as question and answer reveal that this is her brother Orestes. She tells him then who she is and learns why he has come. Together they work out a way of escape for them all. Then, to the temple guards she declares, 'These men are matricides and have defiled by their presence the sacred image of our goddess. We must purify the image and the prisoners in the sea before the sacrifice is carried out.' Down to the sea, with the image in her arms, she proceeds with ritual dignity, the guards following with the two prisoners. Near the shore she orders the soldiers to wait since none may witness the sacred ceremony of purification. Then brother, sister and friend seize their chance of a lifetime; they rush to the creek below where, with oars shipped, ready for flight, Orestes' ship lies hidden. At this moment the soldiers realize they have been hoodwinked and make a desperate attempt to recapture their prisoners. There is a fight round the ship, but Orestes seizes Iphigeneia, wades through the surf and lifts her into the ship, the image safe in her arms. 'And fifty oars struck, and away she flew.' In Gilbert Murray's translation we can feel the thrill of escape as the ship began to run before the wind. The final scene is a peaceful one. Athena appears and names Brauron as the resting place for the sacred image of Artemis. Pausanias states that in his day there was indeed an old image of Artemis at Brauron, but he doubts if it was in fact more than a copy of the original carried off, he says, by Xerxes among his spoil from Athens.

Dr. Papadimitriou's excavation of the site has been more than usually notable, because most of it lay below the modern water level in the marshes around, and also because of the beautiful sculpture and numerous votives he has recovered. The sanctuary lies by a river at the foot of a rocky hill. The temple of Artemis was built on a terrace of rock levelled a few feet above the marshy ground and approached by rock-cut steps. The walls which supported a platform at the east end of the temple where the altar stood are still in position. The rubble fill below the altar contained, besides much ash from an earlier altar, large quantities of sherds from the seventh to the fifth century B.C. and terracotta figurines. The level area below the temple on the rocks was occupied by a Doric colonnaded portico on the north, with wings, which return to the rock terrace on the west, and on the eastern side contained rooms. There were rooms also behind the colonnade on the north side. So the quadrangular sanctuary was completely enclosed. An inscription in the stoa or portico set up in the archonship of Arimnestos fixes its date as before 416 B.C. A propylaea, or entrance gateway, was found behind the north portico to the east, and there was probably another on the western side—a roadway running between them. This road was flanked on the north by a series of bas-relief slabs fixed on the top of low stone pillars, rectangular in section, slotted into the line of bases still *in situ*. This north portico and at least a large part of the wings on the east and west of the quadrangle which date from the the fifth century, were overwhelmed by floods and collapsed. The portico columns have been found and re-erected. Diagonally across the ruined quadrangle a stone roadway was made from the north-west towards the south-east corner. The authorities of the day evidently had given up hope of dealing with a site subject to serious winter flooding, and in the making of this road they used stones from the ruined buildings, some with inscriptions on them; and even some sculpture was incorporated in it. None of these inscriptions or of the sculpture is later than the end of the fourth century B.C. The abandonment of the low-lying quadrangle was not, however, a devastating blow, for on the rocks to the east of the temple and its altar platform above the marsh the line of buildings continued. Among them is the foundation of a sacred house: and perhaps the tomb there is that of Iphigeneia, mentioned by Euripides in his play.

The priestess of the sanctuary of Artemis at Brauron was served by children. Because locally it was held that Brauron was the site of the original sacrifice by Agamemnon and that the substitute animal was a bear, the children of the temple were called the 'bears'. Some pottery fragments show processions of 'bear' priestesses. Two charming sculptured figures of the 'bears' found in the sanctuary are now in the National Museum at Athens. The children are carrying one a hare and the other a dove, and they look extremely happy in their work for the goddess, mistress of the forests and the hills and the wild creatures in them. Several other similar heads and statues have been found. The very fine bas-reliefs of the fifth century are also in the National Museum. One shows Artemis feeding a goat with its three kids by her side, and another a group of deities, Zeus seated by a standing Athena and Apollo with Artemis just arriving in a flurry of windswept drapery. Peat and marsh-land have a surprising capacity to preserve wooden and other perishable objects buried in them, and to the floods which destroyed the sanctuary we owe the preservation of many votive offerings of the fifth century in the form of olive-wood vases. A bone flute, a wooden loom reed, and a bronze mirror with its wooden handle of the late sixth century are other unusual finds. In a cellar under the temple itself nearly 3,000 votive objects were found, including some sixth-century B.C. glass vases.

On the edge of the sanctuary a road bridge has been recently excavated; it is made of long slabs of stone, horizontally set on similar slabs of vertical masonry, and is twenty-seven feet wide. This is a rare and exciting find on a site of the classical period.

The sanctuary is now a lonely place, approached by farm tracks through the vineyards and the corn fields. For this is one of the fertile areas of Attica. The sea is just visible between the hills at the end of the shallow valley—a peaceful place for the tomb of Iphigeneia, and the sanctuary where the little 'bears' served happily.

PART OF THE FAMOUS FRIEZE IN SITU AT THE WEST END OF THE PARTHENON: THE
CAVALRY ESCORT FOR THE PANATHENAIC PROCESSION BEGINS TO MOUNT

*The average depth of the relief is only an inch and a half. That greatest part of the frieze which is in the
British Museum is claimed to be in a better state of preservation than this section, exposed to the weather for
a further 160 years.*

The Temple of Apollo at Delphi, High Above the Pleistos Valley

MARATHON

One makes the journey to Marathon, twenty-four miles north-east of Athens, because in 490 B.C. an Athenian army of 10,000 men marched out from Athens, and then, with ardour unchilled by a week's delay while generals debated, dared here to attack an invading Persian force more than twice its size and threw it back into the sea with a loss of a quarter of its forces. Creasy includes Marathon as one of the decisive battles of the world: there are others who decry this valuation and declare that the Athenians constructed this saga to bolster a position as leaders of Greece and foremost champions of her freedom, and this in the days when they had shamelessly turned the great Confederation of Delos of 250 states into a ruthless Empire. Certainly Plato in saying that the Persians at Marathon numbered half a million men, when in fact the transport in ships in one convoy from Cilicia of one-twentieth of that number was a huge achievement, has made the charge of 'propaganda and absurd exaggeration' a ready one to hold against Athens.

But the Athenians *were* the foremost champions of Greek freedom in the face of Persian aggression, and they had every reason to be proud of their almost single-handed achievement against the giant 'barbarian' empire. True, the battle at first sight was decisive in a limited sense only, in that ten years later Athens and its Acropolis went up in smoke in a second Persian invasion. But, to quote Professor N. G. L. Hammond in *A New History of Greece*, 'It keyed the fighting spirit of Athens to the highest pitch, and it showed to Sparta the conditions under which Greek infantry could defeat Persian infantry. It inspired other Greek States with the will to resist. These consequences were indispensable to the future salvation of Greece. In this sense the battle of Marathon was a decisive event in World history'.

To appreciate the courageous initiative of the Athenians as they stepped boldly up into the vacant position of leadership at this time and, abandoning their walled Acropolis, marched out alone to engage the common enemy on the beaches, we have to recollect the phenomenal spirit of independence which separated Greek cities into distinct States and made concerted action so difficult. Such unions of cities as existed in the early fifth century

67   E

were not political but had a religious purpose: an amphictyony (or council of several States) would be formed to regulate the special sanctuary of some god or an oracular shrine as for Delphi, or for the temple of Poseidon on Poros.

The plain of Marathon, six miles long and about two miles wide, is crescent-shaped, running between a wall of mountains which rise steeply from the level land, and the curving sandy beach on which the Persians landed. The northern end of the plain is all a dangerous marsh; and a much smaller marsh at the southern end gives just enough room for the main road to Athens to pass between it and Mount Agrieliki. The plain is divided into two parts by the river Oenoe, a dry bed in summer; and up its valley a more mountainous way to Athens is possible. The Athenians arrived probably by this latter route to find the Persians already deployed on the beach in battle line, strongly supported by cavalry and archers. The Athenians lacked these latter arms. Their hoplites were equipped for close fighting only, the Persians for the opposite, where cavalry and archers with their long-range arrows would be most effective. Luckily the Athenian with the strongest personality in the group of ten generals who commanded on a daily rota, Miltiades, had had experience of Persian tactics while in the far north of Greece. Half of the Command were for waiting for the Spartans to arrive (Pheidippides had made his famous run from Athens to Sparta with the news of the emergency), and half for action the moment a possibility opened. Four of these generals saw in Miltiades the man of the hour, and handed over their command-day to him. But the threat of the Persian cavalry seemed to make an Athenian advance across the plain simple suicide. Plataeans arrived to reinforce the little army. In the night some brave Ionian Greeks from Asia Minor who had been press-ganged into the Persian army, reached the Athenians with the cheering news that the Persian cavalry had disappeared, perhaps to pasture and water in the northern marshes. At dawn Miltiades gave the order for a swift advance. When the Athenian army reached the barrage of arrows they doubled through it in a charge to close-quarter fighting, for which the Persians were so ill-equipped. In the 'National Gallery' of the ancient agora at Athens, the Stoa Poikile, Polygnotus painted the three phases of this famous victory. First, the close-quarter fighting, then the

68

crush and panic of the fleeing Persians as they were driven into the devouring marshes in the north, and finally the capture of seven of the Persian ships in the chaos of embarkation by the routed enemy. Aeschylus was among those who were portrayed in this scene. Despite the exhilaration and pride of the Athenians in their victory, an elation of spirit which was deep and lasting enough to maintain them on the summit for two generations, they gave the chief honour and thanksgiving to the gods who, they said, had appeared in the battle and helped them. One is reminded of the Angels of Mons in World War I.

The Persian fleet at once sailed round Sunium to land at Phaleron Bay, then the open port of Athens. As they sailed in, they saw the Athenian army, back from Marathon, ready for them twice in one day. That forced march in full armour immediately on top of an utterly exhausting close-quarter battle, was an achievement of the spirit as well as of the body as remarkable as the battle itself.

The mound, raised over the 192 men who died in the battle, is still there, forty feet high and two hundred yards in circumference. The Greeks excavated it in 1890 and found the ashes, charred bones and funeral vases of the dead, eight feet below the present level of the land. Pausanias says that 'every night you may hear horses neighing and men fighting' on the site of the battle. But he warns that to go on purpose to hear these ghostly echoes never brought good to any man. It is odd that the horses neigh, unless it be their cries of frustration that they took no part in the battle!

In the river valley, five miles away, the late Dr. Papadimitriou found the Cave of Pan, a cave with a number of galleries, and stalagmites and stalactites and rocks which Pausanias says are called 'Pan's herd of goats' since they have goat-like shapes. Pan was, it seems, worshipped here and in Attica after the battle, because of his effective appearance in it. But the cave was in use for burials and perhaps cult purposes in all phases of the Bronze Age; and Neolithic vases also were found. There was a gap in its use, however, from the end of the Mycenaean period down to the fifth century B.C. From then onwards till 60 B.C., perhaps for the reason given by Pausanias, the evidences of constant use are numerous all over the site in vases, figurines, lamps and inscriptions.

The plain of Marathon was the scene also of the successful struggle of Theseus to overcome the terrible 'Bull from the sea' which ravaged first Crete—as a punishment sent by Poseidon on King Minos because, though master of the Aegean Sea, he did not honour the god of the sea—and then the mainland of Greece. Mary Renault's novel *The Bull from the Sea* begins excitingly with this episode.

CHAPTER V

Delphi: The Spiritual Centre of Greece

For more than a thousand years, beginning at least as early as the eighth century B.C., a stream of pilgrims zigzagged their way on foot up the rough mountain path to Apollo's sanctuary at Delphi under snowy Parnassus. Many had made long voyages from Greek colonies across the sea, and faced expense and danger through their resolve to make the pilgrimage. Some were private citizens, others officials of their city-states, others again were ambassadors of foreign kings. But for all their differences, a common faith and hope united them. They all had plans or hopes for their future welfare: these they would set before the god of light, and Apollo would tell them, through his oracle, how they might best proceed. Greek states and even foreign kingdoms, like Lydia, might make war or peace, form an alliance, engage in some programme of major public works; a whole population even, like that of Athens in face of the Persian invasion, might evacuate a city; or a man might marry a particular girl, or emigrate to Sicily—all in the faith that Apollo had so guided.

There were other oracles in the Greek world: at Dodona in Epirus the oracle of Zeus was probably the most ancient of all oracles, while that of Zeus Ammon at Siwa in Egypt was of great repute. But Delphi was supreme—an extraordinary, powerful and fascinating institution, and one of the most formative influences in the rise and spread and stability of Greek civilization.

If some giant stage director had the power to move mountains, cut ravines and raise a precipice to make an awesome setting for

Delphi: The Spiritual Centre of Greece

Apollo's oracle, he could not have excelled the scene that nature set. The sanctuary (temenos) is built 1,800 feet up on a steep and narrow shelf on the lower slopes of Mount Parnassus: behind the buildings, the cliffs of the Phaedriades—the Shining Ones—form a 900-foot high perpendicular north wall. To the south the shelf ends abruptly and the olive groves take a dive to the deep Pleistos ravine below. The entire horizon is formed by mountains: across the Pleistos the grim rocky flank of Mount Kirphis rises sheer: to the south-west the peaks of Arcadia are visible across the Gulf of Corinth, while beyond the sea of olive-trees that submerges the whole plain of Krissa between Parnassus and the gulf, runs yet another range of mountains like a rampart in the western sky, guarding the valley-road to Amphissa and the far north. A tremendous panorama, 'a majestic god-touched setting for divination', as Charles Seltman put it.

When Charles Wordsworth, nephew of the poet and head-master of Harrow, was here in 1836, the only evidence he found of ancient building on the site beneath the cliffs was the outline of the stadium. The temple of Apollo, the Treasuries of the various States and many other buildings, not to mention the 3,000 statues which Pliny says were there in his time, all 'had vanished as though they had never been', leaving no vestige of stone behind them. The village of Castri in fact overlaid the sanctuary which had disappeared many feet below the surface in the gradual accumulation of debris inevitable in any human settlement where the Corporation dustman does not call and no main drain runs, and houses are made of sun-dried clay.

It was French enterprise, and French Government money, which recovered Delphi in the last quarter of the nineteenth century, but not without metaphorical dust and heat. The out-raged villagers saw no reason on earth—and, at this stage, none under it either—why they should leave their ancestral homes and move to the new village built by the foreigners half a mile away. In the face of this wrath, the dig was begun under the protection of a detachment of Greek soldiers. Excavation continues today, and still at the hands of the French. Their work has given us one of the greatest and most exciting of ancient Greek sites, and one which we can perhaps most easily rebuild in imagination from the foundations which we see and, in our mind's eye, people with the men and women who for so long gave meaning to the sanctuary, both those who served Apollo, his priests and priestesses and temple attendants, and those who came in faith.

The grandchildren of the once angry villagers of Castri seem now to be very well-pleased with things as they are: they have a village visited by all who come to Greece. One may sit on a hotel or café balcony, built daringly to overhang the Pleistos gorge, enjoy a drink earned by a climb to the stadium, and sometimes look *down* on the back of an eagle doing circuits over the river 1,800 feet below. There are always eagles in the Delphic sky, or at least what the Greeks call eagles. In the up-currents of air caused by the sun on the bright cliffs the progenitors of these modern eagles soared and circled, dived and glided when Apollo's altar smoked with sacrifice: and in a strangely effective way their offspring provide a continuity between then and now as vividly as do the ancient stones and columns, and bridge the gulf of time.

The site is divided horizontally by the road which runs up the valley to Arachova, high up on the far horizon on the watershed, and thence to Athens, and is divided also by the chasm in the cliffs where the Castalian spring still flows. The sanctuary and the Museum are above the road and some hundreds of yards to the west of Castalia; and the other part of the site, Marmaria, is below the road and an equal distance to the east of the famous spring. If we begin a visit to Delphi by drinking Castalia's waters, we shall be in line with ancient practice. The pilgrim of old both had a bath in it (or perhaps a ceremonial lustration), and drank from its stream. And here we hit upon one of the significant points about this wonderful institution. Those who were responsible for the temple and its worship made it clear that a merely external washing was of no avail: for it was the colour of the heart, the purity of mind, that mattered. In the long history of religions it can be seen that Man *vis-à-vis* his god or gods took a long time to learn the simple fact that 'truth in the inward parts' was of more value than a smoking hecatomb upon the grandest altar. 'Stranger,' the priests of Delphi warned, 'when you enter Apollo's sanctuary, be pure in mind. You may be pure, if you but touch the water of the stream. But the seas of all the world cannot wash clean a mind that is evil.' One of the wonders of Delphi is the level of its moral teaching.

When the road at Castalia was being widened in 1959, a fountain-house was discovered which dates from the sixth century B.C. and may prove to be the original Castalian spring of the early period. The ugly rock-cut tank higher up the cleft dates from Roman times.

Marmaria—'marble quarry'—is a sinister name indeed for an ancient site. Many such sites must have had that nickname in the bad old medieval days in Greece. Marmaria meant the place where anyone with a cart and a dissatisfaction with the earth floor of his little house could go and collect, free for the taking, fine square-cut marble blocks for his floor or his front-door step and architrave. Marmaria at Delphi suffered sadly from such pillagers. The Ionic Treasury of the Greek state of Marseilles survives only in foundation and in a single course of white marble, splendidly worked. The white marble circular tholos in the Doric style is another victim: a few columns and their entablature have been set up, but enough to declare its original beauty. The very short and steeply inclined echinus on the capital shows that the building dates from the Hellenistic period, which begins in the late fourth century. The purpose of this tholos is unknown. To judge from the rarity of circular buildings in Greek architecture it would seem that the circular plan had little appeal to the Greek eye. There was a tholos at Epidaurus, another in the Agora at Athens; Queen Arsinoe built one in the sanctuary in Samothrace, and Alexander the Great completed the family 'Folly' of the House of Macedon begun by Philip II at Olympia. There may, of course, be others still to be found.

At the eastern end of Marmaria is the foundation of an archaic temple of Athena Pronaia—that is, presumably, 'before the temple' of Apollo, in the sense of 'guardian'. Her temple, certainly, was the first of the sacred buildings to the pilgrim coming down the Arachova road, one of the three approaches. Herodotus refers to the destruction of this temple by a rock-fall in 480 B.C. The new temple was built further to the west. When excavated, fifteen of the archaic columns were found with the wide swelling echinus typical of the seventh and sixth centuries. But only a few of these survived another rock-fall in 1905: the huge boulders came to rest on the temple ruins.

Several hundred yards to the west and at a higher level is the Gymnasium area, enlarged in Roman times and provided with a practice running track on a now collapsed terrace. The circular plunge-bath for use after training by athletes entered for the Pythian Games is well preserved. These games were second only to the Olympic games in status.

At the main entrance to the walled sanctuary above the road is a small agora, an open space once surrounded by shops: what survives is of Roman workmanship. Here, doubtless, the pilgrims bought the sort of things which tourists buy today, cool drinks and souvenirs, and something else which ancient Greeks used in enormous quantities in all their holy places—little votive offerings, small models and images of bronze or terracotta— and how useful these almost indestructible objects are to the archaeologist who examines their styles, compares them with others and so can often use them to reveal a date.

The paved Sacred Way zigzags uphill and on either hand are the foundations of memorials set up by various States to commemorate victories, or the remains of the so-called Treasuries which many States built there as their pavilions or headquarters. A man from Siphnos, for instance, would report to the Siphnian Treasury and make his appointment with the oracle. Siphnos had rich gold-mines and a specially splendid little building on the Sacred Way. The sculptured frieze from it in the Delphi Museum is one of the most beautiful and best preserved treasures of Archaic art. Pedimental sculpture from this Treasury shows Herakles trying to carry off the sacred tripod and Apollo wresting it from him.

The Athenian Treasury has been rebuilt: it stands at the first turn in the Sacred Way. It looks exactly as the simplest form of temple looked—a rectangular temple in antis, as the architects call one with a porch supported on two Doric columns and on the projecting ends of the long walls. Pausanias, the invaluable antiquary and traveller who wrote detailed descriptions of the famous sites in A.D. 175, says it was built by the Athenians in memory of the defeat of the Persians at Marathon. Some of its stones, which like many thousands of the stones at Delphi are covered with neatly cut inscriptions, were recovered far down towards the Pleistos ravine where earthquakes and the steepness of the slope had sent them tumbling. In the Museum are marble stones from this building inscribed with the Hymn to Apollo set to music, telling how Apollo slew the great snake.

True, the music is late in date, for there is a reference to the attack on Delphi by Gauls which we know occurred in B.C. 279; but it is Greek music, and has been successfully transcribed for modern reproduction on the flute. In 1955, in mist and rain, a chorus of Greek girls from Athens, dressed in the ancient Attic dress, danced in the theatre at Delphi to the somewhat mournful notes of this music—if their stately, almost monumental movement can be described as dancing. And the rain-sodden audience watched and listened, thrilled to feel this living link with an ancient festival across more than two millennia.

The polygonal construction of the long wall which comes into view as the corner is turned, is an anti-earthquake device. Every angle or curve in each stone is fitted with extreme skill into the complementary angle or curve of its neighbour. The whole length of this superb wall is covered by some 700 inscriptions, a register of freed slaves, and a record of decisions by the Council who supervised the sanctuary. The wall, the finest of its kind, is sixth-century work. The delicately designed porch which stood against one section of it was an Athenian war memorial.

The incongruous outcrop of rock between the Treasury and the polygonal wall was left in its crude state in classical times, like a rough boulder in the middle of an exhibition of sculpture, because this was the reputed spot where the Sibyl once uttered prophecies. The Sibyls were mantic itinerants, unattached to any temple, who moved about the country like the earliest 'unofficial' prophets of the Old Testament: their frenzy was popularly regarded as the sign of divine 'possession'.

Of the temple of Apollo, last of a series and dating from the close of the fourth century B.C., only the base and six severely eroded columns, re-erected by the French, are left. But the massiveness of these stones, the great length of the building, and its dominant position on the high terrace conjure up an impressive picture. As he approached the ramp at the eastern end, the worshipper was confronted with the daunting command, inscribed probably upon the architrave, 'KNOW THYSELF': and across the face of the western end the maxim which embodies one of the Greeks' highest values—a deliberate self-control and moderation—'NOTHING IN EXCESS'. The altar of sacrifice outside the Temple to the east has recently been restored. It is of blue 'Eleusinian marble', really a limestone.

Delphi: The Spiritual Centre of Greece

On another terrace high above the temple is a comparatively small theatre, and higher still, though approached by a well-graded path, is the stadium. Here the athletes competed in the Pythian games, presenting their bodies developed and trained to the pitch of perfection in honour of the god. Today the stadium, close under the towering cliffs, surrounded by trees and shrubs of many kinds, carpeted in spring with flowers, is a place of peace and beauty not to be expected in a stadium at all.

How did it all begin? Who chose such a difficult building site, so hard of access, subject to rock-falls, liable to earthquakes? No one in their senses. If we are to attach importance to the tradition reported by Plutarch, Pausanias and Diodorus, we shall believe that the site was fixed by an extraordinary phenomenon experienced first by a single goat-herd and then by all who went to see what he described. He was searching for a lost goat and when he came upon it in a chasm below the cliffs, he found the goat 'possessed' in some awesome frenzy. Instantly the goat-herd, too, was himself 'possessed' by some demonic force and began to utter prophecies. This was strange enough, but wonder grew when others, going to the same spot, were also subject to the same 'possession'. Men felt that here they had contact with a mysterious and tremendous power that could only be divine: and the steep mountain-shelf became a holy place where they believed deity had chosen to have contact with mortal man and to speak his will.

The first established oracle was that of GE, mother-earth, who sustains all things living and embraces them in death: and Delphi was earth's centre, its very navel. Did the sanctuary not hold this precious rock-navel, inscribed with her name 'GES' (of earth), which marked the centre? For Zeus had loosed two eagles from the furthest poles and where they met in flight, there was Earth's navel. An ugly barrel-like stone at the head of the Museum stairs looks like a late edition of the earlier stone perhaps destroyed in one of the calamities which fell at intervals upon Delphi. The worship of Mother Earth appears to date from Minoan days and to spring from that civilization in Crete somewhere about 1600 B.C. Minoan religion was centred upon an Earth-goddess. Snakes are obvious representatives of an underground Earth deity. Snakes appear in the hands of the goddess in Minoan statuettes in Crete: and at Delphi the great snake, Python, lived. In Minoan religious symbolism pairs of birds, heraldically opposed, appear: at Delphi a pair of gold eagles were part of the oracle's regalia. The labrys, the double-axe, was an essential part of religious furniture in Crete: at Delphi the priestly family were the Labryadae. Yet for all these pointers to a Minoan origin, the only material contact with Crete found in the sanctuary excavations is a solitary Minoan drinking vessel, shaped like a lion's head, and precisely similar to one found in the Minoan palace at Knossos in Crete. A Minoan stratum may yet be found, but not below the sanctuary, for excavation has gone to bed-rock. Meanwhile, a large amount of Mycenaean pottery and numerous votive offerings in the form of stylized female figures have been found deep under Apollo's altar and under the archaic temple of Athena Pronaia in the lower site of Marmaria. Some of these are in the long gallery of the Museum and one, dating from about 1500 B.C., shows a nude female figure—nudity in this period was reserved for divinity—seated on a three-legged chair. So the Delphic tripod dates its ancestry back before the Conqueror.

The Conqueror was Apollo. He had to kill the she-dragon before he could set up his oracle in a place already found to be holy. He arrived from Olympus probably in the immigration known as the Dorian Invasion about 1100 B.C., and asserted his authority and his skill as an archer. 'Oh! thou who givest mortal men unfailing trusty oracles, they sing at thy festival of how thou didst seize the sacred tripod, piercing with thy arrows the writhing coils of the monstrous snake.' So went the festal song at the annual dramatic commemoration of the great god's coming. Apollo was to become the most Greek of all the gods, and in their thoughts of him the Greeks reveal to us many of their highest values. They claimed that he was born at Delos. Yet he is probably of Asiatic origin. His title is Lukeios—of Lycia, i.e. of wolf-land. Leto, his mother's name, is thought to be a corruption of Lada, the Lycian for 'woman'. Certainly Apollo was held in great respect by the Ionian Greeks of Western Asia Minor. But whatever his origin, Asiatic or Hyperborean—from the far north—he was swiftly hellenized and, more than that, his seniority in the ranks of the Olympians was considerably back-dated. After his birth he made an official entry to Olympus and,

Delphi: The Spiritual Centre of Greece

with the exception, of course, of Zeus and also of his mother Leto, everyone stood up!

In art Apollo is seen as the ideal of young but developed manhood, beautifully balanced, neither too muscular nor the opposite, and with an inward balance, visible in his expression, to match the mastery his fine body shows. He is calm, purposeful, and clearly in command. The pediment sculpture at Olympia shows all this; and we see there Apollo bringing order out of chaos with a gesture and an expression which is at once calm, authoritative and benevolent. He is a god of light and of law: of music and of archery, one who helps and who heals. But he punishes the law-breaker, for Apollo is clearly a highly civilized and civilizing god and civilization depends on a sound code of laws and an appropriate constitution. So Apollo, through his oracle at Delphi, was active in the setting up of legal codes and in the framing of constitutions. The Greeks, for instance, believed that the constitution of Sparta was proposed to Lycurgus by the oracle at Delphi. The codification of law clearly marks a decisive advance in the development of society. For life is certain misery for the ordinary man if uncertainty as to the law prevails, as it did when only the kings or the mighty in their fortresses knew it and applied it.

Above all, Apollo was a god of prophecy, in the sense that through his oracle human beings believed that they could have their perplexities unravelled and be given divine direction in times of crisis. Unless the utterances of the oracle were on the whole helpful, it is not conceivable that the institution could have lasted a thousand years. Plutarch, himself a priest of Delphi, used this argument of success to support the authenticity of the oracle. 'The oracle has filled the whole sanctuary with the votive offerings and gifts of thanksgiving from barbarians and Greeks alike.' And that no one could gainsay.

The voice through which Apollo's wisdom was thought to come was that of the Pythian priestess. In a cell under the temple she sat on a tripod, where once ran the Cassotis stream: and by her side were the twin golden eagles of Zeus, a statue of Apollo and the tomb of Dionysus (whom Apollo had admitted as a working partner for some months of the year). The priestess on duty was always a middle-aged village woman of religious inclinations and ready to believe that Apollo would use her as his mouthpiece to announce his divine will. She chewed poisonous leaves, and this combination of readiness to serve the god and the effect of cyanide of potassium (in minute doses) produced, it appears, sounds which generally required interpretation by the priest, who doubtless believed that Apollo guided his mind in this sacred duty. After an interval, perhaps of days, the answer was given, generally in hexameter verse. To objectors who said that the verses were often crude and unworthy of the god who was president of the Muses and whose verse one could reasonably expect to surpass that of Homer himself, Plutarch again had the answer. 'Neither the voice, nor the language, nor the metre is of a god: they are the woman's. But the god lights her soul in regard to what will be. What else is inspiration but this?'

The fact must be accepted that Delphi won the respect of men of all ranks from Socrates, Plato, Aristotle, foreign kings, and city councils, down to simple souls who saved the money to journey there to ask about a farm. Delphi had won that reverence by its performance. Even the Christians, in its latest and weakest days, did not deny this performance but declared that the Delphic miracle was of the Devil.

If, however, we look back to earlier days, we may think that we can discover one firm reason for success among much that remains a mystery, in no way less so when the attempt is made by some to explain it all away by using such labels as 'extrasensory perception'. Let us then consider one set of causes for Delphi's great repute. Delphi became, for the Greeks of the whole Mediterranean, metaphorically in the spiritual sphere what it had claimed to be geographically—the centre of the world. And Apollo, god of prophecy, proved himself a panhellenic deity ranking only just below Zeus. This panhellenic character of Delphi is important: for the Greek passion for freedom and for individualism was so excessive that every city wall enclosed a separate state. Under the handicap of this splintering compulsion, the Greeks as a people could never reach their full potential. The few extra-mural institutions where Greek could meet Greek panhellenically won immense support, for they supplied a need, unconscious perhaps but real. Delphi, Olympia, Eleusis, Delos and a few other centres drew Greeks from everywhere.

The influence of the Delphic oracle reached an early peak in the eighth to the sixth centuries B.C., in the age of colonization. Hammond, in his new Greek History, lists 159 Greek colonies founded in those centuries and covering the full extent of the Mediterranean and the Black Sea. To a very large number of these colonists Apollo will have contributed either advice as to the site or a recommendation of the worship of a certain god or goddess as a condition of a colony's success. Colonists did not take the interest of Apollo lightly: indeed they thought of him as their leader; and there was a never-ending flow of embassies to Delphi from across the seas, giving thanks for successful ventures and saying it with statues, or seeking further advice if unsuccessful.

But Delphi gained much more than costly marbles in this thanksgiving traffic. There was an invisible import of high value which was part of the secret of its long influence. The priests, in their contacts with Greeks from everywhere, gained such a knowledge of affairs, political, economic, geographical and social, as no other corporate body in Greece could possess. There was therefore in most cases a factual basis in this Bureau of Information—this Statistical Register—upon which the priests could build an answer, or construct a reasoned judgment on many of the problems presented. Nor is there any reason to doubt that in using their brains on the information available the priests felt they were carrying out the will of Apollo.

There were ups and downs in the oracle's prestige: much was lost, and lost for long, when in the Persian Wars Apollo's oracle advised submission to the barbarian. 'Wretches, why sit ye still? Flee to the ends of the earth. All is lost—get ye away from the sanctuary!' Herodotus, in quoting this, adds: 'Even the terrible oracles which reached the Athenians from Delphi and struck fear into their hearts, failed to persuade them to abandon Hellas to its fate. They had the courage to be faithful to the land and await the coming of the foe.'

Curiously enough in view of the timidity of Delphi in the face of the Persians, the monument of Greek victory was set up in Apollo's sanctuary. This was the serpent column of three intertwined snakes whose heads supported a golden tripod, while in the lower coils were inscribed the names of the states that fought together. Much of this column, taken off to Constantinople as loot by Constantine the Great, still stands in the Hippodrome there.

Delphi: The Spiritual Centre of Greece

In the Peloponnesian War Delphi sided with the Spartans. But in none of the oracle's decisions does Delphi gain more honour than in the Priestess's response to the Spartan embassy sent in the hour of final victory over their bitter enemy and rival. With Athens prostrate, Sparta asked if she should now destroy her enemy and level Athens to the ground. Apollo answered, 'It is not your duty to destroy the central hearth—the undying fire and flame—of Hellas.' No ambiguity in that answer, worthy of a god.

In the Museum at Delphi

Of special interest or beauty—if a short selection must be made—are:

(a) *The Charioteer*, one of the finest of classical bronze figures; offered by POLYZALOS of GELA in Sicily in 478 B.C. in memory of his brother's victory in the chariot race.

(b) *Bronze Relief of the head of a dog*—a melancholy but lovely fragment.

(c) *Little terracotta goddess seated on a tripod, circa* 1500 B.C.

(d) *The archaic VIth-century frieze of the Siphnian Treasury.* The clever composition of this battle between the Gods and the Giants leads the eye from left to right: and we move gaily into the combat with the gods and goddesses, answering to the 'archaic grin' of Apollo and Artemis and the others as they draw their bows and hurl their spears so happily. Archaic sculpture at its high point.

(e) *Marble Statue of the athlete AGIAS by Lysippus (floruit* 328 B.C.). This is a contemporary marble copy of the original bronze statue, but gives a good idea, especially in the head, of how force of character could be combined with technical perfection by a master hand.

(f) *Metope of a group of oxen*, found in the Sicyonian Treasury. This again is archaic work of the VIth century, and is an outstanding example of a very early and successful attempt to compose a rhythmic marching pattern, which would be acceptable in the most 'modernist' quarters.

(g) *Greek musical notation* on a block of marble from the Treasury of the Athenians.

CHAPTER VI

Delos: The Holy Island of the Aegean

Delos, the holy island of the Aegean, in spring is awash with wild flowers: sheets of purple vetch and pale mauve statice, deep blue anchusa and pink mallow, campion and dwarf yellow yarrow, and the dark red poppy which shows up brilliantly against the white marble of the ruined city. All are there in fantastic abundance. Callimachus, the Greek poet of the third century, emphasized another aspect of the island. 'Swept by the gales and grey lies Delos in the midst of the waves.' Wind-swept at times Delos certainly can be, but in the spring one walks this little granite island with a light foot on cushions of colour and revelling in the clean sea breeze. In summer all is burnt brown, but the blue sea remains a glorious background to the ancient white marble city set close to its shore. This is the season when the north wind is apt to rush down the Aegean towards Egypt to fill up the low pressure region there: for Egypt's hot air rises. And then the 'meltemi' winds make a landing at Delos difficult. But even these fierce northerlies bring some benefit, for they have long ago blown away the dust and the insects too. Delos is, and has been for at least fourteen hundred years, an uninhabited island, for the Museum curator and his assistants, together with the staff of the blessed café adjacent (who does not need revival after even the best of museums?) can hardly be classed as inhabitants. So to 'no dust' and 'no insects' we can add 'no roads, no vehicles and no people'. We, and the lizards, share the solitude with the Shades as we wander through their ancient homes. Strangely, we find them warm and almost living still. Nowhere in all Greece is it easier to bring the dead to life than in the houses, big and small, crowded together on the slopes to the theatre.

Delos is the hub of the wheel of the Cycladean islands, the smallest but in history much the most important of them all. From the easily reached summit of its one real hill, Mount Cynthus (370 feet), the encircling islands almost fill the horizon. To the north-east lies Mykonos, looking large and mountainous, its whole length peppered with white spots: these are some of its hundreds of little white-washed chapels, vowed to the Almighty in return for survival from the rage of the sea by fearful seamen in past days. Tinos is visible to the north and if, in the days of sail, a cloud formed and hung over its eastern peak, the visitor on Delos could expect to have to stay where he was until the coming meltemi blew itself out, as Cicero explained in a letter to Atticus. In the north-west, Andros, and, in the west, Syros continue the long count of islands. To the south-west lie Siphnos, once rich in gold mines and, beyond it, Melos. Paros and Naxos to the south and south-east, with Ios between and beyond them, complete the ring of major islands. On a clear day the panorama is superb.

Delos, three miles long and less than one mile wide, lies with its axis north and south. A narrow channel divides it from Rheneia, the island adjacent to the west; and in this channel two small rocky islets act as breakwaters against the heavy seas brought in by the summer northerlies. Thanks to this partial protection, the Delians could build moles and quays, the 'sacred harbour' and the commercial harbour, and make the most of their favourable position in the centre of the Hellenic world, half-way between the mainland of Greece and the Ionian cities on the Asia Minor coast: half-way, too, between Egypt or Syria and the Black Sea. No wonder the little island was to become 'the common mart of all Greece' as Strabo called it.

But we anticipate events: Delos begins with its god. The island was Apollo's birthplace. Zeus himself moored this hitherto roving island with adamantine chains, says tradition, that it might be a secure resting-place for Leto for the birth of Apollo and Artemis. So Apollo's birthplace became a centre of his worship and Delos a meeting-place of Ionian Greeks from Asia Minor and the mainland of Greece; for Apollo was very much at home in the hearts of Ionian Greeks from the twelve cities on the western fringe of Asia Minor. Actually, whether his origin lies in Asia Minor or in the lands far to the north of Greece, the land of the Hyperboreans, is still in dispute.

The Homeric Hymn to Apollo describes his festival: 'Many temples and woody groves and all heights and jutting capes of lofty hills are dear to thee, and rivers that flow to the sea. But in Delos, O Apollo, does thy heart the most rejoice. There, in thy honour, the long-robed Ionians gather together with their children and their noble wives. They delight thee and celebrate thee with boxing and dancing and song whenever they hold festival. A man would say that they were immortal and free for ever from old age who should visit them when the Ionians were gathered together: for he would see the grace of them all, and rejoice his heart seeing the men and the fair-girdled women and their swift ships and their many possessions' (Sir Richard Jebb).

Thus Delos begins as a magnet drawing Greeks together in common worship. But this unifying characteristic of Delos spread from worship to the political field, and the Confederacy of Delos in the fifth century B.C. joined many of the islands and states of Greece together in joint defence against another Persian threat. One might call this the N.A.T.O. of the day.

Athens was the leader in this sensible movement and Aristides 'the Just' its statesman-promoter. The arrangement was that those islands which had considerable fleets, like Samos and Lesbos, would provide ships and crews, while the lesser islands would pay a contribution of money in lieu. This treasure was kept at Delos in the care of Apollo in his temple. But after some years an Athenian expedition against Egypt, then in Persian hands, suffered a disastrous defeat, losing about 100 ships. This naval loss put Athenian command of the Aegean in jeopardy and Samos proposed the transfer of the common treasure from Delos to the safety of the Acropolis at Athens. This may be history, but not as Pericles' enemies saw it. They declared that Pericles had no excuse for the transference, but that this was an act of tyranny in the eyes of Greece and the greatest disgrace to the Athenians. This looks like an example of hind-sight on the part of Plutarch who reported the argument 500 years later. If Samos proposed the transfer, at least it is certain that now came a turning point in the attitude of Athens to her allies. The Confederacy was twisted by Athens into

Empire, and Empire of a tyrannous kind. Delos was now under Athenian control: Athenian officials ran Apollo's shrine, and his festival, with new and magnificent ceremonial.

In the early part of the Peloponnesian War Athens was ravaged by plague and her war effort seriously impaired. People remembered an ancient but long-forgotten oracle which forbade burial on Apollo's sacred island, and assumed that the plague was Apollo's expression of anger at the neglect of the oracle. So every known tomb and grave was opened, and the remains of the dead with the usual vases and other grave furniture were thrown into a common burial pit on Rheneia (the vases, mended, are now in the Mykonos Museum) and henceforward it became an offence either to die or to be born on the sacred island: the pregnant and the dying had to be conveyed across the channel to Rheneia. No good assuring the sick man that this was just a change of air: he knew that soon after this first crossing the grimmer ferryman, Charon, would take him on another.

It was not until the ascendancy in the Eastern Mediterranean of the Ptolemies of Egypt that Delos escaped from Athenian control and felt fully free. From 314 B.C. to 166 B.C. was her finest period, when gifts and dedicatory offerings to Apollo poured into his sanctuary from all parts of the Hellenistic world. But the gain was not only to Apollo. For the centripetal genius of this tiny island was acting in a third field. Delos was becoming a commercial centre of high importance, and the long line of warehouses and quays stretching nearly a mile along the west shore attests it. Some of these 'go-downs' are now only dimly seen below the water, for the coastline has sunk on this western side. So many were the foreign merchants that they built their own temples to their gods: the Egyptians to Serapis and the Egyptian gods at the foot of Mount Cynthus: the Jews had their synagogue in a position somewhat aloof from the Gentiles, on the eastern side of the island: and the Syrian merchants too had their sanctuary.

When Roman Mummius destroyed the greatest commercial centre of all, the city of Corinth, in 146 B.C., Delos was well equipped to take over her lost trade and add it to her own. The island burgeoned as never before.

From the many hundreds of marble inscriptions which have been recovered, the wide area of Delos' influence may be well gauged. For instance, the names are recorded of citizens of eighty-nine states in all parts of the Mediterranean to whom the Senate and People of Delos voted the privilege of becoming a proxenos or public guest, with special rights of honour and of land tenure in the island. There were towards the end of this period very large numbers of Italian merchants living in the city, for Roman power was growing and spreading everywhere. These Italians built their own large so-called agora, in reality an impressively large quadrangular portico and shopping-centre. Delos was proud of its unique position as a centre of trade— proud that, in the season, ten thousand slaves a day could be sold in her slave market, as Strabo says.

But the day of her doom was near. Mithridates, a powerful Asia Minor prince, in rebellion against the power of Rome now intruding into his domains, saw Delos as in effect a rich Roman city, and he sent his fleet to destroy it. Surprise was complete: Menophanes, his admiral, killed the men, carried off the women to slavery and, we are told, 'razed the city to the ground'. There certainly was a period of at least partial restoration, but in Pausanias' day, about A.D. 160, Delos was, he says, uninhabited. He had been commenting on the ruins of Megalopolis, describing the loss of all its beauty and old prosperity and added, 'I am not in the least surprised as I know that Heaven is always willing something new and that all things are being changed by Fortune. Again Delos, once the common mart of Greece, has now no Delian inhabitant.' But in early Byzantine times there were at least a few people probably engaged in salvage on the island; for there are the remains of a very small Byzantine Church close to the agora, with its apse holding the seats of the elders behind the altar, as in the early days was usual. And close to the waterfront a Christian householder, determined to have the symbols of his faith clear over his front door in the island so long sacred to Apollo, cut a cross into the marble in an amateurish way and, with it, a lamb to represent the second person of the Trinity and a crude dove for the third. He also carved a fish, for the five letters of the Greek word for 'fish' are the initial letters of the five words in Greek which mean 'Jesus Christ, of God the Son, Saviour'. It was an exciting moment when, wandering through the narrow streets of the Roman city nearest to the mole, I lighted upon this little domestic challenge to the old pagan gods made by a faithful Christian on the lonely island. His marble architrave now lay on the ground: but it was set off by a cluster of poppies and these danced happily in the wind and sun and gave the stone for me the value of an altar to the Living God.

Delos is the best preserved of all the ancient cities of Greece, and such is the area and the diversity of the site that it falls into seven clear-cut divisions:

1. The Precinct of Apollo and the temple of Artemis.
2. To the north of these, the Agora of the Italians, the terrace of the Lions, the 'Lake', the club-house of the Syrian merchant-guild under Poseidon's protection, and a group of Roman houses.
3. To the south of Apollo's precinct is the Theatre Quarter, Roman streets, shops and houses with the theatre at the end of the main street.
4. Mount Cynthus and its ancient cave sanctuary of Apollo (or is this a structure of Hellenistic date too artfully apeing antiquity?).
5. On the terrace below Mount Cynthus and above and along the ravine known as Inopus, the temples of the Syrian and of the Egyptian gods and more rich houses.
6. On the east side of the island approached by the path just to the north of the Museum and café and distant 600 yards, the gymnasium, the stadium, and a suburb of houses.
7. Along the western shore of the island, the warehouses and quays of the commercial harbour.

The landing today is at a modern mole close to the old sacred harbour and made up of the spoil from the French excavations of the site. If a cruising ship is in the Bay, the path to the Agora is bordered by the bright colours of scarves and carpets, shirts and blouses, skirts and hats and sweaters, brought over in caiques from Mykonos and laid out for sale on the grass and flowers in the most enticing way. He would be an unusually single-minded enthusiast for antiquities who marched to the site with eyes averted from these typical and charming Greek 'souvenirs' and those who sell them. Business is still brisk in the holy island.

The landing mole gives onto a big paved square known as the Agora of the Competaliastae, a union of Roman freedmen and slaves. It is thought by some to have been the old slave market. From here the sacred way, bordered on the left by a fine colonnade given by Philip V of Macedon and once lined with statues, leads north to the propylaea or gateway to Apollo's sanctuary. This large precinct includes the foundations of his three temples, the earliest of the sixth century B.C., with those also of the temple of Artemis, and of a large number of other buildings and porticoes. It is hard to follow the outlines of this complex of sanctuary buildings, but there is enjoyment in the quality of the marble blocks and their incredibly new and clean-cut lines and surfaces. An occasional herm, and Doric columns fully fluted and with no bases, show that this is the Greek and not the Roman section of the city; for Doric-style columns made by the Romans always had bases. In the early days of Apollo's worship the people of Naxos made two dedications of special interest. Parts of their famous twenty-four-foot high statue of Apollo which they set up to greet the pilgrim to Delos, are still in the sanctuary. The statue survived for two thousand years as we can see in a traveller's sketch of the fifteenth century, but evidently an attempt was made to carry it away and it was smashed to pieces in the process. For the enormous block of marble which was its base is now some thirty yards away from the fragment of torso and part of a thigh which is all that remains on the site in the sanctuary. One hand is in the central gallery of the Museum.

The other Naxian dedication is in the second division of the site, to the north of the sanctuary. This is an impressive row of archaic sculptured lions sitting on their haunches, on everlasting guard by the sacred lake where Leto gave birth to the twin deities. Five of the original nine lions are still on guard. A sixth was carried away by the Venetians in the seventeenth century and is sentry at the entrance to the Arsenal in Venice.

The tall-standing Doric columns, with the lower third of each unfluted in the economical Roman fashion (for the sharp edges of Doric flutes are vulnerable) are part of a peristyle in the courtyard of the Beirut shipowners and merchants, the Poseidoniastae. Their building included a chapel to the goddess Roma.

There are several excellent Roman houses in this northern section and a palaestra or physical training school.

The third division, to the south of Apollo's sanctuary and on the right as one enters from the landing mole into the Agora, or market-place, and begins to climb the slope to the theatre and ultimately to Mount Cynthus, contains a large number of shops and the best of the Roman houses. This so-called Theatre Quarter is full of interest and worth a long exploration. Some of the shops still contain what might be called heavy fixtures, vats, marble tables, olive presses, or heavy storage vessels for grain or oil. Between some of the shops a narrow passage will lead into the splendid courtyard or atrium of a rich man's house, with its columns surrounding a shallow impluvium surfaced in mosaic. These impluvia would, it seems, normally have had a few inches only of rain-water in them and this, of course, would well show up the mosaic design, but they are really decorative tank tops, for under all these mosaic surfaces there are deep water tanks cut into the rock. The best of the big houses are those of Dionysus, of the Trident, and beyond and above the theatre, of the Masks and of the Dolphins. The houses get their names from their mosaic floors; two of these are quite exceptionally fine and show Dionysus riding his tiger and, in the House of the Masks, his panther. The design of the Roman house with its central atrium open to the sky lets in air and light and sun but keeps out cold draughts. The Delian houses were of two and occasionally three storeys: all, small as well as big, had drainage connected with the main street sewer system.

The masonry of the theatre outside walls is an excellent example of how the Greeks enjoyed a well-made, well-fitted marble wall: no mortar to hold the stones together; only precision of workmanship, sharp edges to the blocks, a perfect fit, and, out of sight, clamps of bronze, lead or iron.

Mount Cynthus, in the fourth division of the site, is approached up the slope of the old processional way to the slight traces of the temple of Zeus and Athena on the summit. Much of the marble of this temple lies in confusion on the upper slopes of the hill, but there is a late inscription in place on the summit. One climbs Mount Cynthus for the distant view and for the almost airborne sight of the ruins and lay-out of the ancient city below. But half-way up the hill, some fifty yards to the right of the path shortly before it bends, there is a cave sanctuary which was formerly held by many to be perhaps the oldest shrine of Apollo in Greece and to date from Mycenaean times. But the construction of the 'pent-house' roof with its pairs of stones notched into grooves cut in the cave walls tells heavily in favour of a much more sophisticated period of civilization when it was the fashion to copy the archaic in sculpture, and perhaps also in this sort of archaizing 'folly'.

At the foot of Mount Cynthus and to the north—our fifth division of the site—lies another sanctuary area: first, that of Hera, the older foundations dating from the end of the eighth century B.C. and the newer from the fifth, and then close on the north and on the west of the little Hera precinct, the larger establishment of the Egyptian gods with its sixty-yard-long portico round the big court of the Serapion, its temple still containing a now headless statue of Isis. Further to the north is the precinct of the Syrian goddess Atargartis. At a lower level approached by a staircase is the big reservoir of the Inopus gorge, and close to it an earlier shrine of Serapis, with more Roman houses nearby.

For those who have made several visits to this huge site of Delos, it will be worth-while to go across to the east side of the island by the path which leads past the Museum café, to the sixth division of the site, to visit the Gymnasium (in the continental sense), the Stadium and the little suburb of houses close to it. The building nearest to the shore is the Jewish synagogue. There is also an impressive 'works' of some sort in this quarter: a building with marble columns and a fine courtyard, so that though from its many deep bins it is clear that some manufacturing process went on in it, the factory was beautifully housed and no eyesore to the beauty of this stretch of coast.

The seventh division consists of the long line of warehouses and quays running south along the shore for nearly a mile. Many of these structures are submerged by the sinking of the coastline; and a lively imagination is needed to see the lines of cargo vessels from the distant ports of the Mediterranean lying to anchor and with their sterns made fast to the quays, unloading cargoes from their home-ports and then filling up again with the produce of some distant land; every ship adding to the wealth of Delos, sadly short-lived though this wealth proved to be.

From a Greek anthology of the first or early second century A.D., comes this passage describing the personified island's sorrow at the passing of the days of its glory:

'Would I were still drifting before the breath of all winds,

Delos: The Holy Island of the Aegean

rather than that I had been stayed to shelter homeless Leto.
Then had I not so greatly mourned my poverty. Ah! woe is me:
how many Greek ships sail past me, Delos the desolate, whom
once men worshipped. Hera is avenged on me for Leto, with
vengeance late but sore' (translated by Jebb).

The Museum at Delos is small but interesting. The central
hall contains Greek sculpture, most of it archaic; in the many
Kouroi on the one side of the hall and in the Korai on the other
can be read the gradual development of the sculptured male and
female figure from rudimentary origins: and the Egyptian influence of early days is obvious.

The hall on the left carries the development of sculpture
through classical down to Hellenistic and Roman times. Here
too are a number of funeral stelai, bronzes and portrait heads.

It is the right-hand hall which perhaps holds the chief interest.
The typical vases of many periods are set out clearly: the Corinthian with their decorative designs taken from textiles and
oriental carpets, their sphinxes, chimaeras and other unlikely
creatures also reminiscent of oriental art: the black-figured vases
of Attica with their figures from mythology: the red-figured of
the fifth and fourth centuries: the rough unexciting pottery of the
later period, when the terracotta figurines begin to supplant
vases in their interest and charm.

There is a case—the first on the left—which contains several
ivories of Mycenaean work. A soldier standing and holding his
spear and figure-of-eight shield, his head thrown proudly back
so that the line of nose and forehead is horizontal, is an arresting
figure, perfectly fitting the frame of the design. He wears a
helmet of boar-tusks, as described by Homer. Another ivory of
superlative design shows a lion and a griffin in mortal combat.

In this same hall is collected the apparatus of domestic life;
jewellery, kitchen stoves which burnt charcoal, the shopkeepers'
measuring tables for liquids, samples of wall decoration of
Roman houses, their lamps, some of thirty or forty 'wick-
power', and other domestic paraphernalia.

CHAPTER VII

Olympia and the Games

*'Many and wonderful are the sights and the stories
to be seen and heard in Greece: but to an exceptional
degree one feels the hand of the gods in the Eleusinian
Mysteries and in the Olympic Games.'*

This is how Pausanias introduces his description of the sanctuary at Olympia and, departing from his usual technique of describing each building and statue in turn in the logical order as he entered the ancient site, he begins with a description of the central feature, the temple. For Olympia was the chief sanctuary in Greece of Zeus, 'father of gods and men'. So Homer called him and all Greeks reverenced him. A king among gods, he was the protector of kings in early days: then he became the chief civic god, protector of states and households. His throne was on Mount Olympus, the highest peak—nearly 10,000 feet—of all the many mountains in Greece, in the north on the borders of Thessaly and Macedonia: and a suitable place that was for a sky-god whose power controlled the weather. The lightning flash was the sheen on the blades of his double-axe when he whirled it in anger. But he had his sanctuary in a more genial spot, in the pleasant smiling countryside, in the rich low valley where the river Cladeus joins the bigger Alpheus, towards the north-west of the Peloponnese, twenty miles from the port of Katakolo.

As at Delphi, the sanctity of Olympia dated from prehistoric days. Tradition said that here was another oracle of the Earth goddess. Excavation has certainly revealed a Bronze Age occupation of the site, some five feet below the level of the earliest

Greek building, which is the seventh-century temple of Hera. The foundations of two of these Bronze Age apsidal houses are visible in shallow pits a few yards to the east of Hera's temple. The fact that in the temple of Hera there was a sculptured figure of a standing Zeus by the side of seated Hera, as Pausanias saw, suggests that this unusual posture of Zeus was a neat concession by the newly-arrived sky-god and his consort Hera to the dignity of the original but superseded Earth-goddess.

Again as at Delphi, Olympia attracted Greeks from everywhere and the festival in Zeus' honour, held once every four years, was a panhellenic occasion of such sanctity and importance that not even wars were allowed to break the sequence which continued for over a thousand years, from 776 B.C. to A.D. 393, when the Christian Emperor Theodosius closed the sanctuary, for the Games themselves were an integral part of the worship of Zeus.

The Altis—the Grove, as the sanctuary was called—lay on the flat valley floor at the confluence of the rivers and immediately below the steep conical hill of Kronos on the north side. This hill, bare of trees in antiquity, was a convenient grandstand from which to see all that went on inside the walled rectangular sanctuary below. The spectators could watch the splendid processions of priests and officials, of the attendants with the animals for sacrifice, of the athletes and the chariots and horses entered for the races, and of the ambassadors from many states: and as in turn each athlete or chariot team passed the rostrum, they would hear the herald proclaim the name of the competitor, his father's name and that of his city. They could watch the sacrifice on the altar of Zeus and see the blood poured on the traditional tomb of Pelops—a grim ceremony which marked the opening of the festival. The mound is still visible between the temples of Hera and Zeus, but when excavated was found to contain no evidence of a burial at any time.

Ancient opinion differed as to whether Pisa, the area in which the sanctuary lay, or nearby Elis originally controlled the festival, but it is known that Pisa lost control to Elis in 580 B.C. The Pisans claimed that the first games were held by Pelops after the death of their king Oenomaus. Games at the funerals of famous men were an early way of honouring the dead and relieving the tension at the same time. But Pindar, the lyric poet who gained, to our advantage as well as his own, so many commissions to write in honour of the victors at the Games, sided with the Eleans in declaring that Herakles founded the Games. Nevertheless when they fixed the subject for the pedimental sculpture over the entrance to the temple of Zeus, they chose that moment of pause in tension before the start and the violence of the famous (or infamous) chariot race in which Pelops, the challenger, killed King Oenomaus, and himself became king of Pisa.

Pelops had come to Pisa and fallen in love with the beautiful Hippodameia, daughter of the king. But Oenomaus had been told by an oracle that he would be killed by his future son-in-law. To dissuade any admirer of his daughter from any further approach, he devised a cunning plan. A suitor must agree, he said, to his conditions for a marriage: first he must race against him in a chariot race to the Isthmus, and the loser was to forfeit his life. Such were the attractions of Hippodameia that thirteen suitors had already lost their lives in this one-sided race. For the god Ares, father of Oenomaus, had given him horses of a heavenly breed. Pelops, however, was loved by Poseidon, whose functions besides those of being in charge of earthquakes and of water also included lordship over horses. In this capacity Poseidon had given young Pelops a noble pair capable of sustained high speed without overheating, horses divinely supercharged. So far perhaps the odds were equal. But there was a practical strain in Pelops and, for a consideration, he arranged with the royal groom, Myrtilus, that he should extract the split-pin from one of the royal wheels before the race. Thanks to this deplorable lack of sportsmanship, Pelops won the race, the girl and the throne. Piling Pelion on Ossa, he killed Myrtilus also, to forestall any awkwardness. What is more remarkable than this old-fashioned way of founding a dynasty—for Pelops was the founder of the tragic House of Atreus whose son Agamemnon led the Achaean Greeks to Troy and came back victor, only to be murdered by his wife—was the choice of this theme for the sculpture of Zeus' temple, and that in the very place where competitors in the games, and their fathers with them, had to swear to play fair before a statue of Zeus who held a thunderbolt in each hand. The Greek mind was very flexible.

There is considerable evidence that in earliest times kingship was held on an eight-year tenure: and after that period the king had to defend his kingship in a fight to the death with his challenger. Frazer has found evidence that in Crete and in Sparta kingship was once held for eight-year periods. It may be that Pelops was this kind of challenger and that his love for Hippodameia was embroidery applied by a later generation who knew nothing of this dreadful system. According to Plutarch, the early programmes at the Olympic Games included an item 'single armed combat to the death' in conscious or unconscious reminiscence of the old terrible custom. A vivid account of such a ritual killing of a king by a young challenger is given in Mary Renault's novel *The King Must Die*.

But why eight years? The reason is of much interest. The peasant, whether in days ancient or modern, has always been bound by the necessity to plough and cultivate, sow and reap, at the right season and in the right weather. But in primitive days a supernatural complication was added to his difficulties in choosing rightly. The gods of agriculture and the herds, of fertility and growth, would nullify man's effort unless properly propitiated and pleased with the ploughing and the sowing. To ensure the propitious moment, in the absence of a printed calendar, it seemed best to act according to the phases of the moon. For the waxing of the moon meant increase and blessing to man and beast and soil: and its waning the reverse. Such a belief was, and is, common in many primitive communities; and in a more complicated form it was held by at least one startlingly successful English horticulturist who presented a squadron of 'Spitfires' in the War on the proceeds of his lunar system. So the early Greeks, in the words of Rhodius 'tried to conduct their years in accord with the sun, but their months and days with the moon'. This arrangement can only work for a very few years, for there is an accumulating error in that the solar year has $365\frac{1}{4}$ days, and, since the lunar month has on the average $29\frac{1}{2}$ days, the lunar year consists of 354—a difference of eleven days. The first year, the next year, and the year after might successfully be guided by the moon, though the peasant would be getting earlier and earlier in his sowing; but after eight years he would be eighty-eight days ahead of the sun and his farming year quite out of gear. So each ninth year was a 'Great Year', or year of festival, worship and merrymaking; the farmer began his moon-watching afresh with a new count, and the solar year and the lunar year were harmonized. The Pythian festival at Delphi was held originally at eight-year intervals and it is likely that this was also so at Olympia. Strabo (*floruit* 20 B.C.) writes of land redistribution, even in his day, in parts of north-west Greece after eight years of tenure. So it seems there were other reminders, besides a new king, that a new cycle had begun.

The Olympic Festival was held between the harvest and the vintage, in August or early September, a hot dry time of the year but not a busy one for the farmer. Married women were excluded. It is known that there was once a belief in Greece that the presence of married women was dangerous to flocks and herds: in Roman Italy too they were not allowed to attend the festival of the agricultural god Mars Silvanus. The penalty for a married woman found at the Olympic Games was death. Pausanias writes of a mother, Pherenice, whose son was running in an Olympic race: she disguised herself as a trainer and took up a good position in the stadium to watch. Her boy won. In her delight and desire to embrace him, she jumped a barrier, slipped, and revealed her sex. When she proved that her father, her brothers, and now her son had all been Olympic victors, the officials let her go. But the law of Elis was altered to require that all trainers in the stadium must be naked—like the athletes performing there. It appears then that, underlying the Olympic Festival of Zeus, there was an earlier agricultural festival.

There was no actual city at Olympia, but we must imagine the valley turned for the festival period into a vast tented town. Only free-born Greeks could enter the sanctuary and the stadium; but there would be an immense number of miscellaneous folk selling food and drink, fun and entertainment as in a huge country fair; every kind of diversion, high and low, would be available. Herodotus, for instance, we know used this opportunity to 'publish' the first books of his history by reading them in some public place: there would be sculptors with exhibitions of their skill, and poets, both seeking commissions to immortalize the victors in the games: crowds of admirers and critics at the stables of the fine horses from Syracuse or Cyrene: merchants making deals as they found new markets opening as they made new friends from overseas: ambassadors discussing matters of more import than 'form': and, over all, dust and flies and a desperate problem of water supplies—for the rivers were but dangerous stagnant pools amid dried up gravel beds at that time of the year—until in the second century A.D. a good water supply was provided by a rich citizen of Athens, Herodes Atticus. His fountain-house in the sanctuary is close to the temple of Hera.

Now all is peace under the shade of the pine trees planted by the German archaeologists in the eighties of the last century: the purple-pink of the Judas tree glows amid the columns of the gymnasium: dark-red anemones cluster round the fallen masonry and the warm scent of pine needles sweetens the air.

The site divides into three parts: the buildings outside the walled Altis, the Altis itself, and the stadium to the east of it. As one approaches from the bridge over the Cladeus a forest of columns comes into view on the right of the path; first, those of the Gymnasium and the covered practice track, much of which still lies unexcavated under the car park; the portico round the Palaestra for boxing and wrestling practice is next: then, the cluster of foundations of the priests' quarters and the workshop of Pheidias, the sculptor of the huge gold and ivory cult statue of Zeus in his temple. To ensure that his statue would rightly fit its position in the temple, his workshop was given the same measurements as the west end of the temple cella. In the ruins of his workshop, which in the course of time was turned into a Byzantine church, were found recently some of the moulds for casting the gold plates used to fabricate the dress of Zeus, and a drinking cup with the sculptor's name scratched on it. (This is now in the Museum.) Beyond the workshop is the Leonidaion, a very large colonnaded hostel building for distinguished visitors. In the centre of the court is an elaborate fish-pond which would guarantee fresh food for them at least. Turning now to the left— or east—one sees the Council House: this consists of twin, parallel buildings, with apsidal ends, and in the open courtyard between them was an altar and statue of Zeus—the Zeus holding thunderbolts in each hand, before which the oath to obey the rules was taken by each competitor and his father. The penalty for foul play was merely a fine, but the sting lay in that on which the fine was spent. For a bronze statue of Zeus was set up at the entrance to the stadium, and, as each athlete entered, he saw a row of such statues—their bases stand there still—each base having an inscription giving the name of the disgraced athlete, his father's name and that of his city. The Athenians once did not accept the umpire's verdict as to foul play by an Athenian: they refused to pay. When shortly afterwards Athens had need to consult the Delphic Oracle, the reply was given that the god had no dealings with debtors. Athens paid. Most of the fines were incurred by boxers, wrestlers and pancratiasts. These last could fight, naked and unarmed of course, by any means short of biting and gouging out the other man's eyes. One pancratiast was posthumously awarded the olive crown for, in the moment of victory as his opponent gave in, he died.

The dominant feature in the sanctuary was, properly, the great Doric temple of Zeus. The immense stylobate, or platform, on which it stood, still dominates though its great column drums lie on the ground about it in sad humiliation. Was this the result of earthquake or of destructive Christian zeal? It is not known, but it looks like the work of men's hands. At least thanks be to Heaven that sense prevailed when the Parthenon was adopted by Christians as a Church of the Virgin Mary. This happy turn was made also at Syracuse where the Doric columns of Athena's temple still buttress the Cathedral walls. The temple of Zeus was as large as the Parthenon and was completed in 457 B.C. The local stone is coarse and conchiferous, but was covered with stucco, and paint would have been used to pick out detail and in the pediments to provide a dark background to set off the sculptured figures. These are almost complete and form one of the most impressive collections of original marble sculpture that survive.

But the chief glory of this impressive temple, the colossal chryselephantine statue of the god, which was ranked among the 'Seven Wonders of the World', was carried off to Constantinople by the Emperor Theodosius and was accidentally burnt up in a fire in A.D. 475. Other colossal cult statues were made of gold and ivory: it was not its precious material that aroused so much admiration. It was something of much greater value. On the face and in the attitude of this forty-foot-high statue of Zeus seated on a throne there was such a combination of majesty and power with kindliness and benevolence that tough men, like the Roman general Aemilius Paulus, were moved by it. In fact he said that he felt in the presence of the god himself. Other opinions

Frazer has collected and translated are as follows: Quintilian, the Roman rhetorician and teacher, said that the statue strengthened religion: a poet, that either the god came to Pheidias in his studio, or else Pheidias went to the god. Dion Chrysostom considered Pheidias' Zeus as the most beautiful statue on earth. Of this 'serene and kindly Zeus, protector of a united and harmonious Greece, giver of life and breath and all things good, the father of all men', he wrote, 'I feel that any man of heavy heart, bowed beneath a load of misfortune and grief, who had lost even the solace of sleep, if he stood before this statue of the god, would cast aside his troubles and the sorrows that befall us all.' The Christian may surely believe that as through the Hebrew prophets long before the birth of Christ, God revealed stage by stage new facets of His being, so had He revealed to the mind of Pheidias this truth about Himself expressed by the statue of Zeus.

The position of the statue towards the west end of the temple is clearly marked by the blue Eleusinian marble fragments of the base and the sunk rectangular area which was filled with olive oil. This provided a slightly oily vapour which would prevent any decay of the ivory (of which the unclothed parts of the statue's body were made) through the humidity of the sanctuary.

Further to the north of the sanctuary towards the hill of Kronos is Hera's temple, the oldest Doric temple in Greece. It dates from the seventh century B.C.; and the conclusion seems fair from a remark of Pausanias that one of the columns was wooden, and also from the strange variety to be seen in the columns (some with sixteen flutes, others with twenty, some with the wide curving echinus of the archaic period, others with the straighter steeper type of the best fifth-century work) that the temple was constructed originally of timber. As the wooden columns rotted away they were replaced by a Doric column of the then fashionable type. The walls, it will be noticed, are of a construction precisely similar to those of the Minoan palaces of Knossos, Phaestos and Mallia, almost a thousand years older—stone slabs set on edge (orthostates in the architectural jargon) for the bottom four feet where splashing rain or careless people might cause damage to more vulnerable material, and of sun-baked brick above. The building is longer and less broad than later was acceptable in a Doric temple; and the ceiling of the cella—we may be allowed to think of it as the nave provided we remember that a Greek temple was built to house a colossal, that is to say, more than life-size, statue of the cult divinity and not to seat a congregation at any time—was supported by two lines of smaller columns which were engaged by short spur walls with the outer walls. This arrangement, of Egyptian origin and dating from the time when builders had no suitable materials or knowledge of how to make a wide-span ceiling, subdivided the cella into a series of shallow niches all along both sides. They were filled with sculpture. In one niche stood the Hermes of Praxiteles, now a chief exhibit in the Museum and the cynosure of every eye. Its almost perfect condition it owes to the mud-brick walls of the temple. For when there came floods in the sixth century A.D. which drowned the sanctuary and caused the walls to collapse, Hermes lay comfortably in his muddy bed beneath many feet of silt and sand for thirteen centuries.

The Philippeion, or 'Philip's Folly' as it deserves to be called, is near the west end of the temple of Hera: a rare circular marble tholos in the Ionic Order, of which the purpose was to contain gold and ivory statues of Philip and his famous family of the House of Macedon. It is thought that Alexander the Great completed the building. To erect such a personal building in the sanctuary was impious enough, but to put up chryselephantine portrait sculptures was worse, for hitherto those precious materials had been reserved for gods and goddesses. Philip, however, might have objected to these strictures on the ground that the whole sanctuary teemed with sculpture in much of which there was at least an element of personal honour or personal pride, mingled with thanksgiving to Zeus. The inscribed bases of many statues are to be seen especially to the east of the temple of Zeus.

A terrace on the lower slope of the Hill of Kronos overlooks the pathway to the tunnelled entrance of the Stadium. Here are the foundations of one row of State 'Treasuries'; their names indicate the wide attraction of the festival—Selinus (Sicily), Byzantium, Metapontum (Italy), Syracuse, Sybaris (Italy), Cyrene (North Africa). The Stadium was excavated by German archaeologists in 1959–60 with some help from bulldozers. The starting-line had already been laid bare—two parallel grooves cut into a long line of blocks of stone exactly as at Delphi, Corinth and elsewhere. The runners must have used a 'standing-start' with one foot set only six inches behind the other, the toes in the grooves.

The preliminaries of the festival began with the sending out to various parts of Greece of the Spondophoroi, the officials who took the names of competitors and proclaimed the coming sacred truce when all roads to Olympia were declared to be under the aegis of Zeus. The competitors undertook to train for ten months, of which the last would be spent in the palaestra and gymnasium at Olympia.

On the appointed day, a procession of the athletes and officials was formed at Elis and made its way to Olympia, entering only after lustration—a formal washing intended sacramentally to cleanse the soul and prepare it for pure worship. The first of the five festival days was filled up with the scrutiny and identification of the competitors in the Council House, with the oath-taking already mentioned, by sacrifices on six double altars and the pouring of blood on the mound of Pelops, half-way between the two temples. Next morning, in the most impressive of the processions, all concerned with the festival and the Games, priests and athletes, officials and embassies, took part, garlanded and gorgeously arrayed. It was at this time that the crowds heard the Herald's announcements of the names and city of each athlete. One can imagine the beauty and interest of this scene, the pride and hope which welled up in the supporters of each city's athletes as they passed by; and believe that men felt with deep satisfaction that rare sense of the fundamental unity of all Hellas under Zeus which was one of Olympia's great gifts to this divided people.

In the afternoon, another kind of spectacle took place, in the hippodrome of which floods have swept away every trace, the two-horse and four-horse chariot races, the latter an incomparable source of prestige to the victor and his State. It was extremely dangerous and the course was long, twelve circuits, twenty-two tightest possible turns round the mark, between four and five miles in all. Pindar said that only one man in ten could expect to complete the course without damage to himself or his team. Arcesilas, king of Cyrene in North Africa, the city which pioneered the four-horse chariot race, gave the odds as

one in forty. Those who have seen the film *Ben Hur* will understand! A bare-back horse race, and a mule-chariot race which
looked so ugly to the eyes of mid-fifth-century Greeks that it
was then abandoned, and then the crowd moved to the stadium
for a typically Greek event, the Pentathlon. The winner of this
event was the man who was the best 'all-rounder' at running,
jumping, throwing the discus and the javelin, and wrestling.

The third day was the day of full moon, and so of the chief
sacrifices to Zeus, a morning given up to worship and religious
ceremonies in the sanctuary. The afternoon was used for the
boys' races and their wrestling and boxing events. We do not
know the age limit which divided the boys' events from the
'open'. But from an inscription at Nikopolis, where Augustus
established games which were to be both parallel to and of equal
status with the Olympic games, we see that a boy of eighteen
years was ordered by the officials to transfer to the 'open'
boxing because he was too mature; and the stout fellow won the
'open' boxing!

On the morning of the fourth day, the track running events
took place: the stade sprint race of one length of the stadium,
corresponding to our 220 yards: the diaulos—our 440 yards, and
a twelve-lap race—our 3 miles. In the afternoon, the wrestling,
boxing and the horrible pancration finals were held in front of
the altar of Zeus in the sanctuary where the crowd on the hill
could see them. A race in armour, which in the sophisticated
later period must have been treated as a comic relief, concluded
the athletic programme.

Prize-giving, feasting and rejoicing on the fifth day brought
the festival to an end. 'Those who had won no prize, in shame
and misery slipt away by back roads, sadly down in their luck.'
It is a poor spirit which Pindar reports.

Thucydides twice dates a year by giving the name of the
victorious pancratiast, as if we were to say that the League of
Nations settled a certain crisis in the year that Captain Cuttle
won the Derby. Yet not everybody thought so much of the
Olympic Games. Sparta, after a long run of successes, withdrew
on the valid ground that the advantages, so far as training for
war went, were inadequate: Athens withdrew because she regarded over-specialization as a mistake. Euripides is savagely
sarcastic about the 'tribe of athletes, slaves of their bellies, who

know neither how to make money nor to bear poverty. In early manhood they strut about, the darlings of the town: in old age like worn out cloaks, they are flung aside'. Hard words, for it was the people themselves who brought this fate upon their spoilt heroes.

Strange that the very site where all this splendour shone so long was lost and lay unknown beneath the floods and twenty feet of silt, till in 1720 the Bishop of Corfu turned up a squared stone on the sandy waste by the river. Forty years later Chandler turned up more stones and in 1829 French archaeologists recovered a few metopes of Zeus' temple, and the way was opened for the great German excavation of the 'eighties which gave us back this venerable and lovely sanctuary.

Notes on What to Look For in The Olympia Museum

Here is as large a collection of original Greek marble sculpture, as opposed to Roman copies, as can be seen anywhere in Greece outside the National Museum in Athens. No one need avoid this museum on the usually valid plea that museums are exhausting places, for this museum is admirably arranged for easy viewing and does not exhibit too much to be enjoyed.

In the central hall, on the long walls left and right, the sculptures from the east and west pediments of the temple of Zeus (457 B.C.).

1. (a) On the left wall, Zeus stands in the centre, flanked on one side by Oenomaus and his queen, Sterope, and on the other by the young challenger, Pelops, and the king's daughter, Hippodameia, who was to be his prize if he won the chariot race against her father. On the outside of the central group are the chariots and horses; beyond them reclining seers who by their gestures indicate that they clearly see the tremendous significance for the future of the Peloponnese of this impending fateful race of death. A boy, unaware of all this, idly scratches a toe. In the corners, the personified rivers Alpheus and Cladeus. All is still, frozen in the moment before the balance falls.

    (b) In contrast, on the right wall, Apollo has appeared in the midst of a scene of disgraceful violence and bloodshed: drunken centaurs are assaulting the women guests and the boys at the wedding-feast of Pirithous. Theseus helps in the struggle to save the women. But the young god, seen with arm outstretched in a commanding gesture, will surely bring order out of chaos; just as Hellas had beaten down the barbarians in the Persian wars only a few years before. The pride of Greece in this achievement of civilized men is reflected in this superb Apollo. The head has *not* been restored.

(c) On the short walls of this hall, the metopes of the temple of Zeus, depicting the labours of Herakles.

2. On the pedestal at the far end of the hall, the *Winged Victory of Paeonius* (425 B.C.).
This most graceful of all winged Victories stood on a very much higher pedestal to the east of the temple of Zeus. The white flesh in contrast with the once painted and flowing drapery as she so lightly 'touches down' must have added a lovely touch of life. Here is grace and charm, perhaps out of keeping with the grim clash of arms which she directed: we may think the grandeur and the power of the Victory of Samothrace, now in the Louvre, more fitting.

3. In two glass cases, free-standing in this hall, *two archaic VIth-century terracotta figures*, a soldier, and Zeus with a smile of satisfaction carrying off the boy Ganymede to be his cup-bearer. These figures were acroteria, ornaments set on top of the apices of pediments.

4. In a low free-standing glass case in the hall, *the cup of Pheidias*, with his name scratched on it and found recently under the ruins of his workshop.

5. In the alcove beyond the end wall of the main hall and standing in a huge sand-tray to break an earthquake-fall, the *Hermes of Praxiteles* (*floruit* 360 B.C.). That this is a masterpiece is not in question. With supreme confidence the sculptor has done precisely what he wished to do with his material: and the Parian marble has surrendered all its hardness to the master's hand and chisel. The figure has a beauty of body and an easy sensuous grace: but surely also more pride in self than any god should have. Hermes was the gentle messenger who conducted souls to the other world. Does this character appear in him? One questions it.

6. In the small rooms to the left of the entrance, a *collection of bronze griffin heads*, open-beaked and fierce. These strange

but rather majestic objects were a regular export from Anatolia into Greece, and they were fixed as handles to the lips of large bronze cauldrons. The collection of small votive bronze figures and of helmets, weapons and armour in these rooms helps the imagination to fill the empty sanctuary with life.

7. In the corresponding gallery to the right of the entrance, *the helmet of Miltiades*, victor at Marathon, marked with his name and recovered from a well.

Note: a new and bigger museum was, in 1970, nearing completion on the other bank of the river Cladeus, nearer to the Altis.

CHAPTER VIII

Europe's First Great Civilization: Minoan Crete

S t. Paul in his letter to Titus, first bishop of the Church in Crete, quotes a classical Greek maxim that 'the Cretans are always liars'. The poet Callimachus, too, had earlier quoted it, perhaps in scorn of the Cretan tradition that not only was Zeus born in their island but had his tomb there also: as if immortal Zeus were some vegetation god who annually died and rose again in the spring. What would the Father of Gods and men be doing in an island which played no part in the great days of Greek history, stood aloof when the barbarian Persian invaded, and was well known only as a pirates' lair as foul as Cilicia itself? And those Cretans spent their time in feuds and quarrels between their hundred scattered 'villages', and then claimed that once they ruled the Aegean world. To the Greeks the truth seemed rather to be that 'the Cretans are always liars'.

Yet Thucydides, the great historian of Greece, trusted this folk-memory in Crete and wrote that Minos, king of Crete in prehistoric times, was the first to possess a navy and with his fleet made himself master of a great part of the Aegean Sea, colonized many of the islands and, to protect his increasing commerce, went far to rid the seas of pirates. As a result, said Thucydides, the seas were opened for regular traffic.

There were many legends, too, current in classical Greece about Minos and the monster-bull which he kept in the Labyrinth of Knossos, and of how Theseus, the young Athenian prince, went to Crete as one of a party of young men and girls sent as living tribute to the Cretan king, and slew the monster, escaping ingeniously from the dreadful labyrinth with the aid of a clue given him by Ariadne: stories too of Daedalus, inventor of flight with artificial wings of feathers, and of his son Icarus, distinguished as the first airman to suffer a fatal crash; of skilled coppersmiths and ingenious Dactyls. These stories are surely echoes of pride in the new skills, inventiveness and craftsmanship of the Cretans, which excited admiration everywhere in distant days. Beneath this smoke there was indeed real fire—fire smelting bronze and heating metals in the forge and so speeding the rate of Man's development.

Towards the end of the last century scholars began to investigate a few ancient sites in Crete which had been accidentally discovered. One of these was at Knossos, three miles inland from Heraklion on the north coast; another in the Kamares Cave beneath the twin peaks of Mount Ida in central Crete, where the splendid polychrome pottery known now as Kamares ware was found. But a covering curtain of soil kept in the dark all the major visual evidence of this ancient empire till the opening years of this century, when Sir Arthur Evans dramatically revealed by excavation on the hill of Knossos the palace of the Minoan kings and a rich store of their possessions.

While Evans and his team uncovered Knossos, others set to work elsewhere in Crete. The Italian, Halbherr, searched for and at last found Phaestos, the second important Minoan palace and town at the west end of the plain of Messara in the south, where already large numbers of tombs had been found to indicate a centre of population nearby. A Greek archaeologist found a third palace at Mallia, on the north coast twenty-five miles east of Knossos, a place where excavation by the French School of Archaeology fruitfully continues to-day. These seem to have been the chief Minoan centres, but the tale of success in finding Minoan sites is a very long one: it includes cave sanctuaries on mountain-tops in several places with large deposits of votive offerings, royal villas and great houses, farms and impressive royal tombs, even actual towns such as Gournia and Pseira where the houses rise on terraces up the hillsides, and harbour works, paved roads and causeways. It all adds up to evidence enough that the Cretans after all were not liars, and that their island in the second millennium B.C. was not only the centre of a maritime trading empire, as Thucydides believed, but the home of a well-ordered people living happily in remarkable comfort and at a high level of sophistication and taste. Here in fact was Europe's first real civilization, and the range of its visible achievement and interests is astonishingly wide.

The Minoans, as Evans called them after the legendary name of the king or dynasty of kings, were not indigenous Greeks. They were seafarers, probably from Asia Minor but with a knowledge of Egypt and the eastern shores of the Mediterranean. At first—about 2500 B.C.—they settled in small islands, like Mochlos, off the Cretan coast and in places on the north coast where their ships could be safe. But pirate raids were always a danger, and the largest settlements were inland for safety's sake. The fertile Messara plain in the south was quickly occupied, as was Knossos, three miles from its harbours at Amnisos.

Neolithic man was already in the island. He has left traces of his occupation in his houses, tools of bone and stone, hand-made pottery with incised decoration, in the bones of his cattle and of his own people, and in little female figurines of incredible fatness by which he conveyed his sense of wonder at the divine power which gave life and fertility to man and beast and crops. His deity was 'the mother of all living'. Stone foundations of his houses and neat pebbled yards have been found deep under the palace level at Knossos, and it is remarkable that the neolithic levels there were as much as twenty-six feet thick. He liked to build his home with one or two small rooms opening onto a single large room, and this characteristic arrangement was to continue in a much more elaborate form and be the normal fashion in Crete right to the end of the period of his successors, the Bronze Age Minoans.

There are perhaps four special characteristics of the Minoan mind which account for the swift rise of their civilization. The first was the recognition of the value of the sea and ships, both as the best defence and as a means of trading far afield. For having used ships to reach their new home, they had the wisdom not to 'swallow the anchor' and settle snugly on their inland farms, but to use the sea-ways to bring in goods from other and distant places in exchange for their own products. Even in early Minoan times, about 2400 B.C., products of Egypt, Libya and the Cyclades were found in the island settlement at Mochlos, and later their trade extended to Byblos and Ugarit on the Syrian coast, to Sicily and probably to Malta, as well as to numerous places nearer on the Aegean coasts and islands.

Then we shall recognize the Minoan flair for organization and administration, with its implication of discipline. As an instrument of organization they had a hieroglyphic system and later a writing on clay tablets which Evans called 'Linear A'. Still later, about 1450 B.C., a third system of writing, also on clay tablets, was in use. This is the 'Linear B' script and has an importance and interest all its own which will be described in its chronological place in the next chapter.

Then they were great craftsmen. They had copper from Cyprus and could import tin, and so were able to smelt bronze. But more than this, they evidently set a high value on skill in techniques and on design and workmanship. For their arts and crafts centred in the palaces themselves. It may seem strange to us to find workshops as part of the palace buildings, but we should recall that in modern times we again find governments much concerned with the encouragement of advanced technical progress.

Finally, in Minoan times women appear to have had an influence on society to which we may attribute much of the grace and elegance and love of natural beauty, of flowers and colour, of comfort and cleanliness of which, to our amazement and delight, evidence was found in so many varied ways under the dusty soil of Crete. Even the Athenians a thousand years later did not achieve this feminine enrichment of life. The dress and coiffure of the ladies of the palace were extremely elegant. Terracotta statuettes show the Earth Goddess, whom the Minoans worshipped, or it may be her priestess, with snakes held high in each hand, dressed in an elaborate flounced skirt and a tight low-cut bodice which leaves the breasts bare; and this dress and style by its appearance in the frescoes is shown to be customary among Minoan women. Gold jewellery as delicately worked as any seen at any place, beautiful pottery of eggshell thinness, decorative gay frescoes brightening corridors and porches and rooms with painted scenes of cats and birds or flowers and rushes on river banks, baths with running water, and a water-borne sewage system—all these strongly suggest that here lived a people in a thoroughly organized community, equipped for living a full life in a world whose colour and beauty their womenfolk were able to reflect in their homes and in their adornment. The influence of women extended to religious matters also, for they served as priestesses of the Earth Goddess and on the many delicately carved gems, designed for seals or rings, they are portrayed carrying out her ritual.

Remarkably few weapons date from the earlier phases of the Minoan period nor were the palaces at any time surrounded by fortified walls. For the palaces and great houses were not the homes of rival chieftains but centres of organized leadership under the king at Knossos; they were far away in feeling from the grim castles of huge Cyclopean masonry by which the Mycenaean Greeks later in the second millennium B.C. were to hold down their conquests on the mainland. It is true that to meet the possibility of a sudden piratical attempt upon the palace its entrances were guarded and, indeed, altered at one point to be made so narrow that a single guard could hold the entrance while his comrades in the guardroom seized their weapons. In Mycenaean art we find representations of war chariots, a siege or a thrilling lion hunt. But the Minoan artist turns for the subjects of his frescoes, pottery, faience plaques and ornaments to the beauties of the natural scene and the pleasures of a peaceful life. A fresco five feet high of a sheaf of white lilies, another of a cat on the prowl after a bird in the bulrushes, the famous black stone 'Harvester vase' (from the villa of Hagia Triada and now in Room VII in the Heraklion Museum), skilfully cut in relief to illustrate the harvesters returning from the fields, their leader and those behind him singing a full-throated song and one turning to the ranks behind and obviously saying, 'Come on, you fellows, sing up!', or painted sunflowers exploding over the swelling belly of a pot, octopuses sprawling their tentacles over the surface of another jar in a superlatively well-composed design, or again the tall bas-relief of a lordly prince, his waist narrow, his figure and bearing regal, hair long to his waist and a plume of coloured ostrich feathers nodding on his head-dress—all these and many more speak clearly of a joie de vivre in a countryside both beautiful and at peace. The carefree happiness which these scenes suggest is charmingly expressed in a painting of a little crowd of gaily dressed ladies seated and waiting for some spectacle to be presented: their laughter and chatter is all but audible still! Still to be felt, too, is the tenderness of a dappled cow in faience relief suckling her calf and turning her head in motherly concern to lick its back.

A visitor to the museum at Heraklion and the site of the Palace at Knossos may find himself injecting a shot of self-criticism into his sense of wonder at 'Europe's first great civilization', and the apparent grace and gaiety of Minoan life 3,500 years ago. Our vaunted speed of modern progress may look a little slow.

CHAPTER IX

The Palace of Knossos

The palace of Knossos lies on the shoulder of a low hill—
known locally as the 'Gentleman's Head'—which falls on
the east and the south into a narrow valley with higher
ground rising beyond it. Vineyards surround it. The approach
from the main road is through a plantation of young pines which
opens onto the great west court of the palace. Here most fittingly
stands on its pedestal a bronze bust of Sir Arthur Evans whose
skill and enthusiasm, even ardour, sustained over half a long
lifetime, raised up the famous palace to a new existence like a
phoenix from the ashes of its destruction. It was a strange
chance, which Evans had the discernment to seize, that decided
that his hand, and not that of Schliemann, should dig in this
fruitful soil. For in 1878 the news reached Schliemann, then
pioneering at Troy, that a Cretan with the admirably appropriate name of Minos Kalokairinos had accidentally discovered
two storage chambers filled with huge pots on the hill which
was the traditional site of Knossos. Twice in the next few years
Schliemann attempted to buy the site with a view to excavation.
But there were tiresome arguments as to price, for the owner
knew the depth of Schliemann's pocket. Schliemann declined to
buy at the value of 2,500 olive-trees when he could only count
a third of that number, and negotiations were broken off. We
must however be thankful for a merciful deliverance for the
palace of King Minos, for had Schliemann's vast trenches been as
eagerly driven into this hill as into the hill of Troy, the resultant
chaos would surely have deprived the world of one of the most
fascinating and complete archaeological sites in existence.

So in 1899, Dr. Evans (as he then was) of Oxford bought the

site and began to dig—his first big excavation, at the age of forty-eight. For forty-two years, till his death at the age of ninety, Knossos had his heart and consumed his fortune. As a schoolboy in 1919 I listened fascinated by the story Dr. Evans told us and at the slides he showed. Most fortunately I was near the front of our big school hall and I could just hear his lecture; for he was no speaker and for the school at large the inaudible lecture was a dead loss. There might well have been a vastly more serious dead loss; for in his efforts to reach his audience, Evans had come unawares in the dark to the edge of the high stage and suddenly fell heavily to the floor below. It was, of course, the end of his half-finished account: Evans lay inert: we all filed out in fearful silence and foreboding, leaving the great man in the care of the headmaster and staff who seemed as shocked as the poor victim. But what an escape for Knossos and for us all! A schoolboy had however learnt from Dr. Evans a double lesson which has served him well in later life—that there is a wealth of teeming interest in the discoveries of archaeology, and that when he lectures in the dark with slides it is prudent to stand still.

In the excavation of the huge site, first occupied in the Neolithic period and built upon for some 2,500 years before it was abandoned about 1100 B.C. and finally lost, Evans' patience and thoroughness has become a byword. Collating his own finds in and around Knossos and the various strata in which they lay with the changes in style, construction and technique both in respect of building and of pottery, and relating these to objects found of foreign origin, especially Egyptian, where fixed dates are available, he was able to distinguish a long series of periods and give them dates. His scheme with minor changes is still generally in use and for convenience, but in shortened form, is printed here:

Neolithic Period		before 2500 B.C.
Early Minoan Period (E.M.)		2500–2000 B.C.
Middle Minoan Period (M.M.)	I and II	2000–1700 B.C.
	III	1700–1575 B.C.
Late Minoan Period	(L.M.) I and II	1575–1400 B.C.
	III	1400–1100 B.C.

[These dates are of course only approximate.]

The Palace of Knossos

The first palace of Knossos was begun about 2000 B.C. and grew from islands of detached buildings round a central court, the whole on a carefully levelled and terraced site, set off on the northern and western sides by large areas of open pavement. From the ancient main north-south road which joined the northern harbours of Crete to those facing across to Egypt in the south and which ran close by, there were two approaches to the palace, one from the north along a two-hundred-yard stretch of paved road which was bordered by houses, presumably of palace officials, and has survived in excellent order; and another giving access to the south entrance into the palace by a covered stairway which began at the near end of the Minoan causeway to the south. This causeway, which is visible in the vineyard in the ravine to the south of the palace, has stone steps between the piers to prevent water, draining down the hill, from undermining the structure. Nearby is the Caravanserai for travellers and their animals.

Behind a monumental façade, raised on gypsum orthostates, on the west front of the palace lay a series of store-rooms (magazines) to house the wealth and supplies of the royal household. A system of careful administration is shown by archives in hieroglyphic and, later, in Linear A script. There is ample evidence, in the finds of this period, of trade with Egypt and the Levant as well as the Aegean islands. The kernel of the New Palaces is in the Old: the central court, the west court for arrivals, the theatral area, the long store-rooms, the separate quarters for ceremonial, business, religious, domestic, and work-shop use. Important wide stairways and the proliferation of columns are features of both Old and New Palaces.

Already, at this early date, the palace buildings were provided with a full water supply in pipes well fitted together, and with a drainage system to match. The plumbing of prehistoric Knossos is one of the most surprising features of this unpredictable place.

All three of the Old Palaces, at Knossos, Phaestos and Mallia, were built at the same period, soon after 2000 B.C. and, in the following periods, they show signs of repair and rebuilding. All were destroyed about 1700 B.C., probably by one of the destructive earthquakes to which the island has always been so prone.

About 1650 B.C., in the Middle Minoan III period, comes

H

a great spate of building all over Crete: palaces, royal villas, mansions, towns and harbours reflect a greatly increased population and prosperous overseas trading. These are the great days of the New Palaces at Knossos and Phaestos, and Knossos becomes undoubtedly the dominant power in the island. Now came a complete rebuilding of the Palace, partly on the old walls, and the whole of the royal apartments on the east side were replanned round the grand staircase and a system of light-wells. A huge architectural complex, in some places two storeys high and in others three, survives with a highly complicated ground plan to leave us in no surprise that in legend the word 'labyrinth' gained its new meaning here. For 'labyrinth'—the house of the double-axe—is said to derive from 'labrys', a double-axe with a blade facing both right and left, which, found at all sites, cut into pillars in sanctuaries where religious objects were discovered, as designs on vases, and in miniature in gold or silver in sacred caves, was evidently a religious symbol. Though there were additions, renewals and some reconstruction after further disasters, what we see at Knossos is substantially the ruins (with some reconstruction by Sir Arthur Evans) of the seventeenth-century New Palace.

The Cretan palaces share certain marked characteristics. All have a similar complex of buildings set round a central court, twice as long as wide and similarly orientated north and south: all have wide flights of steps beside a level area which do not lead anywhere and can only have been used as spectators' seats, whether for a religious, a regal or a sporting event we do not know. All the palaces have upper storeys in which the larger official rooms were sited, and a system of light-wells, round which ran the staircases, and which provided reflected light and also ventilation, keeping out the cold winds of winter and moderating the summer heat. The same constructional feature is found in all the outside walls: on a stone podium or base at the foot of the wall are set fine, upright stones three or four feet high and above these orthostates the walls are made of sun-baked brick, strengthened at intervals with horizontal and vertical timbers, and plaster-covered. It is interesting to note in the Temple of Hera at Olympia that this identical construction was used there, a thousand years later, and even more interesting to see this half-timber strengthening of sun-baked brick walls still normal practice in the villages of modern Greece. Other features common to the palaces are the placing of the rooms: the domestic quarter entirely separate from the official rooms; the provision of places of worship in the palace; long runs of storage magazines with their 'Ali Baba' pots for keeping oil and wine and corn, together with stone-lined cists in the magazine floors; the presence of workshops in the palace building, and the use of wooden columns wider at the top than at the bottom. A number of these features, it is held, are found in the palace excavated at Beycesultan in Asia Minor.

In his excavation Evans found that after 3,500 years, sun-baked bricks had virtually reverted to soil, and the timbers were little more than distinctive discoloration in it. In a multi-storied building this fact provided a serious problem. He solved it by running concrete beams wherever he found the timber trace, and these he painted the colour of wood. It was his only hope of keeping the upper storeys from collapsing on the lower where they had not already fallen, and so of preserving the authentic shape of the building. His restoration is done in such a way that the original is at once distinguished from the new. There are critics who 'much prefer Phaestos or Mallia', because of the absence there of restoration. Each to his taste: but let us be clear that it would not be possible to visualize those palaces as they were had not parts of the upper walls of sun-baked brick and the timbers of Knossos been so conscientiously and skilfully replaced with modern materials by Evans and his gifted team.

Thanks to the restoration, one may move freely about the palace, up and down staircases, along corridors, into the Throne Room on the west side of the central court, down on the east side to the private apartments of the queen, visit her bathroom, lose oneself repeatedly in this labyrinth of passages, and spend a couple of hours in doing this, half expecting at any moment to come on Ariadne laying the trail of escape for that fine young Greek, Theseus. If one has visited the Heraklion Museum before coming to the palace, it is far easier, in imagination, to people this mass of building with Minoan men and women, beautifully dressed as we see them in the frescoes, the women's long flounced skirts sweeping widely out so that we flatten ourselves against the passage wall to let them pass.

On some of the palace walls, as, for instance, in the South

The Palace of Knossos

Entrance, copies of the frescoes now preserved in the Museum have been placed where once they added so much colour and set such a pleasing and peaceful tone in the centre of government. Frescoes belong to a late phase in Minoan art, and are almost confined to Knossos and to certain of the bigger official houses near the palace.

Anyone looking through the Museum is bound to notice a peculiar interest in the bull in Minoan art. The bull occurs in fresco, is cut in relief on black steatite vases probably once sheathed in thin gold foil, and appears in numerous terra-cotta votive figurines. A fresco copy in the North Entrance Porch at the palace shows a furious bull at full charge with dilated nostril and flashing eye, his head down and turning to toss his enemy. Another, and a complete, fresco identifies the enemy. For here are two young acrobats (perhaps really one shown in two consecutive positions) and a girl, engaged in the dangerous sport of seizing the horns of a charging bull and turning a somersault over his back, to be caught by the stand-in behind the bull. Perhaps the acrobat jumped from above onto the horns. At any rate one bull figurine in the Museum shows a man hanging on each of the horns, with a girl, on her back, spread-eagled between the horns and down over the nose and mouth of the bull. Ivory figurines of an acrobat in the high-dive position, arms outstretched and together in front, and feet together, suggests that the technique was a leap from above at the precisely correct moment. This was a lethal sport indeed—if it was sport at all and not, rather, a ritual—and more suitable therefore to be engaged in by young men and women sent as tribute from subject cities across the sea. This is the line taken by Mary Renault in her exciting novel *The King Must Die*, a book which above others brings the Minoan world to life. It may well be that bull-leaping was a religious exercise, a form of sacrifice. The acrobats would not always live to leap again on another festival day; and when one died, it would be life given to the bull who perhaps was thought to represent the power and vitality of the unseen god; for, when he shook the land with his periodic and terrible quakes, he let out a thunderous roar such as only the very archetype of all bulls could make. In many parts of the palace, and at the royal tomb half a mile away, stylized horns were found. Evans called them 'horns of consecration', so convinced was he that the bull was the representative of powerful deity to the Minoan mind and that the bull games had a ritual significance.

The New Palaces lasted for close on a hundred years. Then, towards the end of the sixteenth century B.C., there came a day of doom in the Aegean Sea. The island of Thera (Santorini), some sixty miles to the north of Crete, blew up in a gigantic volcanic explosion. Thirty-three square miles of the island's centre disappeared in dust, leaving an enormous crater into which the sea cascaded violently, causing waves of prodigious size. That Crete also suffered in this disaster is not guesswork: for (as Marinatos points out in his superbly presented *Crete and Mycenae*) we know what happened when the island of Krakatoa in the East Indies blew up in the last century, and that explosion made a crater only a quarter the size of that at Thera: yet, with the accompanying earthquakes, tidal waves destroyed seaboard towns many miles away. The Krakatoa cataclysm killed 36,000 people: that of Thera played havoc on the north coast of Crete where it engulfed the towns and harbours, mansions and settlements that had grown up during these prosperous years. The palace and town of Mallia were involved in the ruin and were not afterwards reoccupied. Inland, Knossos, Phaestos and the royal villa at Hagia Triada, with many other sites, suffered severe damage from earthquake.

In the following period only the palace at Knossos shows real signs of recovery: in fact there appears to have been a new era of prosperity and development, with restoration and some new building. Knossos remained supreme in the island; for, though some restoration took place at Phaestos, it was not completed and, about 1450 B.C., the palace and the neighbouring royal villa of Hagia Triada close by, were suddenly destroyed, though by what means we do not yet know.

At this point in Cretan history we enter an area of obscurity. We know that a new era which had begun at Knossos after the disaster introduced innovations which reflect an alien influence: a throne room, hitherto unknown in Crete, is built; a new pottery style shows a development towards stylized decoration; hundreds of clay tablets, inscribed in the Linear B script, record inventories and business transactions. At this time, too, many of the frescoes that we know were painted on the plastered walls.

And then, suddenly and finally, about 1400 B.C. or a few years earlier, the palace was destroyed. Fire was the destroyer, and the black, charred surfaces of walls, especially noticeable where the oil stored in the magazines caught alight, are a melancholy witness to it. Was this ruinous fire the result of just one more of the periodic earthquakes occurring in Crete? The others had not caused fire, and the ruin they made had only stimulated better building. There was to be no rebuilding now, but merely a partial reoccupation around the site, and a long-drawn-out decline. Yet Evans saw the ruin as the result of an earthquake. Not so John Pendlebury, his assistant and later Curator of Knossos. (In the War this well-loved philhellene joined with his friends the Cretans and became a member of the Resistance. After a while he was wounded in action and later shot by the Germans.) He held that there was ample evidence that the palace was sacked and burnt, and he believed that the enemy were the mainland Greeks, the Achaeans. He died before he could know of one new vital line of evidence, which might have changed his view as to the enemy.

In 1953 Michael Ventris, architect and amateur archaeologist, broke the cipher of the inscribed tablets, known as Linear B tablets, found in large numbers at Knossos by Evans, and of the similar tablets turned up by Professor Blegen at Pylos, Nestor's Mycenaean palace at the south-west corner of the Peloponnese, by Professor Wace at Mycenae in 1952, and at other Mycenaean sites on the mainland. Ventris and John Chadwick of Cambridge then published their famous book *Documents in Mycenaean Greek* —300 *tablets from Knossos, Pylos and Mycenae*. No one had ever dreamed that the language spoken in the last period of the Palace of Knossos was Greek. This is now the generally accepted conclusion: that the Achaean Greeks—the Mycenaeans—must have been in control at Knossos when the Linear B writing was in use, that is to say, *before* its final destruction by fire about 1400 B.C., for the tablets were found under the stratum of the ruin caused by that disaster.

Professor Palmer of Oxford disputes this conclusion. Did not Evans' assistant, Mackenzie, in his day-to-day log book of work done on the site, report in 1900 that the Linear B tablets were found on the same floor as stirrup-jars of 1200 B.C. style? How then could anyone be sure that the tablets had in fact been in existence before the fire of 1400 B.C. (now the accepted date for the destruction of the palace)? We can only assume that the Greeks were in Crete in the thirteenth century B.C. if this evidence is correct. To which supporters of Evans reply: 'But Evans in 1901 corrected the previous report and wrote that the tablets were found in a deposit one layer below the stirrup-jars, a layer not recognized before and dating to the fifteenth century. The Greeks were therefore in control at Knossos before the palace was finally destroyed.' It may seem strange to the general reader that upon a layer of beaten earth—a floor faintly detectable in a section of excavation—should depend such a big issue as the Greek domination in Knossos two centuries this way or that. But such is the finesse of which modern archaeology is capable. But there is a further point; granted that the Knossos Tablets date before 1400 B.C., how can it be that the Linear B tablets found on the Mycenaean sites on the mainland, at Pylos or at Mycenae, which must be dated 200 years later, are identical with them? Is it credible that the script could undergo no modification in two centuries of use?

Two other pieces of evidence support the conclusion that Greeks controlled Knossos in the fifteenth century B.C.: the throne room is a normal feature of Mycenaean palaces but occurs only at Knossos in Crete; while the Palace style of pottery decoration, also found only at Knossos in Crete in this final period, shows a symmetrical composition and formal treatment of the earlier flower and marine designs which can be matched in Mycenaean vases on the mainland.

In the light of this evidence, the earlier destruction of the palace at Phaestos, already mentioned, may have been the precautionary act of a Mycenaean king at Knossos to eliminate possible trouble from that source.

We are still left with the question 'Who sacked Knossos in 1400 B.C.?' We know from Homer that the Mycenaeans were still in Crete two centuries later: he writes of Idomeneus as leader of the Cretan contingent with the Mycenaean forces attacking Troy in the late thirteenth century B.C., the third in line from Minos to rule Knossos. Idomeneus and his men must have been Mycenaean Greeks. Rivalries and wars between Mycenaean cities there were, and the palace of Knossos could no doubt have been burnt in such a war of rivalry. Alternatively, one might guess at a pirate attack; but why in that case was there no rebuilding of the palace when they had sailed off with their loot? Perhaps survivors of the old Minoan régime worked up a rebellion, successful only in destroying the lovely and lively palace which was the pride of the Bronze Age in Crete. We may yet find the answer, for Minoan Crete seems still to have much to say.

Note

To attempt to write of the Minoan achievement without a description of Minoan pottery is a classic instance of *Hamlet* without the prince. But it is literally true that this pottery must be seen to be believed; and it can be seen in the Heraklion Museum in all its phases. Some attempt, however, will be made in the chapter 'Sorting out the Vases' to enable the Hellenic traveller to pick out the main styles with their periods, not only of Greek vases but also of those of Minoan Crete. For the Minoans excelled in the art of pottery, and in the choice and handling of designs to fit the shapes of their vases they often excelled the later Greek vase painters. This work from the Bronze Age is a joy as well as a wonder.

CHAPTER X

Crete: Gortyna. Phaestos. Mallia

GORTYNA

The interest of the road from Heraklion to Gortyna and Phaestos on the south side of the island begins as it emerges from the streets of the town with the peak of Mount Juktas, the nearby mountain. Who could deny that the peak and its slopes have the form in silhouette of the head of some gargantuan recumbent figure? The Cretans say it is the head of sleeping Zeus. What is certain is that on the mountain summit was a Minoan sanctuary. An altar, a tree and a cluster of tall double-axes with offerings of figurines are the usual finds in these numerous mountain-top sanctuaries. Large storage jars were also found on Mount Juktas.

The road runs past vineyards on both sides of a long valley, slowly climbing to the pass 2,000 feet high. Most of the vineyards produce raisin grapes, and in high summer the day's picking is laid out in a long broad strip on the earth to dry, alongside a similar strip of the day before no longer green but lightly touched with gold. A week's picking makes a strange pattern on a distant hillside—like a huge colour-card of graded shades from green through gold to darkest brown.

Half-way up the pass, on the right of the road, is the flat-topped, steep-sided hill of Prinias, an obvious place for a Greek acropolis, one feels. And this it was found to be. From a seventh-century B.C. temple on the summit came the important frieze of sculptured horsemen in Room N in the Heraklion Museum. The horses proceed in file, long-legged horses and with long narrow

123

bodies but, with their dignified riders, there is a steady movement in the whole stately cavalcade which puts it high amongst
fine archaic sculpture.

The road descends by many hairpin bends into the great fertile
plain of Messara, sheltered by mountains on three sides. As a
long white thread lying across and down the mountain-side the
ancient paved Minoan road is often visible. A dozen threshing
floors, circular and level, pock-mark the nearer hills. Where the
road runs close to a ravine, a Greek will explain that here
Resistance men would ambush Nazi staff cars and hurtle them
over the edge.

Once the plain is reached, the road runs through olive groves
and the only sign that we have reached Gortyna is a ruined
church, close to the road, with just the east end standing. This
was a large sixth-century basilica church of St. Titus, first bishop
in Crete, and reputed to be his burial-place. This is hard to
credit, for Greece is a Christian nation in a literal sense and the
church would not be a neglected ruin if his tomb were really
believed to be in it. But there is somebody perhaps who believes,
for always there are wild flowers in a vase and a faded little ikon
on a stone slab in an alcove in the ruins.

Gortyna was an important Roman city and it is interesting
that the Romans did not consider Crete as an outlying part of
Greece but attached it to their province of Cyrenaica in North
Africa and made Gortyna the provincial capital. The city site has
not been excavated, but solitary columns and chunks of fallen
brick vaulting are visible among the olive trees. Recently a large
Minoan farmhouse was excavated, with a private house-chapel
and an altar with the double-axe symbol upon it.

Archaeologically the chief interest of Gortyna is in the Roman
odeum or music hall. For into the curving back wall of this
building, as a decorative feature and protected now by an admirable brick arcade, a sensible Roman architect incorporated from
an earlier structure the largest Greek inscription yet found. It is
thirty feet long by ten feet high and is part of a code of Greek
Law, dated about 450 B.C. The inscription is thus the most
important and earliest source existing of Greek Law.

The inscription is in boustrophedon lettering, the top line
running from left to right, and the next from right to left and so
continuing, like the oxen with the plough.

While it is clearly an aristocratic code of civil law, openly penalizing slaves more severely than citizens for the same offence, there is much surprising liberalism in it. The individual's rights show advanced thinking, especially where women, debtors and slaves are concerned. For instance a slave can recover damages from a citizen for assault: he can proceed at law against his master: he can own property and marry legally: and, surprisingly, he can marry a free-woman and the offspring will be free.

The excavation of this inscription by Dr. Halbherr in 1884 was highly romantic. Several years earlier he was enjoying the cool water of a mill stream when he noticed the top edge of a worked stone. He cleared the gravel away foot by foot and found under the water what he realized was a discovery of first importance. Quietly he covered it up again and planned to excavate. But there were political difficulties—and it took several years of negotiation before he was allowed to buy the land and divert the stream to find the odeum and this magnificent inscription. Canes grow by the side of the stream and the family in the old farmhouse sell pipes made from them. It is pleasant to walk the path through the olive-trees to the site to the sound of the pipes, and find a small boy making rustic antique music. Theocritus would approve.

PHAESTOS

A few miles further to the west of Gortyna there are now orange groves and all the signs in lush vegetation of abundant water. Three hills lie in the western entrance to the plain, and in 1900 Professor Halbherr here began his search for Phaestos. One of the two western-most hills seemed the likeliest spot. But it turned out otherwise: the hill of Phaestos was the innermost hill. It rises 300 feet, sheer on three sides, and there was room for a town both on and around it. To the north rises Mount Ida, easily identified by its twin peaks 8,000 feet high. The black dot sometimes visible high up below the right-hand peak is the Kamares Cave, the sanctuary in which was found so much of the thin-walled polychrome pottery of about 1800 B.C. known as 'Kamares ware'. The Idaean cave in which tradition says that Zeus spent his infancy is on the far side of Mount Ida, out of sight.

Crete: Gortyna. Phaestos. Mallia

Until Professor Levi of the Italian School of Archaeology began his extraordinarily successful series of excavations in 1952, it had been believed that there were only two successive palaces at Phaestos, the first dating from about 2000 B.C. as at Knossos, and the 'New Palace' from the period after the whole-sale destruction in Crete stemming from the volcanic explosion and earthquake at Thera about 1525 B.C. But Professor Levi, excavating in the south-west corner of the palace site where the ground falls to a level twenty feet lower, has dug into the side of the hill and presented us with parts of two earlier palace buildings of more modest dimensions. His photograph of the new discovery, published in the *Illustrated London News*, clearly shows what the caption described as 'A sight "perhaps unique in the monuments of antiquity": four superimposed palaces in a single glance.'

When the earliest palace was destroyed, presumably by earthquake, for there is no sign of fire or sacking by an enemy nor any break in development, the debris was not cleared away. But, to the great advantage of archaeologists today seeking for artifacts, a layer of concrete was poured over the confused mass of rubble to fill up the gaps and form a new floor level for a fresh building. It is possible in the new excavation to see this process as in a moving picture which came to a standstill: for here, at the lowest palace level, is a heavy mass of concrete which had oozed over the edge of the broken façade wall, with its well-set-up orthostates standing on the projecting podium, down to the courtyard level, and now remains like a frozen waterfall. A number of the finest examples of Middle Minoan II pottery of the Kamares style came from a wall cupboard in the second of these earliest palaces, and other remarkably fine work from the first. These are now in the Heraklion Museum. It should perhaps be noted that Marinatos, in his new book, *Crete and Mycenae*, does not accept that Levi's 'palaces' are more than houses. Yet they certainly have the same monumental outer walls of stone orthostates set up on a heavy stone base as in the accepted palaces on the top of the hill, an entrance hall with seating for visitors, the same—if smaller—storage jars (one of which contained a deposit of grape seeds, the earliest evidence of the vine in Crete), alabaster floors, drainage and, most suggestive of the 'palace', a large store of hieroglyphic and Linear A script tablets. These tablets, with many thousand seal impressions in lumped clay which once sealed the mouth of vases, came from under the layer of concrete which covered the ruins of walls of the earliest period, and were found when Levi opened a stretch of the great court of the last of all the palaces. Judgment perhaps is best reserved.

As at Knossos and at Mallia, there is a large west courtyard at Phaestos with a processional causeway a few inches raised above the paving. Here, too, are walled pits, similar to those at Knossos apparently for the disposal of broken sacrificial vessels. In the north-east corner, at the palace end of a long series of steps for the seating of spectators, are the sanctuary rooms where votives were found. These are close to the splendid stairway which leads up, through an open pillared hall facing on the west court. This feature of Minoan architecture was to be adapted in an improved form by the Greeks of the Classical period and turned into the propylaea with which they dignified the entrance to so many of their public buildings.

Other major features of the Knossos palace are to be found here too: the long galleries of storage magazines, one of the most impressive sights of Phaestos, the private apartments of the prince or governor grouped together this time on the north side where the cool north-west wind—the Phaestos life-saver—would be most effectively enjoyed in the scorching Cretan summer, the hard plaster of the walls (though lacking the bright frescoes of Knossos), and the pillared halls. That there was once a balcony at least on one side of the court was proved when Levi excavated and found stone column bases in a long line. At Knossos, too, it was the Old Palace which had a balcony.

When so many resemblances are observed between Knossos and Phaestos as to suggest a close relationship and not rivalry between them, it is pleasant to learn that identical masons' marks at both sites show that some at least of the workmen built at both places. The town of Phaestos lived on after the last palace was destroyed about 1450 B.C., and a number of Greek houses from the seventh century B.C. onwards covered parts of the ground which concealed the splendid Bronze Age palaces.

MALLIA

For much of the way to Mallia the road runs beside the sea,

till the hills heighten into mountains and a fertile plain widens to give a livelihood with its rich red soil and abundant water. Countless white-sailed windmills turning in the prevailing wind from the sea produce an effect of liveliness and gaiety, enhanced in the spring by acres of yellow corn marigolds in the fields and white birds wheeling in the sky, more numerous here than is usual in the Greek scene. Where the soil is thin and stony, carob-trees flourish and the rocky ground is the home of countless aromatic plants, sage, calaminth, cistus and thyme. Suddenly, with a change of soil, plantations of bananas remind the spring visitor that in the summer the heat is intense, and he will see on his map with some surprise that he is closer here to the Equator than if he were in Tunis or Algeria—and there, in early May, is the barley crop already golden, ready for the scythe.

The Minoan palace, originally found by the Greek Ephor and scholar, Hatzidakis, at the end of World War I, was fully excavated by the French School. Their work has recently been crowned with new success by the excavation of a long crypt hall and associated store-rooms to the west of the palace of which the function is not yet clear, for it is unique in plan in Minoan culture.

The palace buildings are not so extensive as at Knossos and Phaestos but are exactly similar in their essential components. Here, again, are buildings set round a great court: outer walls of fine masonry with the characteristic slab stones on edge standing on a heavy stone base and set in to make, in effect, a step: an entrance from the north through an open pillared hall—a propylon: storage magazines with the large and now familiar pithoi: impressive flights of steps: evidence of a balcony, thirty yards long, on the eastern side of the court, supported by alternate square piers and round columns—for the bases remain to indicate this, to us, unhappy arrangement: a sacred area uniquely furnished with a large circular stone, some four feet in diameter and with perhaps thirty circular depressions close to its circumference; this kernos is thought to have held offerings of all the first-fruits of the land, offerings to the Earth Goddess. There is also the usual labyrinthine complex of rooms and passages, and indications of the main rooms of state on the first floor. Here, also, was a great outer court on the western side. The walls for the most part are exposed rubble and clay, for the plaster covering is gone. It is correct to say that Mallia is not built on the same monumental lines as the greater palaces, but some of the finest gold ornament and jewellery was nevertheless found here. Notable among much beautiful Minoan crafts- manship in the splendid Museum in Heraklion is the Mallia gold pommel of a ceremonial bronze sword. It is circular, and, embossed upon it, an acrobat with curling hair and a finely modelled face rests, in his contortionist act, upon his elbows while with his toes he touches his hair, having bent 'inside out' all the way round in a circle, chest outermost. A gold pendant of two hornets holding a most delicately granulated honeycomb and supporting on their heads a little cage holding a ball, a craftsmen's illogical *tour de force*, is another lovely jewel from Mallia. So, too, is the golden mace in the form of a bounding leopard.

We miss at Mallia the elaborate drainage and water-supply system of Knossos: the authorities there were content to draw water by hand from eight large circular stone reservoirs at the south-west angle of the palace. And though there is a pillar room with the inevitable double-axe symbol, we miss the bull— so far.

So far . . . a Minoan world of fascinating interest and beauty, and the certainty that there is much more of both to come.

CHAPTER XI

Enter the Achaean Greeks: Mycenae. Tiryns. Pylos

At Mycenae we meet the Achaean Greeks, the earliest Greek-speaking people. Their culture is known as Mycenaean because this particular one of the many similar Achaean settlements was to become the most important, and, in its latest phase, to have a strong king, Agamemnon, who was accepted as leader of the great expeditionary army, made up of contingents from many places under their own leaders, which sailed to the famous siege of Troy. It was at Mycenae that Schliemann discovered in the Royal Grave Circle a treasure of gold and beauty of workmanship that is a highlight of this civilization.

These Achaean Greeks were moving in from the North Balkans between 2100 and 1600 B.C. and settling in a country and climate more pleasing than the wet and densely-wooded forest lands they had left behind. They were hunters and enjoyed the hunt; and being physically taller and stronger than the Mediterranean people who had earlier crossed the Aegean from Asia Minor, they were ready to use their weapons on men who resisted their advance. Where they settled, these Achaean Greeks built themselves fortresses and by their inherent qualities of energy, drive, intelligence and a martial spirit, they were able to develop and spread their distinctive culture. Contact with the Minoan civilization in the Aegean and beyond must have come early, for precious objects found in the Mycenaean palaces—metalwork, fine vases and engraved gems—show Cretan artistic

AT DELOS: 'DIONYSUS ON HIS PANTHER'—FLOOR-MOSAIC IN THE HOUSE OF THE MASKS
(100 B.C.)

This may well be the finest Roman mosaic to survive from the period ending with the first century B.C. Some of the marble tesserae are minute: for instance, the soft folds of the drapery, astonishing in a mosaic.

IN THE ALTIS AT OLYMPIA: THE TEMPLE OF HERA (600 B.C.)
*Note the early form of wall construction (as in the Minoan palaces): orthostates
on a podium. Above this first massive course, the wall was of sun-baked brick and
half-timber. The Hermes of Praxiteles stood towards the far east end of the cella*

HIGH ON THE SIDE OF THE ACROPOLIS AT PHILERIMOS IN RHODES
A fountain-house of the late Classical period: one of the very few preserved.

design, if not always workmanship. In their great days, after the fall of Knossos, the Mycenaeans spread their trade and influence far and wide from Sicily to Asia Minor and Syria and from Egypt to the Black Sea; and in all this Mycenae itself played a dominant role, for we read that the king of the great Hittite Empire addressed the Achaean king as 'brother'.

We can see the remains of the splendid citadels the Achaean warrior-chiefs built to maintain their position—Mycenae is the best of them all—and we can admire the beauty of their finest treasures because they were buried with them in deep graves now excavated. More than that, we can enter into their civilization, question their morals and manners, campaign with them at Troy, sail the seas with them, enter their homes and eat with them, know them and enjoy them, in the poems of Homer. True, he wrote his epics five hundred years after they had gone—gone as they had come, with fire and sword, but this time as the victims—yet, where archaeology can be a check, Homer's picture of Mycenaean life is found to be in true colour. This memory of Mycenaean life was kept green in the episodic lays of minstrels moving from place to place and living by their songs; and Homer in the eighth century B.C. transmuted the songs into his epics. The more we see of the Mycenaean sites and, in the National Museum at Athens, feast our eyes upon their wonderful weapons inlaid with gold and silver, their jewellery, gold cups and treasures, the more eagerly will many of us turn again to Homer to seek this golden age of Mycenaean Greece restored to life. But there is now a school of thought which denies that Homer reflects much of Mycenaean life. That 'all things are in a state of flux' is an uncomfortable present truth observed by the philosopher Heraclitus about 500 B.C.

MYCENAE

Mycenae is a fortified hill-top on the lower slopes of a twin-peaked mountain, six miles inland from Argos and commanding the road to Corinth, the Isthmus and the northern half of Greece. The earliest occupiers of this defensible site came at the beginning of the Bronze Age (about 2600 B.C. in southern Greece). Their non-hellenic origin is shown by the name they gave their home, as well as by evidence from objects and pottery from Early Bronze Age levels. Place names terminating with -enai, -ssos, -ttos, and -inthos are pre-hellenic. Other such names are Athenai, Knossos, Hymettos, Corinth and Olynthos.

In the Middle Bronze period (2000–1600 B.C.) comes the first Achaean settlement which litters this level with its characteristic pottery—the plain monochrome grey 'Minyan' ware (so called because it was first found in Minyan Orchomenos in Boeotia) that marks the settlements on many sites on the southward move of the Achaean Greeks.

By the sixteenth century B.C. Mycenae is strong and wealthy. The king has a palace and he and his chief officers are protected by fortification walls; but their horizon is by no means limited to the mountains that surround the rich plain of Argos. The Mycenaeans have already acquired a fine store of gold. Marinatos suggests that this was Egyptian gold, the pay given to these Mycenaean warrior adventurers, adept with the long sword and the spear, who went, perhaps in ships of the great Cretan navy, as mercenaries to help Egypt in its war against the Hyksos and were rewarded in the traditional Egyptian manner. It is certain that at this time Cretan art forms and craftsmanship appear at Mycenae. For the Mycenaeans, far from local in outlook and tough warriors though they were, saw the comforts and elegance of Minoan culture and adopted much of it at home. But they kept their distinctive palace architecture: the megaron, the big rectangular room with the long walls extended to form a porch and with its central hearth, and throne for the king against the wall on the right; and the fortification walls. Though pottery decorative designs were in general Minoan, the Mycenaeans developed some shapes of their own, such as the tall-stemmed two-handled wine-cup, a shape destined to survive and appear in a refined form as the lovely kylix of the best Attic period. It appears very likely that, in the fifty years before the destruction of Knossos, Mycenaean Greek was in use there, for the Linear B tablets found in the palace ruins are generally thought to belong to that period. Other innovations at Knossos in the period 1450–1400 B.C. that were not reflected in the rest of Crete, and which strongly suggest Mycenaean influence, are the introduction of a throne room for the king, as was normal in Mycenaean palaces on the mainland, and the beginning of that stiffening and stylization of the old, free-moving naturalistic

designs of pottery decoration which is to be the mark of Mycenaean vases all over the Aegean and eastern Mediterranean in
the heyday of Mycenaean power.

There is no evidence that Knossos was taken by force as a
preliminary to these changes: Mycenaean control there might
well have come about by the marriage of a Mycenaean leader
and a Minoan princess. With the collapse of the Minoan empire,
the wealth and power of Mycenae, now the strong centre of a
common culture in Greece and beyond, grew rapidly.

The fortifications—half a mile in circuit—date in their present
form from 1350–1300 B.C. when the citadel was enlarged and
strengthened. Except at the main entrance they are built of
large boulders, in a wall between sixteen and thirty feet thick.
The main entrance is the Lion Gate and here the masonry is of a
high order; very large square-cut conglomerate stones, nearly
two feet thick, are laid in level courses. Two single upright
stones and a huge horizontal slab laid across them make an
entrance way: and above it, in a relieving triangular space, there
is a thin slab carved with two lionesses which, with their front
paws on two altars, stand heraldically on guard on either side of
a typical Minoan column. The lions probably symbolize the
power of royalty and the single column the near presence from
on high of the deity to protect. The early sculptor has done well
in his modelling of these muscular lions, which are among the
oldest monumental sculptures in Europe.

Disagreeing with the scholars as to the meaning of Pausanias'
reference to the tombs of Agamemnon and his entourage,
Schliemann believed that he would find them inside the walls of
the acropolis. His eagle eye spotted the signs of a grave-circle
close inside the Lion Gate and, with a strong labour force of
125 men, he went down in places more than thirty feet to discover five royal family vaults with the bodies in them of twelve
men and three women and perhaps two children. Many of the
bodies were smothered in gold and jewellery and surrounded by
golden goblets, diadems, necklaces, toilet-boxes, swords and
daggers of bronze inlaid with gold and silver, decorative discs
of gold with repoussé designs of butterflies, cuttlefish, spirals
and the like, with articles, too, of crystal, silver, bronze and
ivory. It was a find of enormous importance, for the beauty of
the work, the variety of objects and the sheer wealth displayed,

proved the existence of a high state of civilization in the mainland a thousand years before the great days of Athens. How right
Homer had been to speak of Mycenae 'rich in gold'. When
Schliemann found that a splendid gold mask, fitting tightly over
one face, had in fact preserved the face itself, he was deeply
moved. 'I have gazed upon the face of Agamemnon,' he tele-
graphed to the King of Greece. But, as at Troy, he had got his
dates wrong. These graves all date about 1550 B.C.: Agamemnon
was murdered about 1240 B.C. Horace was right: there were
indeed great men before Agamemnon but they lack a poet to tell
us more of their story. At least we can be sure that these
honoured dead were of royal blood and loved beautiful things.

Beyond the grave-circle, Schliemann excavated a large house,
known now as the South House, which he took to be Agamemnon's palace, but again he was mistaken. The royal palace was
later discovered to be on the highest point of the acropolis. A
long ramp from the Lion Gate leads up to the steep summit and
the propylon to a large open court. There are similar courts at
Tiryns and Pylos and, a millennium later, the ordinary Greek
house (as can be seen at Priene or Olynthus) also has an open
court onto which the main room opens. The megaron has a
double porch, the inner one perhaps acting as a waiting-room.
The stone bases on which stood the wooden columns to hold up
the roof are still *in situ* and here and there patches of the original
floor survive. The ruins of Agamemnon's palace are certainly
meagre, but before or after a visit to Mycenae a reading of
Aeschylus' *Agamemnon* will rebuild its walls. He would be a dull
dog who could not in imagination stand in this courtyard and
join in the welcome home of the 'King of men' from the wars,
with a shudder notice the cold kiss of Clytemnestra and the
invisible link joining her to Aegisthus, and impotent, as in a
nightmare, even to shout a warning, see Agamemnon pass to his
bath and his doom.

But there are other features at Mycenae which do not require
a mental reconstruction; the postern gate in the north wall, the
sally-port in the furthest eastern corner of the circuit walls, and,
opposite it, in this same semi-enclosure which was the latest
addition to the fortification system, the entrance to a stairway
which with a hundred steps leads down in a tunnel under the
wall itself to a deep underground spring. In a siege the unending

water supply of the citadel would be a severe puzzle to the enemy. The steps end suddenly in a six-foot drop into what was once a tank and is now a trap for the unwary who rely on a box of matches to light their descent.

Outside the citadel walls, where the road bends sharply 150 yards from the Lion Gate, a second grave-circle was discovered in 1952 by Dr. Papadimitriou. Here are twenty-five graves of the same Middle Bronze period as those of Schliemann's discovery inside the citadel, and they have produced almost similar treasures of which the most charming and surprising is a pale blue crystal bowl in the form of a duck. The late Professor Wace of the British School also had much success at this time in the excavation of several Mycenaean houses, in one of which fifty-eight Linear B tablets were found, by the roadside not far from this second grave-circle. Two other adjacent houses also produced Linear B tablets, in addition to carved ivories for the decoration of furniture. The significance of these finds of Linear B writing in ordinary houses is that it now seems incorrect to assume that the art of reading and writing was confined to Government scribes working in the palaces, as had hitherto been thought.

But the finest monumental stone construction of the Bronze Age in Europe is still to be described. It is the so-called Treasury of Atreus, in reality a royal tomb, and the best preserved, the largest and the best constructed of nine tholos-type tombs in the immediate neighbourhood. It is a circular beehive tomb, nearly fifty feet in diameter and forty-seven and a half feet high at the apex, built into the hillside on the left side of the approach road and 300 yards lower down the hill than the newly-found houses. The entrance is a wide corridor forty yards long, between walls of large squared stone which grow higher and higher as the corridor drives into the hillside till the eighteen-foot-high doorway is reached. This is wider at the bottom than at the top, like the Egyptian pylon, and was flanked by engaged columns, tapered in the Minoan manner and decorated with a chevron pattern. Parts of these columns are now in the British Museum after lying forgotten and effectively lost for a generation in the basement of an Irish country house. The son and grandson of the house did not, it seems, share the grandfather's interest in curious stones he had gathered up on a tour in Greece in the

early nineteenth century. The lintel of this magnificently pro-
portioned doorway consists of two enormous stones, the inner
one is twenty-nine feet long and weighs 120 tons. One wonders
whether a Mycenaean architect had watched some huge construction in Egypt and so learnt how with the use of sand,
rollers, wedges and—last but not least essential—complete discipline among the huge team of labourers working to signalled
orders, such vast weights could be precisely controlled by
human minds and muscle. Over the lintel is a triangular space,
once filled with a light slab probably sculptured as at the Lion
Gate and as also in Egyptian practice where this method to
relieve the lintel of excessive weight was first used. It is worth
noting the construction in this triangular space: a corbel system—the overlapping stones cannot fall because of the great
weight above holding them in position. This, in fact, is how the
whole dome-like beehive effect is obtained in the chamber itself.
Each circular course of masonry overlaps the course below until
at the top a single stone crowns the whole. In the construction a
cylindrical pit was first dug, and as the stones in their circular,
overlapping courses were laid, heavy boulders and earth were
placed to fill up the space between the walls of the pit and the
outer faces of the stones of the chamber. Finally the pit and the
chamber in it were covered over with a mound of soil and the
tomb looked like a simple tumulus. When the overlapping edges
of the stones in the interior were smoothed away, the walls were
faced with bronze plates. The nail holes and some of the nails are
there to indicate that Homer was not exaggerating when he
describes, for instance, the palace of Alcinous 'in bright splendour like the sun with its brazen walls'. A small rectangular
chamber opens out of the main room, on the right; this was
perhaps used to house the first burial when the tomb was
reopened later for a second.

The corbel construction of the tholos is not so safe as a true
dome and the majority of these tombs have, at least partially,
collapsed. The tholos 'tomb of Clytemnestra' is near the second
grave-circle and, indeed, in building impinged on it: its topmost
part has been restored. Close to it is the collapsed 'tomb of
Aegisthus'.

A tholos tomb of about 1550 B.C. was found at Knossos, but
most of this type are in the Peloponnese, a few in Thessaly, and

a fine but collapsed one in Orchomenos—the 'tomb of Minyas'. They date in Greece from about 1500 B.C. and fall out of architecture about 1300 B.C. From the evidence of pottery fragments the Treasury of Atreus is dated between 1330 and 1300 B.C. Parallel construction has been found in Ireland and in the Sardinian Nuraghi: but these latter remarkable buildings are above ground, have two and three storeys and were lived in as domestic fortresses. In many of them a ladder to reach the stairs at first-floor level was a necessity. The verdict of some experts at least is that the tholos tomb was a Mycenaean invention.

Their victory over Troy, like so many victories in the world's history, did not introduce a long period of peace for the Mycenaean contingents. The united army broke up: some men returned to the various settlements centring on their fortress palaces, while others went adventuring. Within a very few years all those fortresses had gone up in flames except only that on the Acropolis at Athens. The Dorians—men of iron—had arrived. It was the ending of the Bronze Age. Unlike the first wave of Greek-speakers—the Achaeans who appreciated the culture of the more advanced Minoans and made much of it their own—this great migration of Dorians, also Greek-speakers, did not have any taste for the Mycenaean civilization. They were destroyers, superior in force but not in culture to those they overcame, and a long dark age ensued.

TIRYNS

Like a great whale's back intruding on the surface of a calm sea, the dark hillock of Tiryns rises from the serene plain of Argos, looking quite out of place. Tiryns is a grim fortress of large, black limestone boulders, many weighing several tons apiece, built in the late Bronze Age, now a mile from the sea which once came close to its walls, and commanding the road from Nauplion to Argos and Mycenae. Pausanias regarded these walls as a phenomenon more amazing than the pyramids of Egypt—which shows how the ancient Baedeker exaggerated. But he is right in calling attention to the extraordinary size of the stones used. They were not quarried in the usual sense, but taken from the slopes of mountains near Mycenae, where similar rocks are everywhere to be seen. Homer had dubbed Tiryns 'great-walled', and, since it seemed that only a race of giants could have handled such stones, the Greeks called these walls 'cyclopean'.

Such a site was sure to be settled in the earliest days before the plain was drained, and it is no surprise that neolithic fragments indicate such an early settlement. Moreover, the name of the place, terminating in -inthos, points to a pre-Greek origin.

Schliemann undertook a first excavation at Tiryns and sank many trial shafts which brought to light some of the palace walls. It was not until 1400 B.C. that Tiryns began to assume its present form. Certainly there were large buildings on the summit before that date. One of them was a circular building ninety feet in diameter, itself built over the foundations of a still older building. No traces of these are now visible, but in the excavation much detail of the rare circular building was recorded.

The great days of Tiryns, then, were those of Achaean rule when further inland the warrior kings of Mycenae held a broad sway. Perhaps a prince of the royal house lived here, guarding the route from the sea to his father's palace up in the hills. The huge walls were built in stages, each extending the fortified area. In the last stage, the whole of the northern part of the hill, less high than the fortified and terraced summit previously walled in, was given walls, and so provided for the safety, in a crisis, of the whole population of the city who lived around the hill on the plain. This was about 1300 B.C. when, significantly, new fortifications were built on other Mycenaean sites. Danger was in the air. At this time too, at Tiryns the magazines, or underground storage galleries, were constructed. These, in comparatively recent centuries, have been used as sheep pens and the stone walls polished by the constant movement of the sheep. Since the polish extends several feet up the wall, a gradual deepening of the deposit on the ground must be assumed.

In 1962 a tunnel was found under the extreme north-western wall of the latest area of fortification, by which the defenders could have secret access, as at Mycenae, to an underground source of water outside the walls.

The fortress was entered by a long ramp, supported on a wall of cyclopean masonry, which led up below the high walls and turned into a narrow passage between two towers before reaching the actual gateway. Thus, all the way an attacker would be exposed, on his right side undefended by his shield, to the fire of the defenders on the walls and towers. Once inside, the attacker found he was still overlooked and that there was still another gateway to pass through. Beyond that was an outer propylon (part of the palace buildings rather than of a fortress), a large court, a second propylon and an inner court, surrounded on three sides by columns, and then the megaron of the palace itself.

The megaron at Tiryns is very similar to those of Mycenae and Pylos. There is, in fact, such a similarity between the fortification walls, the gateway arrangements at the end of a long passage, and the details of the megaron at Mycenae and Tiryns, that it would seem the same supervisors and workmen built both palaces and citadels.

There are two smaller megara and two small courts in front of them, which some authorities consider to be women's quarters. But Wace holds that there is no evidence that the three megara ever existed at the same time. To the left of the main megaron is a bathroom, its floor a single enormous flat stone.

Tiryns lost its palace buildings and the beauty of its patterned floors and frescoed walls in the general destruction inflicted upon all the major Mycenaean sites by the Dorian invaders; but the town of Tiryns around the fortress hill continued to exist and in due course, in the crisis of the Persian invasion, sent its contingent to Plataea. The name of Tiryns is on the honour roll of all the thirty-one states who fought at Plataea against the barbarian invaders, engraved upon the bronze serpent-column supporting the golden tripod that the Spartans set up at Delphi as a thank-offering, and later looted to Constantinople.

But the pride of the Tirynthians during the years that followed was too much for the neighbouring, larger city of Argos to bear, and Tiryns was destroyed.

There is no grace or charm, no benefit of scenery at Tiryns, only a grim undertone of force and struggle for existence, to which the modern Greek prison at the foot of the citadel seems to send an echo.

PYLOS

Homer makes it clear that Agamemnon, lord of Golden Mycenae, included in his expeditionary force for the assault on

Enter the Achaean Greeks: Mycenae. Tiryns. Pylos

Troy contingents from all over the southern Peloponnese. Fragments of Mycenaean pottery, turned up by the plough, confirm that large areas of the south-west of the Peloponnese were once occupied by Mycenaeans. It is a beautiful part of Greece and, because it is mountainous and lies in the path of the prevalent westerlies which have crossed a long stretch of sea to reach this land, the rainfall is good. There is deep soil in the valleys and in May 'they stand so thick with corn that they do laugh and sing'.

Just where in that region Homer's Pylos lay, no one could say with certainty—not even Strabo, the historian and geographer of the first century A.D. He could not distinguish it among three places called Pylos. All that was known was that, according to Homer, somewhere near the sea in the far south-west of the Peloponnese stood the palace of Nestor. He was the friend of Odysseus, and famous for his wisdom and his great age. He had won fame for his part in the Trojan Wars, but he contributed more than wisdom, having taken his men in no less than ninety 'black ships'.

Nestor had safely returned home after the war, but Odysseus had failed to make Ithaca. At last Telemachus, Odysseus' son, urged on by Athena disguised as Mentor, sailed away to search for him and, first, to inquire of his father's wise old comrade-in-arms what news he might have of him. In the third book of the Odyssey, the party lands on the sandy beach of Pylos at the moment of the sacrifice of ninety bulls by a huge gathering of Nestor's men. 'There sat Nestor with his sons, while the banquet of wine and meats was prepared around them.' The strangers are welcomed and fed handsomely, 'sitting on downy fleeces on the sand'. Prompted by the ever-active and helpful Athena, the nervous Telemachus braces himself to make his speech of inquiry for his father. Nestor, alas, has no firm news to give, but many a tale of heroism and hardship to recount. But he builds up the young man's confidence and promises him a chariot to Sparta so that he may question Menelaus. And first—he is no threadbare pauper: he has blankets and warm bedding for all in his palace—he insists that the son of his old friend must sleep indoors in comfort like a gentleman. It is a charming scene which Homer paints—of simple courtesy and homely welcome and assistance in a setting of a rich well-ordered community. At Pylos (and at Tiryns too) there is a bathroom on the ground floor near the megaron; for to offer, and to give, a bath to the honoured guest on arrival was part of the traditional hospitality of the Achaeans. Homer in *Odyssey*, Book III, writes:

'During the sacrifice beautiful Polycaste, the youngest grown daughter of Nestor son of Neleus, had given Telemachus his bath, washing him and anointing him with rich olive oil before she draped him in a seemly tunic and cloak: so that he came forth from the bath-cabinet with the body of an immortal.'

Translation by T. E. SHAW (Lawrence of Arabia)

In 1839 Christopher Wordsworth, after visiting Pylos and recalling this Homeric story in his book, wrote that one would willingly exchange some historic battlefield for a fixed spot with which to associate old Nestor and his delightful hospitality. Exactly 100 years later Professor Blegen of Cincinnati University found that spot. He has now uncovered a large palace building of Mycenaean type together with 600 clay tablets inscribed in Linear B, which, with other evidence, proved that here indeed was a seat of Government and, beyond reasonable doubt, the palace of Nestor. It is about five miles away, in a north-easterly direction, from the sandy northern beach of Navarino Bay, at Epano Englianos.

The palace stands on the steep-sided shoulder of a long hill with deep valleys on either side. From it Nestor could look out to sea over the long and beautiful bay, and, nearer, to his harbour at the foot of a precipitous hill by the shore. In medieval days this hill was to be the perfect site for the castle of the Regent of Morea, Nicholas of St. Omer, and later for the Genoese, the Venetians, the Turks, and, finally, Morosini, all of whom desired it and fought successfully for it.

The palace foundations and low walls are now covered over by a huge plastic roof to preserve them, but, despite this twentieth-century structure which looks like a 'bus garage, the place in its spring dress is beautiful, and the bee-orchids and the wild flowers under the olive-trees are a constant diversion from the study of antiquities.

On the very first day of the excavation, Blegen had found the archives room, containing some hundreds of clay tablets, well-preserved by having been burnt hard in the fire which had clearly consumed the whole palace. This find proved to be of the utmost importance, for the inscriptions on the tablets were

in the same script as those Evans had found at Knossos in Crete
and called Linear B. These Pylos tablets from a flourishing
Mycenaean site, though found in a context two centuries later
than those found at Knossos, are an important link in the chain
of evidence that, in the last years of the palace of Knossos before
its destruction in about 1400 B.C., the Mycenaeans were dominant at Knossos, for Ventris and Chadwick have shown that the
language of them all is Greek.

There are two palaces proper, an older and smaller building
with its megaron (the ceiling of which was carried by four
columns), an entrance hall, domestic quarters, and a staircase to
the upper storey; and the later, much more substantial and
bigger palace. This was built as a homogeneous unit and to the
highest standards of structure and lay-out of Mycenaean times.
The ground-floor contained forty-five halls, rooms, porticoes,
lobbies, courts, stairways, bathroom—the bath is *in situ*, as also
the chilly, stone bath-mat—and, of course, the megaron; and
this building had an upper storey. The lower walls are of stone
blocks coated with plaster; the upper walls were probably of
sun-baked brick, also plastered, and, as in half-timbered Tudor
houses, heavy beams of timber were used vertically and horizontally to hold and strengthen the brick construction. Evidence of
painted decoration on the walls was found throughout the
palace and the subjects include compositions of human figures,
floral designs, animals and marine creatures and even griffins,
and there is a warrior in a boar's tusk helmet as described by
Homer.

The megaron roof was supported by four fluted columns and,
in the centre, is a noble hearth, decorated with a flame design.
On a side wall there is the platform for the throne. The plaster
walls were decorated with paintings—among these, one of a
splendid griffin on guard beside the throne. In the Queen's hall
the griffin is again seen. As it appears also on seal impressions,
it may be that the griffin was a badge of the Royal House of
Pylos.

In a pantry no less than 600 pots were found; in another,
some hundreds of kylixes (wine-cups) lay as they had fallen
when the shelving collapsed. In two magazines some fifty giant
pithoi had been stored, and many others in a wine storage
building outside the palace.

Enter the Achaean Greeks: Mycenae. Tiryns. Pylos

The palace buildings did not last long. The whole period of use falls in the Late Mycenaean period. This is the evidence of the pottery. In Troy VIIA (Priam's Troy), also excavated by Professor Blegen, Mycenaean pottery of the period known as Late Helladic IIIA and IIIB was found: at Nestor's palace the pottery is only of L.H. IIIB and IIIC type. It is concluded, therefore, that the fire which destroyed Nestor's palace burnt it out not long after the fall of Troy—i.e. about 1200 B.C.

The main gateway to the palace area was also excavated, with foundations of guard houses on either side of the steep paved road. A hundred and fifty yards outside the gateway, the first of numerous tholos or beehive tombs, was found. The 'dome' had, however, collapsed, but it has now been restored. Some thirty such tombs are now known in the Pylos area. The building of the dome is effected by the use of the corbel principle: each course of masonry slightly overlaps the course below it, so that the building rises to a single capping stone. The 'beehive' is then covered with soil, the entrance being at the end of a dromos, or stone-lined passage, running horizontally into the side of the mound.

One particular tholos was recently excavated by Lord William Taylour who recognized minute sherds of Mycenaean pottery on what was then a level drying-floor for currants. Burials of Mycenaean date were found only nine inches below the surface. Beneath the original floor level of the tholos four large pottery jars each contained a complete skeleton. Though this form of burial was at an early period—c. 2000 B.C.—common in Crete, this was the first such discovery in a Mycenaean tholos. Twenty-five weapons—rapiers, swords and daggers—came from this tomb, and a quantity of beads, including some of amber from the Baltic.

Pylos stands high in the list of important archaeological discoveries, and, though the walls that remain are only two or three feet high, we should be able to raise them in imagination and people the courts and balconies, the pantries and the megaron, with gay and courteous folk with a welcome to inquiring visitors from across the sea.

CHAPTER XII

Troy: The Nine Cities

*'What's not destroy'd by Time's devouring hand?
Where's Troy, and where's the Maypole in the Strand?'*

The Eighteenth-century poet was well in advance of his time. His question implied that Troy, though lost, did once exist, whereas most scholars even a century and a half later, in the 'seventies, denied it and thought of Troy as existing only in the legendary epics of Homer and Virgil and in the imagination of Roman Emperors who dutifully broke their travels in their eastern Empire to sacrifice on the traditional tomb of a mythical Achilles. It was Schliemann who put Troy on the map in 1870 and in doing so both fulfilled the ambition of his boyhood, fired by the incomparable stories told him by his father from Homer's *Iliad*, and made an immortal name as a pioneer archaeologist. His full, strange and romantic story is well told by Robert Payne in *The Gold of Troy*. It is true that Schliemann excavated more like an enthusiastic mastodon than a scrupulous scientist, but his success at the hill of Hissarlik where he uncovered Troy, and at Mycenae and Tiryns, seems to require a touch of magic in his uninstructed intuition.

Of the few scholars who did believe in the reality of Troy, the majority favoured Bunarbashi as the likely hill, five miles from Hissarlik to the south-east; for in this area there are many springs, some hot, some cold, yet in close conjunction, and Homer had mentioned this phenomenon in setting his scene for Troy. Homer, however, was writing a poem, not a geography

book. Schliemann unerringly chose Hissarlik (despite the fact
that 'hot and cold' were not laid on!). It is a low hill on the edge
of a flat plain, three miles inland at the entrance of the Dardanelles on the Asiatic side. Here we can now say that

> '*Odysseus drunk delight of battle with his peers*
> *far on the ringing plains of windy Troy.*'

Not that Schliemann correctly recognized in the chaos of his
excavations the actual walls of Priam's Troy. There have proved
to be nine settlements, some mere villages, others cities, one
upon another. The much more scientific German archaeologist,
Dörpfeld, assisted Schliemann in his later work and did much to
clarify results. Professor Charles Blegen and his fellow-Ameri-
cans have done an important re-excavation of the site, which was
seriously disturbed in the first early work of Schliemann; indeed,
some of the evidence was lost for ever in the zeal which drove
enormous trenches into the hillside. Some idea of the mountain
of spoil removed by Schliemann's large labour force is given by
the height of several pyramids of soil and stone which he pur-
posely left untouched, and which rise above the present level of
the ground to indicate the original height before he removed the
top of the hill.

It is not feasible for the visitor to sort out the foundation lines
of all the nine cities of Troy, superimposed as they are in ever-
widening rings, one upon another. From no position can the
whole be seen at one time, and the hills and valleys of excavation
produce a confused and ugly effect. But to stand on the acropolis
of Troy and look out across the plains of the Scamander and
Simois—now only minor streams—to the distant sea, takes the
gaze over the long battlefields of Achaeans and Trojans and the
encampments of the army and the stockaded ships. It is not
beyond the imagination to visualize the duel of Hector and grim
Achilles below, as one stands near Andromache tense upon the
walls, till the fateful saga completes its sadness and the dead
Hector is dragged by the feet behind the victor's chariot, his long
hair trailing in the dust.

The few small walls of the first settlement (Troy I: 3000–
2500 B.C.) are distinguished by the comparative smallness of the
stones used (not much bigger than modern bricks) and they are
laid only roughly in horizontal courses, nor are they cut with

flat surfaces. The lowest course leans to the right, the course above to the left, an alternating herringbone pattern. The pottery is black, and the wheel not yet in use. These walls—or the bases of them—can be seen half-way down the valley in the hillside which runs down to the plain on the north side of the hill.

Troy II (2500–2100 B.C.) is a true fortified acropolis. It is only 100 yards in diameter, but this is enough to contain the megaron or palace of the king, the temple of the patron goddess and the houses of the court. In times of trouble this citadel would of course be filled with fighting men and some proportion of the people crowded into temporary housing. We shall find evidence for this in Troy VIIA. The fortification walls of Troy II, their courses roughly laid with small unsquared stones, are in many places visible to a considerable height, and one of the site's most interesting features is a stone ramp on the southwest side which leads up to a gateway in the wall. Schliemann, always ready to jump to a picturesque conclusion, supposed this to be the slope up which the Trojans dragged the wooden horse packed with Greek commando troops after the Greeks had left it on the plain and sailed away—but only to hide in waiting behind the island of Tenedos. But Schliemann's dating was all wrong. Troy II was 1,000 years older than Priam's Troy which is identified as VIIA. The great find of gold and jewellery which he called 'Priam's Treasure' and which he smuggled out of Turkey, came from the level of Troy II. This citadel was destroyed by fire.

Troy III and Troy IV were nothing more than village settlements, but the pottery shows development: the jugs have long necks and single handles appear on some pots.

Troy V (1800–1700 B.C.) shows the beginning of decoration in pottery, pale though it is. But Troy VI (1700–1275 B.C.) is a fine city and a new one built by new people. Here are signs of prosperity and power and of trading with Mycenaean Greece. The encircling wall encloses a much larger area and the wall itself is a fine construction. The stones are squared and skilfully laid in clear courses, but it is only the lower part of the wall which survives. This shows the 'batter', the inclined slope towards the bottom of a wall which was to be used in so many medieval fortifications. It has been suggested that this inclined base has a practical military purpose beyond that of adding

AT KNOSSOS IN CRETE: PORTICO ON A BASTION AT THE NARROW
NORTH ENTRANCE-PASSAGE TO THE PALACE OF MINOS, 1600 B.C.
(restored)

*On the wall behind the Minoan columns is a reproduction of the fresco of a charging
bull. The original (now in the Heraklion museum) was in situ on the portico wall
when Greeks of the Geometric period lived close round the abandoned palace ruins,
for with its fallen wall the fresco was found above the level of Greek dwellings.*

IN CORFU AT PALAEOKASTRITZA

*There is a sheltered harbour between the two headlands, and a second lies to the left
of the picture. The headlands are joined to the mainland by a neck of level land. It is
a place of luxuriant gardens. Here are the topographical features which fit Homer's
picture of King Alcinous' palace to which Nausicaa led the shipwrecked Odysseus.*

strength. A boulder dropped from the battlements at the top of the main vertical walls at the moment when the enemy sought to apply scaling ladders or to use a battering ram, would strike the incline and fly out into the face of the enemy instead of dropping dead upon the earth. The walls are built in straight runs until a change of angle is required. A close examination will show how the masons effected this with no loss of strength. Towers were provided at intervals by which to enfilade attack. These are not bonded into the wall, because, being higher and heavier than the wall, if their foundations settled under their weight they would have damaged the wall, had they been engaged with it. These masons of the sixth city knew their job. There is a specially fine tower—or the base of it—at the north-easterly point in the circuit, and here there is a narrow stair-way which the agile may still descend and, looking back and up, feel that Homer rightly called Troy 'well-walled, well-towered and high-gated'. A main road runs in from the south gate: it was paved and had a central buried drain down the centre. On the left is a house with two internal pillars to support the roof: and wall cupboards such as occur in Minoan palaces. The local pottery is grey Minyan, undecorated, and there is much imported Mycenaean ware. This fine city was destroyed by earthquake and fire.

Troy VIIA is a poor, hasty and cheap rebuilding of their stricken and splendid stronghold by the survivors. The evidence is clear enough that in the short lifetime of Troy VIIA trade between Troy and Mycenaean Greece steeply decreased, per-haps stopped: that the number of people living now inside the fortifications enormously increased, so that numerous small rooms of light construction were crowded in; and, most sig-nificant, great stores of food and oil and other supplies were 'laid in', big pithoi being sunk into the ground below floor level to give room for living or for additional storage. In several of the houses close up to the walls these unusual storage chambers survive. This overcrowded Troy VIIA was 'ruthlessly laid waste by the hand of man who completed his work of destruction by fire'. So writes Professor Blegen. And the date? Somewhere between 1240 B.C. and 1200 B.C.

This, then, was Priam's Troy which saw the danger coming and crowded the people into the acropolis whose walls they had quickly and urgently repaired where the earthquake had damaged them. But it was a vain effort, even if it lasted ten years. Yet the defence, as Homer tells the story, was so stout-hearted as to put the adjective 'Trojan' into our dictionaries as a term of admiration for great and enduring effort. The pathos of Homer's description of the farewell of Hector, the young warrior prince, to his wife Andromache before he entered into that single combat with Achilles which he knew in his bones would be his last battle, still tugs at the heart-strings; and in Virgil's *Aeneid* we watch with bated breath as that good son, Aeneas, staggers out of the smoke and flame of the burning city with his old father Anchises on his back and his household gods in his bag, to venture the long escape which will take him right across the Mediterranean by way of Carthage and the warm welcome of Queen Dido, eventually to Latium to be the founder of the Roman State.

Troy VIII emerges after a long blank period. No pottery of the years 1100 B.C. to 700 B.C. was found. Over the ashes of Priam's Troy there was indeed some crude hand-made pottery of the kind found in Danubian sites of 1200–1100 B.C., signs of a temporary settlement by an alien folk, but no new city was built till the Ilium of 700 B.C. We find the lustrous black Attic pottery of the sixth and fifth centuries and the familiar architectural fragments, capitals and columns of the Doric order. These are of such a level of excellence as to suggest considerable prosperity in the Greek city.

Troy IX was a Hellenistic city, furnished with temples, theatre, odeum, bouleuterion and doubtless all the other amenities of the day, and it lasted through the Roman imperial period, to fade away about A.D. 400. Close to the little theatre, which is an odeum or music-hall for a comparatively small audience, there are Roman period altars, and the marble drums of Corinthian columns. Troy in Imperial Roman days must have been of importance to have been furnished with marble in its public buildings. Another Roman sector of the site is to the north-west. There is a path down to the plain in this corner of the site outside the perimeter of the walls: and half-way down the hillside in an open court are a pair of wells—the well-heads built up in masonry. No doubt the area was paved; here is an opportunity to compare the regular courses of heavily rusticated

Roman masonry with the earlier Trojan work. Doubtless the Roman city spread far outside the walls. To the east, several hundred yards from the city wall, there have been found traces of a large theatre in a natural hollow of the hillside overlooking the plain.

The root cause for this long series of cities lies in geography. Sailing ships from the south found it hard to stem the adverse current running through the narrows of the Dardanelles, and cargoes would be off-loaded on the Asiatic shore to the east of the Dardanelles, transported overland to a point above the narrows and loaded into ships from northern and Black Sea ports for the completion of the journey north. Troy was in a position to protect this overland route, and charge for the protection. A strong city on the hill of Hissarlik was a paying proposition both for sea traders and for the Trojans of all periods. Not that the Romans, when it came to their turn to take over the city of Troy, were actuated by purely commercial motives; they felt an immense veneration for the town of their origin—as they liked to believe it. Julius Caesar paid a visit to this city of his ancestor Iulus, son of Aeneas; and various financial and other privileges were granted to the historic city. Nero added to them; Antoninus Pius confirmed them; and Caracalla set up a colossal bronze Achilles on the mound by the sea at the entrance to the Dardanelles which was his reputed grave. There was a Bishop of Ilium for several hundred years; but then the name dropped out as the city declined. The day came when the famous city fell clean out of history into legend, and goats grazed on the bare and rounded hillock where nine Troys had stood.

A question is often asked as to the whereabouts of the two rivers, Simois and Scamander. There are two water-courses, marked by their lines of rather scraggly willows: one to the north, Simois, and the other, larger, to the west, Scamander. But on this alluvial plain winter floods are normal, and the rivers must have changed their courses more than once. Strabo and Pliny in their accounts of the rivers' courses hardly help, the latter even asserting that the Scamander was navigable. No geologist could agree that it was ever open to ships.

There are, however, other landmarks mentioned by Homer of a more stable kind. From our stand on the hill of Hissarlik we see in the far north-west the mountain-top of the island of Samothrace, towering over nearer Imbros, and thirty miles to the south-east Mount Ida is often visible: the grand-stands from which the gods, Zeus on Mount Ida and Poseidon on the peak of Samothrace, watched the long-drawn siege and the battles of mortal men who have entered immortality in Homer's *Iliad*.

CHAPTER XIII

In Search of Odysseus in Corfu and Ithaca

CORFU

For the traveller approaching by ship from Venice, the island of Corfu is likely to be the front door to Greece—for Greece is not to be thought of as only the mainland, and her islands are to be counted in hundreds—and a lovely entry it is. Corfu is the most northerly of the Ionian Islands and lies, at its nearest point, only two miles from the north-west tip of the mainland of Greece. Across the huge sheltered bay stand the high ranges where 'Arethusa arose from her couch of snows in the Acroceraunian mountains'. Corfu, too, has its mountain range to catch the moisture-laden westerlies and call down their showers to water the deep valleys which score its sides and produce such a wealth of olives, figs, oranges and lemons, vines and maize.

The fertility of the island has long been famous. Even Homer wrote of the well-watered gardens of King Alcinous, ruler of the Phaeacians. For Corfu is claimed to be Homer's Scheria, where Odysseus was washed ashore from his wreck and escorted to the Royal Palace. On emerging exhausted from the rough sea, he had gone to sleep in the shade and was later awakened by the laughter of girls as Princess Nausicaa played a ball-game with her laundry-maids during a break in the laundering process. The poor man had lost, in the sinking of his ship, everything he once stood up in; but here might be help if he could decently summon it. So he plucked a spray of leaves and sallied forth. Away went the servants with a shriek: only the regal Nausicaa stood her ground. Odysseus made a splendid explanation of his plight,

discreetly observing that, if Nausicaa were not the goddess
Artemis herself, then her mortal beauty was the loveliest thing
he had ever seen and exactly reminded him of a fresh young
sapling palm-tree which had made a deep impression on him
when he saw it in the island of Delos! Nausicaa responded
admirably. 'Sir, your manners prove that you are no rascal and
no fool. Clothes and everything else you need will be given you.
My father is the king.' Before the laundry cart moves off,
Odysseus tidies himself and now looks much better for his toilet,
in which Athena had invisibly assisted him. His bushy locks now
hung from his head 'thick as the petals of the hyacinth in bloom'
(Rieu's translation). Nausicaa describes the town and the twin
harbours and the narrow level ground between them, the high
ramparts, the palace itself, and the vegetable garden. The
exciting point of all this is that Palaeokastritsa, on the open
rocky western coast, fits this description so well that we may say
that, even if Odysseus was never here after all, at least Homer
knew of it.

In any event, Palaeokastritsa is one of the most beautiful
corners of Greece. The long mountain-side sweeps down to the
sea with a varied texture and colour of orchard greens and grey-
green olive-trees, with random dark cypresses growing tall and
slender among the plantations; and the downward sweep ends in
high cliffs of colour-streaked rock, except where twin peninsulas
jut out from a level stretch of land. Between these steep and
rocky natural citadels is a perfect harbour with a sandy beach,
and, beyond the southern citadel, a second harbour and a second
sandy beach. Away to the south runs the long mountain wall,
torn and battered where it meets a sea always angry when the
west wind rides. Some seven miles away to the south, at Ermoni,
a river falls into the sea, making clean, clear pools in the rock
ledges of the cliff as it cascades down. Homer must have known
this place, and so provided Nausicaa with a mule-cart for the
laundry baskets. For it is much too far from the palace to carry the
washing. We are indeed in Homer's footsteps, but archaeology
has found no trace—may we say 'yet'?—of those of Alcinous on
these rocky peninsulas. The only building there is that of a
monastery, old and white, with vine-shaded courts and flower-
decked porticoes—in summer paradise enough, especially with
lobsters from their rocky haunts below as plentiful as sprats.

In Search of Odysseus in Corfu and Ithaca

The Greeks on the east coast of the island, with a cheerful disregard of probability, claim that Alcinous' palace was on the peninsula at Corfu city itself. Are there not twin harbours there? And, a few miles to the north, a river runs into the sea where still on Mondays the local ladies beat their washing on the stones. But no. Drifting in a gale from the west, Odysseus must make his landing on the island's western shore, and not on the beach of the sheltered channel on the eastern side.

The Corfu Channel offered shelter from the strongest westerlies and was therefore a useful waiting-place for shipping making the crossing to Sicily and Italy and the numerous Greek colonies of Magna Graecia. So Corcyra (as we know it in Greek History) came into being. It was founded in 734 B.C. as a colony by those great traders and seafarers, the Corinthians; and the economic success its geographical position gave it was probably the root cause of the quarrels and wars with the mother-city which distinguish its history. For the city quickly accumulated wealth and power to the point of provocation. It was in fact a renewal of this long-standing competitive jealousy which led to the outbreak of the Peloponnesian war—the tragedy of tragedies for all philhellenists. Stung by a naval defeat at the competent hands of Corcyra, Corinth mobilized her allies and a large fleet for revenge. Even the hardy Corcyraean seamen quailed at the odds against them: they sought Athenian help. Athens, unwilling that a Corinthian naval victory should add the Corcyraean fleet to the resources of a rival maritime power, answered the appeal. Corinth counter-appealed to Sparta. Hinc illae lacrimae.

For so long as Corfu's sheltered harbours gave security to ships—all through the centuries when navigators had to wait for favourable winds—the history of the island is written round its geographical position. Each power that rose and used the much-furrowed route between east and west in the Mediterranean, desired to possess this valuable stretch of sheltered water. And so the people of Corfu have been constantly involved in wars and in occupation by stronger powers . . . Spartans, Macedonians, King Pyrrhus, pirates, Romans, Byzantines, Venetians, Napoleon . . . but never Turks. Even the British at one time held the island, from 1815 to 1864; and the evidence for this, and for the architectural good taste of the Lord High Commissioner, Sir Thomas Maitland, confronts the surprised visitor, as he steps on to the town quay, in the Georgian neo-classic style Government House of white Malta stone. Possibly destined to last longer than the Georgian building as evidence that the British were here, is the curious existence of the cult of cricket on this stony island, its rules and customs observed as keenly as on an English village green, but played perhaps with more dust and heat—of both kinds.

Classical remains on the island are scanty and are mostly confined to the Corfu Museum. The chief exhibit is a sixth-century B.C. temple pedimental sculpture group, aesthetically of singular ugliness, but interesting as an example of archaic style and its conventions. The gorgon-headed Artemis is seen full-face and her body too is shown in its widest aspect, while the legs are in profile. She appears to be kneeling on one knee, but that is the early convention for running at full speed.

The visit to the Achilleion—so called because of a colossal modern bronze statue of Achilles in the garden of the palace—is worth-while for the view over the island and, across the straits, to the mountains of the mainland. The palace, built in 1890, was used as his summer residence by Kaiser Wilhelm II, who was a lover of Greece and liked to spend a foreign holiday here. It is furnished in the grand style—'de style pseudo-grec'. To walk round this morgue of faded majesty was to see a classic example of bathos. But Fortune's revolving wheel has recently turned it into a casino.

From the peninsula of Kanoni—'Battery Point'—one looks across the water to a minute island, Pontikonisi (Mouse Island), entirely occupied by a church, a small monastery, a handful of nuns, and a group of clustered cypress-trees which complete a memorably beautiful scene.

ITHACA

Gratitude is not the commonest of virtues. We are so apt to take things for granted. And when one whole people does feel grateful to the people of another nation, it is difficult for them to find a way to show their thanks. But the people of Ithaca succeeded, and their gratitude was wholly uncontaminated by what Sir Robert Walpole called 'a lively sense of future favours'. In 1953 the chief town of the island, Vathy, lost ninety per cent of its buildings and very many lives in a series of earthquakes. The Royal Navy was quick to bring help—unmeasured help. Eighteen months later, a first ship-load of Hellenic travellers called at Ithaca, just to visit the island home of Odysseus. Ithaca has one of the heaviest annual rainfalls of Greece. Much of the year's supply was being delivered as we sailed into the Gulf of Molo, bordered by mountains whose tops were hidden in low cloud. We turned sharply to port to enter a narrow sea-loch. It might have been the west coast of Scotland in August. Rocky hillsides rose straight out of the water, and boulders lay about at random everywhere among the scrub. Only the tall cypress-trees among the rocks and an occasional square white house suggested that this was Greece.

The loch widened to a circle, the sheltered Bay of Vathy, and through the drizzle appeared ahead the remains of the waterfront houses and the ruined town of Vathy. In the open space in the centre, the market-square, the townspeople had gathered in the rain, each under his umbrella—a wide sea of them—to welcome the English tourists; but to give and not to get. As we landed, and to our complete surprise, a Greek man or woman who 'spoke English' was allotted to each two or three passengers, and the whole company moved off to a reception in the temporary hutments brought by the Royal Navy. Here they said it with flowers and wine, nuts and oranges, and warm speeches. Afterwards, as we dispersed, children would dart out from gardens and press flowers into our hands. A whole island with a single thought, beautifully expressed. In all this we had forgotten Odysseus, but we shall always remember Ithaca.

The rain had stopped, the cloud was higher, and the sun struggling to penetrate it. Now I walked the road to the Gulf, surely in the footsteps of Odysseus, revelling in the scents of the aromatic rock plants and herbs which beautify the hills of Greece. Across the still and glassy blue-green water of the Gulf rose the splendid mountain Anoi, the feature of the northern half of Ithaca. In front of me was the narrow mountain which is the isthmus joining the southern mountain mass to the northern. Here, high on the narrow top of the isthmus Schliemann had excavated, hoping to find the palace of Odysseus. There are cyclopean walls and a very small acropolis, and Schliemann found traces of 190 houses within the walls. But Aetos, as the place is called, cannot be the site we want to find. For it does not fit into Homer's description and location of Odysseus' palace, which people would pass 'on their way to the city'. When we ask 'where, then, did Homer—if not Odysseus himself—place Odysseus' palace?', we find that Schliemann's assistant, Dörpfeld, has thrown an offensive red herring into the court and, to his satisfaction and that of some other scholars, proved that Homer's Ithaca was not our Ithaca—and that of classical antiquity—but was, in fact, Leucas to the north of it: and he states that Homer's description of Odysseus' Ithaca fits the topography of Leucas better than that of our Ithaca. To explain the change of names, Dörpfeld suggests that, in a migration from their old home forced upon them by population pressure as new tribes came down from the north through Epirus, the Ithacans of what is now called Leucas occupied 'our' island and brought the old name of their home with them; and that this happened after the time of Odysseus. And the *Encyclopaedia Britannica* concludes, 'no amount of ingenuity can fully reconcile the descriptions in the *Odyssey* with the actual topography of the island of Ithaca. Leucas fits Homeric descriptions better.'

But the conclusion that Odysseus' palace must be looked for in what is now called Leucas is a red rag to many bulls—scholars and lovers of Homer and of this most beautiful island of Ithaca. One of the most sensitive was the one-time British Ambassador to Rome, Sir Rennel Rodd, whose book *Homer's Ithaca* is as charming as it is convincing that Dörpfeld's red herring is a regrettable mistake; and the excavations of the British School at Athens in the years before World War I, while they do not prove that the tradition of antiquity is right, leave the door wide open for Odysseus to enter into his heritage in Ithaca, as we know it. There is a sheltered bay to the north-west of the island where now there is no town, yet the name of the place is Polis (city). Here have been found cyclopean walls of Mycenaean type, pottery and graves and worked stones, fountains and all the evidence that here, too, was a city, with a harbour, and with some of the best land for cultivation on the plateau above. The old city at Polis overlooks the Ithaca Channel which lies between Ithaca and the bigger island of Cephallonia to the west. Homer writes 'there is a rocky island in the midst of the sea, between Ithaca and rugged Samos' (there is a harbour in Cephallonia with cyclopean walls on land still called Same), 'Asteris, a little island. And in it is a harbour with double access, affording safe lying for ships. There the Achaeans remained in ambush for Telemachus on his return from Nestor's Pylos'. For the suitors of Penelope 'had murder in their hearts' (Rieu) for the son of Odysseus who believed that Penelope's husband was still alive and would return. Telemachus would naturally sail up the Ithaca Channel from Pylos, if his father's palace was near Polis. Is there a little island in the Channel? Yes! opposite Polis. True it has no double entry to its sandy beach. But ambush could be laid there.

As for other natural features in Homer's description, the Raven Rock (Korax), the fountain of Arethusa, the oak-trees on the high slopes, on whose acorns Eumaeus' pigs did well, all are there to be seen and enjoyed, in the southern half of the island. Odysseus was carried ashore asleep by the friendly seamen of King Alcinous and left in a lonely cove, named Phorcys, where they had been able to run their ship ashore on the sand and not be noticed—a cove from which Mount Neriton was visible. When he awoke, he did not know where he was. 'Over there you can see the vaulted roof of the cave of the Naiads'; said Athena, disguised as a shepherd boy, 'there you may hide your goods while we decide what must next be done. For this is Ithaca.' The little Bay of Dhexia, the first to the west of Vathy, is the likely landing place. For, high above it, though not as close as Homer implies, is a cave which otherwise excellently corresponds to his description. It is three-quarters of a mile up the mountain slopes, has two entrances, as Homer said; one faces north and the other, at the far end of the cave, has a hole in the roof for the gods to use. The 'high looms of stone where the mountain nymphs wove their robes', are there as stalagmites: the drip of water has worn hollows in the rock shelves which are the 'mixing-bowls'. An ancient altar stands on the floor. This had been a place of ancient worship, without a doubt; and equally without a doubt, Homer had once climbed up and seen it.

Homer had surely been to Palaeokastritsa in Corfu. The evidence is good, and to be seen, that he was once in Ithaca too. The *Encyclopaedia*, in its next edition, should at least open the door it shut in Odysseus' face. For our part, let us cast that red herring into the turquoise sea; and rejoice with Odysseus in the lasting, unspoilt beauty of the rugged domain that was his.

CHAPTER XIV

Sailing Past History: The Battle of Actium. Preveza and Nicopolis. Dodona: The Oracle of Zeus

On its course from Corfu to Athens through the Corinth Canal, the ship passes the sites of three of history's great naval battles—Actium, Lepanto and Salamis. The sea-bed must be littered still with the wreckage, the bronze rams, iron anchors and weapons and armour, even if the wooden ships have lost much of their timbers. The exploration of the sea-bed —underwater archaeology—has only just begun: it is going to bring very great rewards in many seas.

Before we sail past the entrance to the Ambracian gulf, where Antony and Cleopatra fought with Octavian and lost the chance of empire, two small islands, Paxos and Antipaxos, remind us of a strange story Plutarch tells in his essay *De Oraculis*. In the days of the Emperor Tiberius, a passenger and cargo ship was sailing slowly on a calm sea, passing Paxos and bound for Rome. It was late evening: some passengers had gone to bed, others were still drinking their dinner wine. They were all startled by a great shout from across the water, addressed to the Egyptian helmsman who had never been to Paxos and whose name was unknown to most of the passengers. 'Thamus'—that was in fact his name—'Thamus, when you pass the point Palodes, announce that Great Pan is dead.' The helmsman and all on deck were disturbed and puzzled. How was Thamus' name known? Some spirit, some divinity must be behind this; Thamus was in doubt whether to obey or not. He was alarmed, and finally decided that he would cry out the weird news only if the sea remained calm and the wind light. They drifted past Palodes, so Thamus shouted out, 'Great Pan is dead!' At once a multitude of mysterious voices and cries of wailing arose from the shore, and the alarm on the ship increased. The news of this strange episode spread rapidly on the ship's arrival at the port of Rome, and the Emperor sent for Thamus to hear his account of it. This story comes from a pagan source, and is not Christian propaganda. But Christians would like to know the date when all this happened. It was in Tiberius' reign that another great shout was raised: this cry was from a Cross—'tetelestai'—'it is accomplished'.

THE BATTLE OF ACTIUM

The mainland mountains drop to a wide plain as the ship approaches Leucas, technically an island, if a bridge across a narrow waterway to the mainland does not forbid the name. The entrance to the Ambracian Gulf is narrow and the Gulf is almost an inland sea twenty miles across. At the south entrance Antony's huge army was encamped, drawn from all parts of the East. King Bocchus of Libya and the kings of Upper Cilicia and Cappadocia were with him; Herod the Jew had sent a contingent; there were Arabian forces and men from Pontus on the Black Sea—in all, 100,000 men and 12,000 cavalry. His fleet numbered 500 ships, and, among the host, in charge of her big squadron of sixty ships, was Cleopatra herself. But there was disorganization in Antony's camp. He had not yet been able to embark his fighting men; he pretended that he had, and kept the oarsmen on deck, armed. Nor were the ships fully manned, and the local countrymen were press-ganged to fill the gaps. So mesmerized was the man by the attractions of the woman that, though his commanders advised a land battle where they were stronger, he determined to fight it out at sea, as a compliment to Cleopatra and her squadron. Domitius Ahenobarbus, an old friend, in disgust went over to Caesar. To demonstrate his contempt for the deserter and his own complete confidence in victory, Antony had his orderlies and luggage sent across after him!

Octavian's fleet was half the size of Antony's; his ships were smaller and faster. It was to be like the story of the Armada. The omens were good for Octavian. He had met a local man with a donkey during the awful days of waiting for a gale to die down, and had asked him his name. 'My name is Prosper, sir, and my donkey's Victor.' The place where this brief encounter took place was later marked by a bronze statue of Eutychus and his donkey, Nikon. During these days, a commando of Octavian's forces slipped across the channel in the dark, found its way to Antony but, in error, seized his companion, and in the confusion Antony made safe away.

The early stages of the great sea battle were a ding-dong affair, for Octavian's ships were too light to ram the far heavier, though clumsy, enemy ships. 'The engagement was like the storming of a town,' writes Plutarch, as several smaller ships fastened themselves to some great ship and soldiers with javelins, swords and firebrands tried to take or sink it. With the issue still in balance, Cleopatra suddenly led her powerful squadron out of the battle, crashing through the turmoil, and to the general amazement, set sail for the south. Antony's fleet still greatly outnumbered Octavian's, but at this crisis—to quote Plutarch in the Langhornes' translation—'Antony forgot both the general and the man; and as some author has pleasantly observed "that a lover's soul lives in the body of his mistress", so as if he had been absolutely incorporated with her, he suffered her to carry him soul and body away. No sooner did he see her vessel hoisting sail, than forgetting every other object, forgetting those brave friends that were shedding their blood in his cause, he took a five-oared galley and followed her who was the first cause and now the accomplisher of his ruin.

No script writer for a film could pack in more pathos than the bare facts lay on. Cleopatra turned her ship to wait for Antony. He climbed aboard, but both were so ashamed that neither could look the other in the face. The woman retired below; the man sat alone in the bow of the ship, head in hand, for three days and nights.

Octavian took 300 enemy ships. A return of the gale put an end to the fight. Antony's army, intact on the shore, simply did not believe that their commander had deserted them. They expressed complete loyalty to Antony and rejected with disdain all overtures for surrender, supposing that their gallant commander had been caught by the gale and would return when it was possible. It took a week for his outrageous behaviour to sink into their loyal hearts. Then they followed their officers into Octavian's camp.

First Philippi, 42 B.C.; then Actium, 31 B.C., and Octavian was master of the Roman world and set to be its first Emperor.

PREVEZA AND NIKOPOLIS

Preveza is the small port inside the entrance to the Ambracian Gulf on the north side, where the road to Jannina, the capital of Epirus, begins. Preveza and Epirus in the north remained in Turkish hands until 1912. The north road soon enters a large area of overgrown Roman and Byzantine ruins, waiting for full excavation. But this site is low on the Greek list, for there was no ancient Greek town here and indeed no need for any town at all. Augustus (as Octavian was entitled when he became Emperor) created a new city, Nikopolis—Victory City—to commemorate his decisive victory at Actium.

To populate this preposterous and unnecessary city, he ruthlessly moved in people from a number of towns which had grown up where economic and geographical conditions were favourable. Naupactus, at the narrows in the entrance to the Gulf of Corinth, was one such city. It was depopulated. Nikopolis was provided with a magnificent theatre, which is among the best in Greece. But it is overgrown now and in a dangerous condition as to its masonry; also it is said to be full of snakes. The stadium, exceptionally, is rounded at both ends; it was the scene of an athletic festival which Augustus commanded should be regarded as on a par with the festival of Olympian Zeus, and with the same rules and procedures. Here and there, far and wide, emerging over the tops of the dense and universal scrub, can be seen walls and parts of brick vaulting, towers and aqueducts. St. Paul was attracted to Nikopolis, and in his Epistle to Titus says that, when he sends a messenger to him, Titus is to make haste and join him in Nikopolis where he has determined to spend the winter. The city was probably extremely Roman in more than architecture, and it was St. Paul's great aim to bring the Gospel to the rulers of the world.

The unnatural city did not last long. The Emperor Julian made a first effort to restore its life in A.D. 362. But Goths broke it up. Justinian tried again in A.D. 530: and it was for 300 years the metropolis of Old Epirus, and a flourishing Byzantine city. On the floor of a large basilica church, one of the best preserved of early Christian mosaics has been excavated and preserved under cover. It sets out to portray the Universe and the Earth, with its trees, flowers, animals, fish, fruit, birds and Man. Several other large basilica churches of early date have recently been excavated outside that quarter of the city which Justinian provided with new walls, reducing the size of the new city to fit the diminished population. A Roman building constructed round a colonnaded portico appears to have been used as the bishop's palace. A fine basilica church is adjacent to it.

In the ninth century a combination of disasters brought the city to an end: a Bulgar attack, an earthquake, and a subsidence into the sea of a section of the city. Because the city fell quickly under these three violent blows, it is likely that there is a wealth of architecture and sculpture too, not to mention the more durable paraphernalia of domestic life, lying about under the earth and the tangled scrub which hides Nikopolis today.

To Dodona—The Oracle of Zeus

The road to the north from Nikopolis now crosses a fertile plain where in summer whole families camp in tents and shanties and work in the fields; and, after some twenty-five miles, enters the mountains and runs alongside a swiftly flowing river often shaded by immense plane-trees. The scenery is increasingly magnificent, the valley narrow, the mountains higher and more rugged. When the road reaches the watershed at 2,100 feet, a vast panorama opens—a high plain bordered by range after range of mountains, with the Lake of Jannina spread out in the distance below.

This is an area of Greece which has always been handicapped by the sheer physical difficulty of farming and living in the valleys, often so steep-sided that there is little room on the valley floor for more than the river. One such river, which makes for the sea through gloomy gorges, is the Acheron; at places in its course it runs underground—clearly to Hades, thought the Greeks. Epirus has been backward and out of touch with the main centres of life through lack of easy communications and in ancient times a deficiency of harbours on the ironbound coast where the mountains fall steeply into the sea. Nor is the climate ideal, for the rainfall is heavy and the winters cold. Aristotle observed that Deucalion's flood began here. Yet Epirus was important in antiquity as a main channel for great migrations of peoples coming from the north and slowly making their way southwards to easier lands. But there was an early period when large-scale settlement took place here, and Dodona was its centre. Aristotle held that Dodona was the cradle of the Hellenic people. Certainly Zeus had an old oracle here, and his priests were called Helloi (as well as Selloi) and the region Hellopia: and the name 'Hellenes' spread south in the Dorian invasion, while Homer couples the form 'Panhellenes' with Achaeans to cover all Greeks.

The Oracle of Zeus was very early established and widely honoured, the oldest oracle in Greece and once the only one. In the *Iliad*, Achilles prays to Zeus of Dodona to protect Patroclus, and the wily Odysseus knew the right place to go to when he wanted first-class advice. Herodotus gives two accounts of the origin of the oracle which he had heard, and then gives his own view. Priests of Zeus in Egyptian Thebes told him that long ago the Phoenicians had stolen two priestesses from their temple and had sold them, one in Libya and one in Hellas; and that both priestesses, now slaves, had taught divination. But the Prophetesses of Dodona had a more picturesque account of their origin: two black doves had flown from Thebes, one to Libya and one to Dodona, to Hellas, land of the Hellenes; and the Dodona dove settled in a tree and in human speech ordered a place of divination to be established, a divine order promptly obeyed. Similarly, the black dove in Libya caused an oracle of Zeus Ammon to be set up. Herodotus is down to earth in his more credible explanation that the doves were in fact the black Egyptian women, who as slaves worked as they had been accustomed to work, at divination; and that they had been called 'doves' because of the strange sounds they made before they had learnt to speak Greek.

The place of divination was evidently under some fine tree, for a tradition grew up at Dodona that Zeus uttered his will and gave his answers to questions through the rustling of leaves in an oak-tree. Coins of Dodona bear an oak-tree; Aeschylus and Sophocles refer to 'the speaking oaks' and 'the many voices of the leaves'. A later addition to the oracular apparatus was a

L

bronze cauldron placed beside a bronze statue of a boy equipped
with a whip which moved in the breeze to touch the cauldron;
its resonant bombinations were interpreted by the Selloi, the
bare-footed priests, or by the aged priestesses, the Graiai. The
Selloi believed they drew their inspiration from the Powers of
the Earth (from which all oracles derived) and so, to keep closer
touch with the earth, went bare-footed.

The location of the ancient site of Dodona was unknown until
M. Carapanos made a successful excavation in 1878, and found
clear evidence in a number of lead tablets on which were written
both the question of the seeker and the god's answer. The
majority of the questions are personal. 'Will my neighbour pay
his debt to me?' is typical. But the renown of the oracle was
wide-spread, and it is known that Croesus, king of Lydia, sent
there for guidance. Though the oracle of Zeus at Dodona, from
the seventh century B.C. onwards, was far surpassed by that of
Pythian Apollo at Delphi, yet it maintained the second position
in repute, with the Libyan oracle of Zeus Ammon as the third.

The valley where Dodona was excavated reminds one of a
Swiss mountain valley; there is, of course, the river, but it runs
through a pleasant and fertile countryside in strong contrast
with the steep and stony mountain range which walls it in on
the western side. To reach it, we descend from the plateau on
the east by a road which plunges downward in a series of hair-
pin bends; and, at the edge of the valley and the cornfields,
where the eastern mountains rise sharply, is Dodona. There is a
theatre, dating from the time of Pyrrhus, king of Epirus in the
third century B.C.; it is larger than that at Epidaurus but not so
well preserved. Bulldozers have recently cleared the orchestra;
and it appears that in Roman times the stage arrangements were
altered to make room for gladiatorial combats and all the bloody
slaughter of men and wild beasts which made a Roman holiday.

The walls of the theatre rise high and are nobly built. Close to
the theatre wall, the stadium was unearthed in 1960. Carapanos
had found the foundations of two temple buildings to the east of
the theatre, one of which had a precinct wall all round it; it may
be that the ancient oak-tree grew in the court outside this temple.
A third foundation is that of a temple upon which an early
basilica church was later built. Since the building of a church on
top of the destroyed temple of an older religion implies the

victory of the new, it is perhaps more likely that the temple below this basilica is the site of the original oracle of Zeus.

We know from literary sources of three destructive attacks upon Dodona. The first came in 220 B.C., when the temple was destroyed by Aetolians in a war against the Achaean League; another was made by the Roman Aemilius Paulus in 168 B.C. in a dreadful mood of revenge for support given to enemies of Rome, revenge which destroyed seventy towns and sent 150,000 Epirotes into slavery; and, again, in 88 B.C., it was attacked by allies of Mithridates. Excavation, three feet down below the alluvial soil, showed a level of burnt earth, brick debris, wood ashes and human bones. The Selloi, it seems, defended the sanctuary to the end. But Dodona rose again from the ashes; and coins with the famous oak-tree as a type, together with the evidence of Pausanias, show a revival at the end of the first century A.D. The Greek Archaeological Service has found that the end of the theatre came at the close of the fourth century A.D. by deliberate destruction, presumably at the reforming hands of Christian zealots. The apostle Paul's injunction to 'overcome evil with good' was at this period apt to be applied in the sense of a good and hearty demolition. We know that the Christian faith had early reached Epirus, and that among the bishops at the Council of Ephesus in A.D. 431 was Theodorus, Bishop of Dodona.

CHAPTER XV

Approach to Corinth: The Gulf of Corinth. The Corinth Canal. Old Corinth

As the ship enters the Gulf of Patras, making towards the narrows which are the gateway to the Gulf of Corinth, the wise passenger stays on deck. For the grandeur of mountains and sea in combination is here incomparable. To port is Missolonghi, famous in modern Greek history for its heroic defence against overwhelming Turkish forces by the Greek patriots in the War of Independence. The Greeks had 4,000 men, the Turks ten times as many. Finally, in 1826, the defenders broke out to fight again in the mountains, leaving an engineer to blow up the store of gunpowder and himself. He took with him in the explosion some 3,000 old men and women and children, for whom this end was deemed more merciful than slavery. Byron, who had championed the cause of Greece and won its heart—it still beats fast and warmly at the sound of his name— had died here two years before.

These waters cover the wrecks of the second of the great sea-battles, that of LEPANTO in 1571. At this time the Mongolian nomadic peoples and the kindred Turks were at a peak of power from China across Asia to Russia, Hungary and North Africa. They well might go on to sweep through all Europe, as the Turkish ships then swept the Mediterranean. In this crisis for Europe and Christendom, an allied fleet of 300 ships was raised by the Papal States, Venice, Genoa, Spain and the Knights of St. John in Malta, and young volunteers from most of the noble families of Italy and Spain were on board; so was Cervantes, author of *Don Quixote*, who was to lose an arm in battle to hold up the advance of 'the invincible Turk'. The commander-in-chief was Don Juan, aged twenty-four. With a view to tactical and fighting efficiency alone, he divided the fleet into five squadrons, ignoring nationality. Ali Pasha also had 300 ships, lying at anchor off Lepanto (Naupactus) in the narrows. It was a fearful battle, and fearful issues depended on it. The casualties were enormous: 8,000 Christians and 25,000 Turks were lost in this last battle in history in which both sides used vessels propelled by oars. One happy outcome of this carnage of men and ships was the liberation of 15,000 Christian galley-slaves in the Turkish fleet which was annihilated as a fighting force.

Down to the south, before the narrows, lies PATRAS, the third port of Greece after Piraeus and Salonika. Currants and wine are its chief exports. Patras did not play a notable part in Greek history, though it had the courage to resist Sparta and side with Athens in the Peloponnesian War. Augustus revived the city by settling there veterans from the legions with him at Actium. The Roman Odeum survives as almost the sole relic of its past. A late and unreliable tradition says that St. Andrew, the first to answer the call of Jesus, was martyred at Patras in A.D. 60. At all events, someone's much revered body, subdivided into convenient units, was in Byzantine times distributed far and wide in those relic-hunting days. The chief authentic glory of Patras, however, remains secure: it was the first town in 1821 to answer the call to rebellion against the Turk, and in those cruel days that was a brave step indeed.

NAUPACTUS (Lepanto to the Franks), at the narrows on the north side, is a charming little town. The mountains rise beyond it, and on the lowest slope above the town the Venetian fortress walls still stand. The little circular harbour is a miniature fortress, protected by walls and twin towers at the entrance. At the beginning of the first Peloponnesian War Athens prudently ensured the support of Naupactus by settling there refugees she had rescued from Messenia; here was a safe base for the Athenian fleet when operating in the Corinthian Gulf and western waters.

To sail the Corinthian Gulf is to enjoy some of the loveliest scenery in Greece. To port, the mountains rise straight up from the sea and there is hardly a house to be seen till the Gulf of

Itea opens and Parnassus rises 8,000 feet in the distance, with Delphi briefly visible on a shelf 2,000 feet up its side. But to starboard, the mountains of the Peloponnese sweep down more gently and there is room for cultivation in the rich soil. Vine-yards and orange-groves and the homes of those who tend them, plane-trees and oleanders and rivers give this well-cared-for side of the Gulf an air of genial ease, absent on the rugged face of the mountains across the sea. East of the Gulf of Itea on the north side, 6,000 feet high

> *'Helicon breaks down*
> *in cliffs to the sea.'*

The number of times the poets of Greece, Rome and England have used the music of that name to invoke the Muses, whose haunt it was, has yet to be recorded. The next big mountain further east on the north shore is Cithaeron, where the hunter Actaeon, on his lawful occasions with his hounds, had the ill-luck to chance on Artemis bathing in a mountain pool. Angered that mortal eyes should see her beauty, she turned him into a stag, and his own hounds tore him to pieces.

When Corinth begins to be visible ahead, there will be a peninsula and a headland to port. This is PERACHORA, where the late Humfry Payne so successfully excavated a sanctuary of Hera, and a wealth of bronze and pottery and ivories. The remains of an ancient city were brought to light, foundations of three temples from the ninth, eighth and sixth centuries, and remains too of the classical and Hellenistic periods. In few other places had so much beauty and interest in the countless votive offerings been found. The dust of excavation has been turned to gold in the charming books of Dilys Powell, formerly Humfry Payne's wife.

Opposite to Perachora on the southern shore, to the west, was SICYON. Its flat-topped acropolis, above a broad flat terrace, can be made out two miles inland. It is not a beautiful site and not worth a visit, except by the specialist. The theatre is com-paratively well preserved, but not much else; and the whole place is, by nature, a gaunt piece of country. It is all the more surprising that, in antiquity, Sicyon was a famous centre of the arts of painting and sculpture. Apelles, who painted many royal portraits—of Philip, Alexander, and Ptolemy—came from

Ephesus to study at Sicyon, and Lysippus, one of the greatest of
Greek sculptors of the late portrait-era of sculpture, was a
Sicyonian. If the metopes of 'Europa and the bull' and 'the
cattle-drovers', found in the Treasury of the Sicyonians are
Sicyonian work, they are examples of an early sculptor of Sicyon
powerfully conveying movement in the one, and producing a
beautifully repetitive rhythm in the other—'the march of the
cattle-drovers' (see page 82).

Had we landed at Patras, as do many travellers coming from
Italy, and taken train or car to Athens by the road along the
coast, we would have arrived at the banks of the Styx, and,
without the services of old Charon, crossed it easily—by the
bridge. If we had time to visit the waterfall, the highest in
Greece, and to penetrate the dark gorges, described as gloomy,
scraggy and perpendicular, through which this sinister stream
flows, we might agree with the sombre ancient view of this river
of death. But the *Guide Bleu* states that 'the place is unlikely to
fulfil the traveller's expectations', the reality presumably being
less horrific than the ideas of the ancients and ourselves about it.

THE CORINTH CANAL

Corinth was essentially a commercial city. Its position made
it so, for it lay at the crossroads of both Greek and international
trade. All land traffic from north to south in Greece must cross
the Isthmus; and, in the days of sail and small ships (when seamen
liked to stop for the night and haul their ships up the beach on
rollers), such were the perils of the long voyage round the south
of Greece with its series of rocky headlands and the turbulent
waters associated with the winds off high promontories, that it
actually paid traders and seamen, bound West from the Aegean
and Asia Minor ports or East from the Gulf of Corinth, to un-
load, carry the cargoes overland and reload into other ships on
the far side. This was an expensive process in time and in
labour, and Periander, tyrant of Corinth (625–585 B.C.) devised
a better way. He built a portage trackway for carrying the ship
itself with its cargo stowed. This diolkos was excavated in 1957
by N. Verdelis for 1,600 yards of its length. It is a cambered
stone trackway, made of large squared stones and with twin
grooves of four feet six inch gauge. The track enters the water,

and, at the western end, was noticed under the surface first by an American archaeologist, Fowler, in 1930. Evidently the ship floated on to a submerged carriage fitted with projections to slide in the grooves, and was then dragged up high and dry and so pulled across the Isthmus. The diolkos, towards the western end, is visible from the ship just as it enters the canal proper. One expects and hopes that dividends, as well as honour, were paid to Periander for this life-saving, time-saving and money-making invention; for pottery dug up on the track confirms the date, already believed to be that of Periander from the type of letters used as masons' marks on some of the diolkos stones.

Though Periander is said to have thought of it (Diog. Laert. I. 99), Nero was the first man to attempt the cutting of a canal. He employed a labour force of 6,000 Jewish prisoners, kindly provided by his general, Vespasian. He personally turned the first sod. Some half-million cubic yards were dug when the project was abandoned. In 1893, the French and the Greeks completed the canal, having found that they could use Nero's cuttings which had been correctly set out on the best route across the 7,000 yards' width of the Isthmus. The canal was blocked by German bombs during the war, and the single road bridge and the railway bridge were destroyed. The maximum height of the canal walls is 261 feet, the depth of water twenty-six feet, and the width seventy-five feet at the floor level. Ten million tons of spoil were removed, so that Nero with his achievement of half a million tons did well. The canal shortens the journey from the Adriatic to Piraeus by nearly 200 miles.

OLD CORINTH

Spread out below the towering mass of Acrocorinth—a backcloth 1,850 feet high—approached by the marble-surfaced Lechaeum road up from the sea, encircled by walls six miles in length, or eleven miles if the walls of Acrocorinth are included, Corinth in Imperial Roman days had probably the most impressive and handsome centre of any city in Greece. They are the remains of this Roman Corinth only that survive, with one striking exception—the temple of Apollo. For the wealthy but unlovable Greek commercial city was razed to the ground in 146 B.C. by Roman Mummius, and for 100 years was unoccupied except by the equivalent of rag-and-bone men salvaging what they could from the ruins, and robbing the tombs of their treasures.

From the eighth century B.C. Corinth began its rise to become the major industrial and commercial city of Greece. Pottery, perfume and bronzes were its own chief products, and in early days they were carried in her own ships the length and breadth of the Mediterranean world. For the cargo-ships of all nations, Phoenician, Syrian, Egyptian and in time Roman crowded her two harbours, Cenchreae on the Aegean side of the Isthmus and Lechaeum on the west, and the city took on a cosmopolitan air, strongly flavoured with the colour and scents of the East. Traders and seamen, white, brown and black, rubbed shoulders here, exchanged their goods, made their profits and, doubtless, spent some of it on the pleasures of a city widely known for its immorality. Plato in the Republic used the phrase 'Corinthian girl' as the equivalent of prostitute; and that is what the thousand temple-girls were, in their role as attendants of the temple of Aphrodite on the summit of Acrocorinth.

We could fairly apply to Corinth and its destruction in 146 B.C., the passage in the Revelation of St. John the Divine in which he foresaw the eventual doom of Rome:

'The kings of the earth who have lived deliciously with her shall lament, and the merchants of the earth shall weep, for no man buyeth their merchandise any more: the merchandise of gold and silver and precious stones and fine linen and purple and silk and all manner of vessels of ivory and precious wood and of bronze and iron: and cinnamon and odours and ointments and frankincense and wine and oil and fine flour and beasts and sheep and horses and chariots and slaves and souls of men. For in one hour so great riches is come to nought. And every ship-master, and all the company in ships and sailors cast dust on their heads and cried weeping and wailing, "Alas! that great city, wherein were made rich all that had ships in the sea! For in one hour she is made desolate."'

But a city at this geographically natural traffic centre was inevitable, and it is not surprising that in 44 B.C. Julius Caesar rebuilt the city, and on a majestic scale. For instance, the South Stoa or colonnade of shops, bounding the agora on the side nearest to Acrocorinth, is the longest colonnade we know in

Greece; the theatre, rebuilt on the site of the old Greek theatre, and arranged for gladiatorial shows, held 15,000 people; but the 'Façade of the Captives', where the Lechaeum road enters the agora, is magnificent merely for display. It is nothing but a decorated free-standing wall. All the public buildings were highly expensive and at least one was really beautiful—the fountain of Peirene. This was the gift of Herodes Atticus, the Athenian millionaire benefactor who was a personal friend of the Emperor Hadrian, and like him in his delight in beautifying cities with his wealth. Peirene's cool waters still flow today and splash unceasingly in their underground cisterns as of old. Enough is left of the walls of the court, once a setting for a statue of the donor's wife, in whose memory the fountain house was so beautifully designed and built, for us to visualize the pool and fountains which filled the central space and the surrounding pavements with their ranges of marble seats in the shade for exhausted shoppers.

Where everything is Roman, it is strange to find that the most important building which survives erect is a part of the sixth-century B.C. Greek temple of Apollo. Did a genuine respect or some superstitious fear of Nemesis stay the bull-dozing hand of Mummius? The temple's seven archaic, monolithic columns with their architrave, stand in stark austerity on higher ground above the agora, silhouetted against the northern sky. The repose, strength and simplicity of the early Doric temple must have made a startling impression of permanency upon the milling crowds in the business and political centre of this luxurious and easy-living city, and suggested that maybe there were values beyond the ephemeral interests of Pleasure, here in Corinth so amply provided.

In the centre of the agora, on the east-west line (right-left to one looking down from the temple) is a raised tribunal—the bema—where the Roman proconsul would make an official appearance from time to time. It was here that his enemies brought the Apostle Paul before Gallio. But 'Gallio cared for none of these things'. So, at the bema, we are in the footsteps of that fearless Apostle.

Another special point of interest is the triglyph wall, and its secret entrance through a hinged triglyph to give a back-door access—in a tunnel—to a sacred spring and oracular altar. A small hole in the roof of the tunnel and in the floor of the shrine would allow a hidden voice to give profound responses to questions put in faith to the oracle. That the water should sometimes emerge from the spring coloured red or white at the command—and signal—of the priest strikes one as a regrettable possibility. More to be commended is another use of running water under the long row of shops in the south colonnade. A vertical shaft from each shop down to this underground stream provided hanging-space for perishable food in the cool air.

Close to the east side of the agora in this area can be seen the starting-lines of the old Greek stadium, lines cut into stone slabs as at Olympia, Delphi and elsewhere. So complete was the work of Mummius that the new city-centre could be planted right on top of the earlier stadium.

The large theatre and the odeum, or small music hall, are easily missed, being out of sight from the agora. They are on the north slope of the hill where it drops down to the plain and the sea, only a stone's throw from the Museum but in the direction opposite to that leading to the agora.

The hideous rock-cut structure and cow-shed near the car-park is the sad ruin of Glauke's fountain, once, of course, faced with marble.

The Museum's best possession is a splendid collection of vases of the chief periods of Greek pottery. Corinthian ware is naturally very well represented, and the influence of the East, drawn from the patterns and designs of oriental textiles and carpets, can be clearly seen. Most of the sculpture in the Museum is of Roman date.

CHAPTER XVI

Epidaurus: The Sanctuary of Asclepius

Epidaurus lies in a wide and wooded valley, alone and very peaceful in the north-east of the Peloponnese off the road from Nauplia to the Saronic Gulf. It is a lovely place to visit, and its theatre is the best-preserved and by far the most beautiful of all Greek theatres. The peculiar quality of Epidaurus does not lie in the acres of somewhat confused low walls and old foundations, but in its power still to bring refreshment to mind and body, tired by crowds and cities. It was famous in the Greek world and beyond as the sanctuary of the healing god, Asclepius. Sick people from all over Greece, who had given up hope of cures either by medicine or by natural means, came to Asclepius for divine help. By the god's skill in divination he would diagnose and cure, they believed. It is not possible that the faith of the sick went entirely unrewarded; for this great institution for healing could surely not have lasted for eight hundred years unless it had been of service.

The origins of Asclepius are in dispute, for there are various versions of his story. Hesiod and Pindar both declare Asclepius to have been the son of Apollo—himself a healer—and of Coronis; and they describe a unique birth. Coronis, before her child by Apollo was born, married a mortal. When Apollo heard of this, he asked Artemis to kill the pregnant Coronis and the husband. While the bodies were being consumed on the funeral pyre, Apollo snatched away his son (in the first caesarian) and handed the baby over to the centaur Chiron, on Mount Pelion, to be brought up and taught the art of medicine. The

Epidaurus: The Sanctuary of Asclepius

setting of this ancient story is northern Greece. The local tradition at Epidaurus, expressed on a marble stele of the fourth century B.C., while claiming that Coronis was a local girl, admitted that the rites at Epidaurus and at Tricca in Thessaly were similar. We know that while the cult of Asclepius was introduced to Cos and a new sanctuary was established there (Hippocrates taught medicine at Cos), the tradition at Cos was that Asclepius came from Tricca. To Homer, Asclepius is a physician of Thessaly, who sent his two doctor sons to Troy because he could not himself manage to leave his practice to go to the war.

It looks as if Asclepius began as an unusually good healer in the north, was turned into a demi-god and brought to Epidaurus, and there, in the fifth century B.C., was thought worthy of divine honours. In the fourth century he was given a temple at Epidaurus, and the devotion of a great number of people. Pindar writes (460 B.C.):

> '*And all who came Asclepius cured;*
> *those whom some taint of nature had laid low,*
> *and those whose limbs were wounded by the blow*
> *of far-flung stone or bronzen-gleaming sword,*
> *whom summer suns too fiercely smite;*
> *and whom the freezing winters bite;*
> *relieving each peculiar pain*
> *and cleansing all from scar and blain.*
> *And one he healed with skills benign,*
> *and one with soothing anodyne,*
> *with simples too their flesh he bound,*
> *or with the keen-edged knife restored the festering wound.*

(From *The Third Pythian Ode*, translated by C. J. BILLSON.)

This passage shows a variety of ills being dealt with in various ways, including surgery. This last point is corroborated by a sculptured stele which shows surgical instruments. It is clear that faith in the divine powers of Asclepius was called for, and was given. On the site we can see the traces of 'the sacred dormitory'. This is not to be taken for a hospital ward. Its function was different. Here, after lustrations to purify the body and, no doubt, after prayer to orientate the mind to surrender to the divine power, the sick man went to sleep in the expectation that the god would come to him, would speak to him through a dream and show him the way back to health. Perhaps the god would show himself under the form of a snake. Harmless yellow snakes were kept in the sanctuary and believed to be messengers of the god with a beneficial lick to their tongues.

The part played by snakes in the sanctuaries of Asclepius perhaps points to a belief in the healing powers of underworld deities, so that there may be a chthonian origin to Asclepius. If so, the strange underground maze-like foundations of a circular building—the tholos—may have been the place where libations were poured to the powers of the underworld. That curious crypts at Knossos and Phaestos were places for libation ceremonies to the earth-powers and perhaps the earthquake-making powers is widely accepted. There is also a theory which joins the maze and the snake-pit in a horrifying combination of therapeutic significance for the mentally sick. The patient—if the theory is correct—was introduced into the outer circuit of the maze and in darkness felt his tortuous way towards the centre where a faint shaft of light encouraged. As he stepped over the last high threshold of the central cell, his hope was that Asclepius would cure at a single stroke. And, doubtless, he sometimes did, for the patient now found himself stepping among the snakes in the darkness in the snake-pit itself; and we know of the therapeutic value of shock-treatment in certain forms of disorder. Shell-shock *has* been cured by a road accident!

Over this maze (or was it the snake-pit?) was built in 360 B.C. a beautiful and costly circular building. Inscriptions record its cost. The architect Polyclitus the younger used black marble from Argos and white marble from Paros. On a stepped circular platform there was a colonnade of twenty-six Doric columns; then a circular wall with a single doorway; inside, another circular colonnade of fourteen Corinthian columns. One Corinthian capital, perhaps the prototype, was found carefully packed and buried in a chamber three feet below the then ground level. It is in the Museum, and is of great beauty of design and of simpler workmanship than the ever more elaborate Corinthian capitals developed in Hellenistic and Roman times.

The theatre was built by the same Polyclitus who designed the circular building. The acoustics are remarkable; even the striking of a match in the centre of the orchestra is easily audible at the highest of the fifty-four tiers of seats. A speaker, on the other hand, standing in the orchestra, hears the sounds of his voice sharply returned to him, more like the rattle of musketry than vox humana. It seems to me that the face of the stone seating, given a concave curve like the reflector of an electric fire, may perhaps neatly reflect the sound in a plane wave, so that the next sound wave from the speaker has a passage uninterrupted by any 'mush' of sound filling the cavea, or auditorium. To require the architect of a Greek theatre in his design to go beyond audibility, vision and seating for the necessary numbers, and to clothe the difficult shape of a high-tiered stone semicircle with beauty too, would seem to be asking too much. Yet Polyclitus added it. The slope of the auditorium is less steep than it is, for instance, at Pergamum or Aspendos, yet steeper than at Syracuse. It is evidently at the precisely 'right' angle for, to a unique degree, the shape itself and the patterning and texture of light and shade on the stonework of the huge auditorium both contribute to a very fine effect.

Among other buildings whose outlines are still visible, are a large hostel of 140 rooms, set round four courtyards, the physiological department for curative bathing, for which arrangements of the water supply can be seen, a gymnasium, a small music hall, the temple of Artemis close to the bigger temple of Asclepius, the dormitory, and the Roman baths. Apart from the theatre, which is in use for an annual dramatic festival, the buildings are now little more than foundation outlines.

The Museum. Some of our knowledge of the treatment of patients and of the cure of ailments comes from inscriptions. Some of the cures are not credible: for instance, that of the woman Cleo who had been pregnant for five years, and who at last, at Epidaurus, gave birth to her son. He at once ran off to the nearest fountain and had a bath.

Then there is the case of the man with a paralysed arm who was told to go to the mountain-side, fetch the largest stone he saw and throw it over the sanctuary wall. That he successfully carried out instructions is 'proved' by the presence of an oddly-shaped stone still lying in the sanctuary and conveniently provided with a hole as a hand-hold.

Another inscription records the recovery of his sight by

Thyson, a blind boy of Hermion, when one of the dogs about the temple licked his eyes.

Apart from the inscriptions, some of which are mentioned by Strabo and Pausanias, the chief contents of the Museum are architectural fragments and clever reconstructions in plaster which give a clear idea of the beauty of the buildings. Before a visit to the underground maze which served as the foundation of the tholos and is all that now remains, it is well worth-while to examine the reconstructed sections of it. It is one of the earliest buildings in the Corinthian order.

The very fine bas-relief of Asclepius is no longer in his sanctuary but in the National Museum at Athens. His face is all benevolence and serenity. Indeed this sculpture seems to have been, in its effect of gentle sympathy with the ills that afflict mankind, very like that of the great Zeus at Olympia, the supreme work of Pheidias. Athenagoras states that the temple statue at Epidaurus was the work of Pheidias: the surviving bas-relief might well be a copy of it in miniature. It could be that the bearded Christ of Christian art owes something in likeness to the widely revered bearded god of healing, whose sympathy with men and women was portrayed in his statues which were the central features of the innumerable Asklepieia all round the Aegean Sea.

Asclepius' sanctuary at Epidaurus had immense renown, which even stretched to Rome. There was an outbreak of plague at Rome in 293 B.C. and, in their distress, the Senate sent an embassy to Epidaurus calling for the serpent of Asclepius. Later a sanctuary of the god was set up at Rome.

CHAPTER XVII

Sparta

The Hellenic traveller who knows his Thucydides will not expect to see much of ancient Sparta outside the Museum. The historian might have been writing to warn the traveller of the distant future. 'Suppose the city of Sparta to be deserted, and nothing left but the temples and the ground plan, distant ages would be very unwilling to believe that the power of the Lacedaemonians was at all equal to their fame. And yet they own two-fifths of the Peloponnesus and are acknowledged leaders of the whole. But their city is not regularly built, and has no splendid temples or public buildings: it rather resembles a straggling village and would make a poor show.' Thucydides went on to say that, by contrast, Athens, if similarly deserted and visited by later ages, would look so magnificent that people would suppose her to have been doubly as powerful as she actually was.

It was natural for Sparta and Athens to be compared, for they were the two outstanding states in Greece in the greatest period of her history. But they were poles apart politically and ideologically: Athens, the birthplace and training-ground of democracy; and Sparta, the very citadel of an aristocratic conservatism (though with a limited element of democracy) maintained by an extraordinary code of rigid convention governing the lives of the citizens, and by a secret police organization to keep the non-citizen majority in control and subjection: Athens, living by maritime trade, expansionist by necessity and by temperament, mind and eye open to every new thought and thing; Sparta, a land-power, despising the wealth that trade would bring, and serving with utter devotion their own brand of ordered society

Sparta

which, by the provision of a huge slave labour force, left the citizens free to devote their lives to public service as part of a superb military machine: Athens, giving pride and pleasure to its people and to the outside world by the splendour of its public buildings and festivals, and in its expression of beauty and quest for truth in literature, drama, sculpture, music and philosophy; Sparta, expressing its soul in purest devotion to the preservation of the state by the military virtues, and finding its pleasures in the expertise of the barrack square, the control of the infantry phalanx and the comradeship of the mess table. It is not denied that satisfactions in this field are real, and as intense as those of the other kind; one only notes that they are different and appeal to a different temperament. As both these great States developed power and leadership, gathering allies till one half of Greece was ranged against the other, a dreadful clash of arms became inevitable. It was a trial of land-power versus sea-power. Sparta won: and for a generation the lights of Athens were dimmed.

For most of us Pericles was right when he proudly called Athens 'the School of Hellas'. Yet, while the adjective 'Spartan' has won a place as a valid word in the Oxford English Dictionary, there is no parallel 'Athenian' there to express the grace of the civilized and balanced citizen, equipped in intellect, outlook, spirit and physique to create (after ample debate) and to enjoy the 'good life' with his fellow-citizens. Perhaps the emergence of the term 'Spartan' into the English language is due to the deep-seated admiration all men feel for courage and hardihood: and to a unique and formidable degree the Spartans achieved these qualities. To their attainment they directed their education, their social habits and their life-long endeavour. All Greece admired and trembled at their terrible efficiency and sacrificial courage as fighting men. The holding of the pass at Thermopylae against the Persian hordes by King Leonidas and his 300 Spartiates till all were dead, was not the work of any sudden new spiritual fervour, but the result of Spartan tradition, education, training and character. Over their burial mound, the authorities set up a memorial with the apt words on it:

> 'Go, tell the Spartans, thou that passest by,
> that here, obedient to their laws, we lie.'

And the word 'Spartan' lives on in our language to denote grim

courage and 'hard-lying', in the naval sense of tough living conditions in a small warship where there is no room for personal
comfort and the chief concern of all is the armament and the
working of the ship in battle. In ancient Sparta, by virtue of the
successful Dorian invasion of the Peloponnese in the late twelfth
century B.C. and the subsequent domination of all Laconia and,
later, Messenia by the Spartan tribes, the owners of the land
were the comparatively small number of full citizens, the Spartiates: and the architect of their constitution, Lycurgus, designed
it with the sole purpose of maintaining them as a military caste,
invincible in the face of external enemies, and at home, powerful
enough and for ever on the alert to keep in subjection the Helots,
the original population of the conquered territories, now the vast
slave labour force of the State. Given land, therefore, and slaves
to provide all the means of livelihood, the Spartiates were free
to govern the State and to train themselves, insatiably, for war. To
Plato the Spartan constitution had the elements of the Ideal State.

In his life of Lycurgus (of whose date he admits he has no
knowledge) Plutarch gives numerous instances of ingenious
devices to discourage all that might soften soldiers or weaken
the structure of discipline. Money was deemed a danger, and
so was made of large slabs of brittle iron, useless for any other
purpose and of so low a value that a whole room would be
required to store the equivalent of £300 in our currency, and a
yoke of oxen to remove it. This currency had, of course, no
circulation outside Sparta and trade beyond its frontiers was
thereby made difficult. Again, 'citizens were forbidden to eat at
home or to fatten like voracious animals in private'; they ate at
common tables where, adds Xenophon, 'it was like a college,
for the young were being instructed by the old, and hearing of
great deeds done in the past, the young would be incited themselves to improve upon that performance in their own day'.
By unwritten law 'the doors and woodwork of houses were
wrought with no tool but the axe and the saw'. Plutarch explains
that if the house was so plain, 'no man could be so absurd as to
bring in bedsteads with silver feet, purple bedspreads, golden
cups and the train of expense that follows these'. Hard-lying—
all along the line! The womenfolk, Plutarch tells us, proved
troublesome because, owing to the absence so often of their men
on active service, they assumed great power and independence,

being left sole mistresses at home. But the great lawgiver dared to grasp even that nettle, and designed regulations 'to take away the excessive tenderness and delicacy of the sex—the consequence of a recluse life'. To reduce this delicacy and also to improve health, the unmarried women were required to engage in athletics. The charming statue of the Spartan running girl, now in the Vatican Museum, suggests a failure in the first aim of this policy.

There are numerous references in literature to the drastic methods of Spartan education. At birth a boy child was scrutinized by the Elders, and the decision to rear or to expose on Mount Taygetus was theirs, not the parents'! At the age of seven, the boy was enrolled in a large boarding school where food was hard to come by and the acquiring of it by clever stealth was encouraged, provided only that, if caught, the boy was mercilessly punished; the beds were rushes on the floor or out of doors, washing and baths a rarity, and lessons in the academic sense concerned only with reading and writing at a rough level. But skilled repartee and a terse answer were considered manly accomplishments. The aim was to make disciplined, strong men-at-arms who would be good comrades, able to endure pain, hunger, cold, long marches, and be ambitious only to be true to the Spartan tradition of utmost loyalty to the State. Training continued without remission until, at the age of thirty, the young Spartan who had passed every test became a full citizen.

Plutarch tells the story of a boy's theft, hidden to the moment of an agonizing death; and he believes the truth of it. 'A boy having stolen a fox and carrying it under his garment, suffered the creature to tear out his bowels with his teeth and claws, choosing rather to die than be detected by people standing near him. Nor does this appear incredible if we consider what their young men can endure to this day; for we have seen more than one of them expire under the lash at the altar of Artemis Orthia.'

The sanctuary of this Spartan goddess is one of the very few ancient sites to have been discovered in Sparta. It was on low ground by the river Eurotas. Pausanias' description provided a clue to the discovery of the sanctuary by the British School of Archaeology; for he wrote, 'the place named Marshy is sacred to Artemis Orthia. They say the wooden image there is that which once Orestes and Iphigeneia stole out of the Tauric land' (the Crimea) 'and that it was brought to Sparta because Orestes was king there.' About 600 B.C. the place was flooded and a thick layer of sand deposited over the whole site. Excavation has brought to light the foundations of several sacred buildings, some above and others below the sand layer, together with many hundreds of lead figurines and bronze votives and much of the typical Laconian pottery from the ninth century to the mid-sixth century B.C. The sand level has proved invaluable in the dating of the objects found. The cult of Artemis Orthia and the ordeal by savage thrashing which young boys had to endure before her altar have been the subject of much speculation. A contest of agility, cunning and daring may have evolved out of an ancient ritual, but it is clear that it provided a crucial test in the training of Spartan youths, which called for unflinching endurance of pain from the whips of the servants of the goddess. It is said that Lycurgus introduced this variant as a useful sub-stitute for earlier human sacrifices. The latest building on the site proved to be a grand-stand, built in the Roman period in the court before the temple of Artemis, for the comfort of spectators who liked to watch the proceedings; for Pausanias tells us that the altar had to be splashed with blood before the goddess was satisfied. Some authorities hold that this appalling exhibition of cruelty was a revival, after a long period of abeyance, to suit the decadence of Roman times.

Yet it is certain that such was Spartan devotion to the duties owed to their gods that awful risks were taken in the observance of prescribed worship. In 490 B.C. when news reached Sparta that the barbarian Persians had landed on Greek soil and the war of survival had begun, it happened that the religious festival of Apollo Carneius was in progress, with several days still to run. The Spartans could not bring themselves to cut it short: they would march to battle with the invader the moment the moon was full and the festival duly ended. And what a march it was—140 miles in three days to Athens! They were too late to fight, but they went on to Marathon to inspect the battle-field, saw the 6,000 Persian dead, and took notice of the enemy's equipment and weapons with a professional eye on a future encounter.

Sparta

In the Sparta Museum there is a collection of prizes dedicated to Artemis Orthia by boys successful in leading their teams in various contests at the festivals. These were for warlike exercises and tests of endurance, and there were also contests in music and dancing, doubtless of a martial kind, and in declamation. The prizes are sickle-shaped knives, set in stone slabs which bear descriptions of the contest and the names of the winning captain and team. If one recollects the harsh methods of the Spartan training of youth, these prizes received by boys and then dedicated by them to the demanding goddess, evoke a complex of emotions in which detestation and admiration, horror and compassion are all mingled.

One of the most interesting conclusions of historians, supported by archaeological study, is that in Sparta the militarized state hitherto described in this chapter was a relatively late development. The early history of Sparta seems to have been similar to that of other Greek states where kings and an aristocracy governed. In the seventh century B.C. Spartan music and poetry were of a high order; their own poet Tyrtaeus had written elegiacs on martial themes, used long afterwards for battle-songs and for contests at the festivals, while Terpander of Lesbos and Alcman of Sardis had found inspiration in Sparta. Precious objects and jewellery were imported, and Sparta had wide contacts overseas where the excellence of her own craftsmanship was well known. Her economic development follows a normal pattern until the middle of the sixth century. Then comes a decline.

In the late eighth century Sparta had conquered the land of Messenia to the west of the Taygetus range, had divided the territory into lots for each Spartan citizen, and enslaved the Messenians who were forced to work the land for their masters. This unhappy subject population was now dangerously large, and a bitterly-fought revolt which inevitably broke out in the seventh century had nearly resulted in the defeat of Sparta. The State recovered however and it was some time before a rigid system of government was introduced and Spartan life given the in-turned, martial character for which it was famous in classical times.

It is a classic irony that this all-embracing effort to mould life to the one end of service to the State should have cracked at the moment of apparent victory in its greatest test. The Spartans beat the Athenians to their knees in the tragic thirty-years' long Peloponnesian War which ended in 404 B.C. But their training failed when Spartans were exposed to the different tasks which victory in war lays upon the victor. Dispersed in various centres of Greece and Asia Minor for tasks of administration and government or diplomacy *vis-à-vis* the Persians, Spartan leadership did not match the hour. Men who had scorned money and luxury at home in loyal obedience to the law, now in some pleasant, rich, semi-oriental city of Asia Minor, far from the hard life of the mess, fell willing victims to easy living and bribery. At this period Sparta was helping Cyrus in his attempt on the throne of Persia. The wide stage of the Aegean world and Asia Minor was too big for Spartans. The goddess of Victory had given them the palm, but the fruits were a slow poison undermining character.

Laconia, the Spartans' homeland, remains probably little altered in appearance apart from the orange groves. Scenically it seems to fit the tough open-air Spartan temperament. The valley of the river Eurotas is so wide and long that perhaps twenty or thirty villages are visible at one time—tight clusters of white buildings among the olive groves, wheatfields and vineyards, and the rocky hill-pastures on the lower slopes of the mountain ranges. Taygetus, the western wall to this great domain, is a grim and tremendous mountain, much crevassed and with dark gorges cutting deeply into its sides. To the east is another mountain range, the Parnon. Geographically one large area, there was no need for a great city in such a valley: Sparta's scattered settlements would feel at one together, in sight of each other and all guarded by these great mountain bastions. Through all their long period of power in the sixth and fifth centuries B.C. they never built walls round the central settlement where their temples lay. 'It is men, not walls, that make a city,' as Lycurgus rightly said.

MISTRA

MISTRA, three miles from modern Sparta, is a dead Byzantine city, built up the side of a steep mountain and crowned with a Frankish castle. Its sad ruins recall Les Baux in Provence. It will be described in the chapter on Byzantine Greece.

CHAPTER XVIII

Lesser Sites in the Peloponnese: Bassae. Sphacteria. Nauplia. Asine

BASSAE—THE TEMPLE OF APOLLO

Four thousand feet up in the heart of the mountains of Arcadia at Bassae there is a temple of Apollo which every specialist in Greek architecture desires to see, so many are the variations there on the Doric theme. The non-specialist traveller, preparing himself for a visit, will find that there are views of differing emphasis about this remarkable temple in its lonely mountain site.

Pausanias writes, 'On Mount Cotilius, forty furlongs from the city of Phigalia, is a place called Bassae and the temple of Apollo the Succourer, built of stone, including the roof. After the temple at Tegea, this temple may be placed first of all the temples in the whole of the Peloponnese for the beauty of its stone and the symmetry of its proportions. Apollo acquired the title "Succourer" from the help he gave in time of plague.'

Edward Hutton's reaction in his book *A Glimpse of Greece* is delight in the temple's setting. He describes the rough, steep road to Bassae (this is now open to motor traffic), and the bleak, stony hillsides with only occasional plane-trees and oaks; then 'suddenly, on turning a corner and coming up beyond one of the numerous threshing floors, we caught sight of the temple, standing there against the eastern sky-line, in a saddle between two hill-tops, roofless and without its pediments, but otherwise serenely perfect. The temple looks as though it had risen by magic out of the rock of the mountain upon which it stands'. Hutton's last point is precisely right; for it is a basic criterion of excellence in a building that it should be completely at home in its environment. But rocks of the mountain and the temple stones and columns made from them are of a sombre colour. Hutton did not worry about that; but Sir James Frazer, while gazing with wonder on the regiment of mountain peaks to the south, with vistas here and there, through openings in the ranges, to Taygetus' snowy pinnacles and to the flat-topped Ithome and the distant sea, was overcome by the melancholy of this spectacular loneliness, the dead, colourless temple of the same cold grey as the surrounding rocks, and the awful silence of the place; and he mused unhappily on 'the transitoriness of human greatness and the vanity of human faith'. But is not human history like a torch race? When the torch, all ablaze, has been successfully passed to the next runner, the scene of the race is bound to change.

The temple was the work of Ictinus who also designed the later Parthenon. Externally, it is in the Doric Order, internally in the Ionic, but it included a single Corinthian column and capital on the centre line of the cella. This is probably the earliest use of the Corinthian capital, and in a unique and strange position. There were fifteen columns on the sides and six at the ends of the temple. The axis of the building is north-south, again unique. Seeing that there was in fact no room on the site for the normal east-west orientation, it is fanciful to suppose that the temple was intentionally sited to face north towards Delphi, Apollo's central sanctuary, or towards the land of the Hyperboreans in the far north from which, some said, Apollo had come. The columns have entasis, but that is the only optical refinement in the building; they do not, for instance, lean inwards, nor is the platform or stylobate given the slight upward curve of the Parthenon stylobate. The columns have three annuli, or rings, below the echinus, an Archaic feature. Archaic, too, is the ratio of the great length of the temple to its width. Another oddity is the use of thicker columns and wider capitals on the north side than elsewhere. Indeed the building is full of eccentricities and interest.

The interior is like the sixth-century temple of Hera at Olympia, for the sides of the cella are divided into alcoves by short spur walls. At Bassae these end in engaged Ionic columns with fantastically large bases, double the diameter of the column. There are five columns and spur walls each side, four at right-angles to the outer walls, as would be expected, but the fifth on either side is set diagonally. Midway between the ends of these diagonal spurs was the central Corinthian column. The position of this central column was for long a problem to the archaeologists. How could it rationally be placed right in front of the cult statue? Then the statue must have faced to one side, perhaps to the east, to the rising sun through the oddly placed doorway in the long wall? It was argued that the statue could not have stood in front of the Corinthian column because the cella appeared not to have been roofed except behind the central column, and a cult statue was always under cover. But Professor Dinsmoor solved the problem. Holes have been found in the architrave to take the ends of roof beams: the cella was roofed in after all, and the cult statue of bronze, twelve feet high, had stood in full view in front of the column. Curtains were hung behind the statue and gave privacy to the unusual additional space behind, from which the door on the east side led out to the peristyle. It is suggested that in this room an oracle might have given responses.

All round the interior of the cella ran some hundred feet of frieze sculptured with a battle of Lapiths and Centaurs, and of Greeks and Amazons, both subjects common in architectural sculpture because the Greeks delighted in thus symbolizing the Hellenic victory over barbarism in the Persian invasions. This frieze is now in the British Museum. A careful inspection shows that, when completed, it was found to be too long to fit the cella walls; slices here and there were cut off to make it fit the space. This process amputated some of the tails of the centaurs. Archaeologists seem to miss very little!

There were also sculptured metopes over the inner porches, north and south. No pedimental sculpture survives, but there is evidence of a plinth course to take sculpture, and it is believed that Augustus may have taken it to Rome. For, in the Garden of Sallust there, certain Greek pedimental sculptures of the death of the sons and daughters of Niobe, slain by Apollo and Artemis, have been excavated: in period and style (they show kinship with the Olympia pedimental sculpture) and in size and theme they fit the requirements of a group for one at least of the Bassae pediments. The style of the frieze and the metope sculptures is that of 420 B.C., but the main structure must antedate the Parthenon and must be regarded as the work of Ictinus in his younger and experimental days, perhaps about 450 B.C.

Apart from the great architectural interest of Apollo's temple, its chosen position, high on the roof of the Peloponnesian world and commanding so magnificent a panorama, takes us into the mind of the Greeks as they gave thanksgiving and worship to Apollo the Succourer.

SPHACTERIA

The Hellenic traveller lands at Navarino with his mind on Pylos, old Nestor and that prehistoric period of Greek history each year coming nearer to dropping the prefix 'pre-'; but he will learn with satisfaction, if he is one of those who take the side of Athens in the war against Sparta, that the long island, which lies from end to end of the great bay of Navarino and makes it the finest harbour in Greece, is Sphacteria. And that name brings to mind a minor but fascinating Athenian success in the long war story; for in this island Spartan troops actually surrendered to the Athenians, a rare event indeed for these formidable troops. He will look at the highest point of the cliffs at the north end and visualize the final stand of the Spartans. In 425 B.C. the Athenians had established a fort just inside the north entrance to the bay, only forty-six miles from Sparta and had defied all the Spartan efforts to capture it. The Spartans then landed on Sphacteria, but the Athenians successfully outwitted this manœuvre and finally killed or captured the entire force. There is a fine account of this commando operation in Thucydides, Book IV, 1–41.

It is clear from Thucydides' account that both sides distinguished themselves by their courage: and that in the end more was at stake in this hard-fought struggle than the mere possession of territory. It was indeed a daring and brilliant idea of the Athenian, Demosthenes, to draw off Spartan troops from Attica and the Spartan fleet from their attacks on Corcyra, allied to Athens, by planting a force so close to Sparta itself. The plan was successful in both immediate objectives, and it led to a third—to provide a rallying point for the Messenians and any others who wanted actively to express opposition to the hard Spartan masters who controlled them.

But, as the Sphacteria affair developed, another consideration began to dominate men's minds. After the Spartan landing on the island, an Athenian fleet in a surprise attack decisively defeated the Spartan fleet supporting and victualling their land force. This was now, therefore, completely cut off, except when daring swimmers under cover of night could swim in with supplies from the mainland. The Spartans proposed an armistice, and even an alliance with Athens. But here was a chance for the Athenians, so Cleon the demagogue led them to think, to break for ever the formidable legend of Spartan military invincibility, of which one of the expressions was a preference for death instead of surrender. To lay this ghost and force unconditional surrender seemed to be of immense advantage to Athens—and to Cleon. The Spartan offer of peace was thrown away: and the ultimate fall of Athens followed on this terrible misjudgment.

Weeks passed and the blockaded Spartans, 420 in number, still declined to surrender. Cleon, at Athens, began to lose men's confidence: to recover 'face', he personally led a reinforcing party and landed on the island with 800 infantry. The Spartans fought with traditional courage against odds but were out-manoeuvred. A final Athenian attack was chivalrously held up for an offer of quarter. The Spartan commander was dead, his second-in-command wounded; the third in command requested permission to contact some senior officer on the mainland to ask what Spartan honour required in these appalling circumstances. He was told to consult the safety of the survivors. This was an unexpected and merciful decision. Of the 420 men who had fought so well, 128 had been killed, and 292 surrendered. They were taken to Athens by the triumphant Cleon. But, for the ultimate survival of Athens as a great power and influence in Greece, the acceptance of Sparta's offer of peace would have been perhaps an infinitely greater triumph.

NAVARINO BAY

Here was fought the strange and famous 'accidental' naval battle in 1827 which helped Greece to gain her independence.

Nearly 200 warships of Turkey, France, Russia and Great Britain had concentrated here, not to fight a battle but to negotiate a truce. But somebody fired a shot and, in the vast mêlée of fighting ships locked together, a fearful slaughter of ships and men ensued, and the Turkish fleet was almost entirely destroyed.

NAUPLIA

'The stranger should approach Nauplia reverently—not as a tourist, but as a pilgrim.' That is the authentic voice of Greek patriotism—and patriots are beyond count in Greece. This veneration springs from the part played by Nauplia in the struggle with the Turks for independence in the climacteric years 1821 to 1833. The Turks surrendered the keys of the great fortress in 1821 and the fighting hero, Kolokotronis—'the Old Man of Morea'—stooped in tears to kiss them. His equestrian statue keeps his honoured name secure. Here the Greek Government was established from 1829 to 1834, and Otho confirmed as the first king of the Hellenes in 1832. Athens was then a decayed market town of a mere three hundred houses, and Nauplia might well have been the capital of modern Greece, had not memories of Athens' ancient glory, and faith in its new future, prevailed.

The town is built by the sea in terraces on the side of the old acropolis, which in turn became a Venetian and then a Turkish fortress. It lies at the foot of the precipitous and massive Palamedes rock, 700 feet high, which is also crowned with Venetian fortification walls. Besides Turks and Venetians, Byzantine Greeks and Franks also had their day at Nauplia.

Five hundred yards out from the waterfront is the beautiful little islet of Bourdzi, an old Venetian fort and now a hotel. The mountains across the bay, and the long plain of Argos, itself hemmed in by more distant mountains, and the little island in the foreground make a lovely picture. The town has many pleasant stone balconied buildings, a good Museum which houses pottery and other finds from Tiryns, Mycenae and Asine, and is well cared for and obviously—and rightly—proud of itself.

ASINE

Kastraki Rock—'Castle Rock'—is a steep-sided, small, scrub-covered peninsula on the north side of the Bay of Argos, about four miles east of Nauplia. It gets its name from a Venetian tower on the high point and from some 300 yards of the ancient walls which cut across the neck of the peninsula and which gave protection on the landward side to the little town of Asine. There was a settlement here in Neolithic times and through the Mycenaean and the subsequent centuries until 720 B.C., when it was destroyed by its jealous and more powerful neighbour, Argos. After a long gap of several centuries, life returned to Asine in Hellenistic and Roman Imperial days.

People of all these periods have left as evidence their graves, their bones and their funerary vessels, together with the foundations of their homes. Archaeologically, the site is for the specialist, which is a way of saying that, apart from walls and towers (of the Hellenistic period) and tombs and house foundations, there is not much of antiquity that a visitor would notice. Moreover, the path to the summit is awkward.

But the place itself is beautiful. Close by the old walls on the beach is a taberna, and on a shady terrace the wine of the vineyards all about. While the younger members of the family crouch in Mycenaean tombs hollowed in the rock, climb the hillside and mistake for some ancient structure an Italian gun-position from World War II, or search in the scrub towards the top of the hill on the seaward side for the remains of a Hellenistic olive-press, let us, with retsina in our glasses, ruminate on the curious history of this high-spirited and tiny town which had a great respect for its remote ancestry, and was determined to preserve its special identity though the heavens fell. They were a prehellenic people who came from the north of the Gulf of Corinth, where, they said, they had been driven from their homes by Herakles. For a time, keeping together, they had taken refuge on the slopes of Parnassus; then they had crossed the Gulf and had been settled by Eurystheus, an enemy of Herakles, on this rocky peninsula.

We hear of Asine in Homer's *Iliad*, in the list of cities which contributed ships for the Achaean expedition to Troy. With 'Tiryns of the great walls' is coupled 'Asine, which dominates the gulf' of Argos. This suggestion of power must refer to Asine's control of sea-borne trade; and the contents of Mycenaean tombs with their jewellery and ivories, show that she took advantage of her position, her harbour, her ships and her determined men in the days when Mycenaean Greece traded far and wide.

Strabo and Pausanias tell of the ultimate fate of these people in the late eighth century B.C. They incurred the wrath of Argos by siding with the Spartans in a quarrel between Argos and Sparta. After the withdrawal of the Spartans, Argos recovered strength and savagely paid off old scores. But, though the Argives destroyed their town, the inhabitants of Asine had managed a complete evacuation and had sailed away, as two thousand years before they had sailed away from one home to find another. The Spartans repaid their debt and settled them in Messenia at Koroni, a new Asine, strikingly like the Asine they had left. This evacuation accounts for the gap in the findings of the Swedish archaeologists in 1922 and subsequent years. On the small site, only a few hundred yards in diameter, they found sherds of all periods of pottery from 2600 B.C. to Roman times, the Archaic and Classical periods excepted. Thirty-three tons of sherds were packed up and sent to Sweden for sorting and examination—an estimated two and a half million pieces. The gap in the pottery sequence shows that the evacuated city remained deserted for 400 years. When it was inhabited again, its new citizens could not claim that their ancestors once fought against that new-comer, Herakles!

CHAPTER XIX

A Chapter of Islands

I. AEGINA: HYDRA: POROS

Three of the many Aegean islands can be visited from Athens within one day—Aegina, Hydra and Poros, in the Saronic Gulf. Each yields its own delight, and the ferry-steamer sails close enough to the mountainous tree-clad coastline for the passenger to enjoy both land and sea.

At AEGINA one walks a dusty path up through the pine-woods to the sanctuary of a primitive local goddess Aphaia, later identified with Athena. The Doric temple is finely sited on the hill-top overlooking the sea. Since some of the pedimental sculpture is of the pre-Persian war period, and some of it post-war, the exact date of the building is not clear. Perhaps it was the quick completion of the temple which was taken in hand after the Battle of Salamis 480 B.C. as an act of thanksgiving for the victory in which the Aegina squadron was held to have played a decisive part. Most of the columns stand: it is an impressive and beautiful sight.

Actually, it was the third temple on this hill-top, each larger than its predecessor, and all three altars, in various states of ruin, are visible at the east end. The seventh-century altar is by the side of the entrance ramp to the temple; the altar of the next century at the foot of the ramp; and that of the latest temple, a large, high structure still further to the east and on the main axis of the building. The excavation at the west end has been left open in order to show the foundation of an apsidal Bronze Age building over which the later temples were built. That the

THE THEATRE AT EPIDAURUS (340 B.C.)

*The best preserved and most beautiful of all Greek theatres—to seat 16,000 people.
The extraordinary audibility, even 54 rows up, of words spoken from the orchestra
in a normal tone is a perpetual surprise and fascination.*

DETAIL AT DELPHI

*On this Ionic column, once thirty feet or more high, stood a sculptured figure perhaps,
or a tripod, for the inscribed base showing that it was a monument has been found.
The detail of the capital, out of sight of the spectator in ancient days, was not out of
the mind of the maker. The eighty-yards long terrace wall of the temple of Apollo,
called the Pelargikon (sixth century B.C.), with its stones intricately fitted together,
is covered with neat inscriptions.*

IN MYKONOS (OR ALMOST
ANYWHERE ELSE IN
GREECE)

*The spars can be rotated to
reduce or increase the sail
area; probably the inspiration
of the Wykeham-Martin furl-
ing jib, of blessed assistance
to smaller yachts in waters
far from the Aegean.*

AT SKIATHOS: AN AN-
CIENT WINE AMPHORA
FROM THE SEA, IN
MODERN HANDS

*Fishing boats and caiques are
often named after the Apostles
and the Saints. The nearest
boat is ingeniously named 'the
Forerunner' so that St. John
the Baptist may bless it, and
the fisherman also may
proudly feel that his boat
leads the fleet home.*

sanctuary was originally a late Mycenaean one is shown by the terracotta votive figurines found at this level. These are of women and of animals, so that it seems that the primitive Aphaia was seen as the goddess of fertility. The last of the temples required an increase in the area of the sanctuary, and a new propylon. The foundations of both of these gateways, the old and the new, can be traced; and that of the old, closer to the temple, is of unusual interest. For it can be seen on the pavement that the columns were octagonal and must have been wooden. The foundations on the right of the two entrance gateways are those of the priests' quarters.

The columns of the temple, mostly monolithic, are badly weathered, as might be expected on this high site above the sea. A few of them still keep patches of the stucco with which they were covered. This stucco is also to be seen in the propylon, and on the floor of the temple itself (where it is coloured red) and in a cistern at the north-east corner of the peribolos (the enclosure). It is a remarkable plaster indeed which can last so long.

As we enter we might notice the holes in the eastern columns where a system of bronze grilles safeguarded the treasury inside the temple. In the main cella where the statue of Athena Aphaia stood, a point of interest is the double row of columns in two tiers supporting the roof and dividing the cella into three aisles. Curiously, a doorway was made, off centre, at the back of the cult-statue into the opisthodomos; and to secure the opisthodomos, used in all probability for storing the treasure, another metal grille ran across from anta to anta at the west end of the building.

It is the sculpture in the pediments which above all has made this temple famous. It is now in the Glyptothek at Munich. In 1811 Cockerell paid £40 to the local people for the pediment sculptures which were in their hands. After a series of adventures and changes of ownership, they were bought by the Prince of Bavaria for 10,000 sequins. In both east and west gables the scenes are similar, indeed almost exactly so. Athena in the centre, invisible to the combatants, watches over a battle of Greeks and Trojans. The triangular space is fully filled by fighting men in all the attitudes of close combat, alive and dead, in well-composed groups in lively action, some falling, some on one knee drawing their bows. Herakles, from the east front, wearing his invariable lion-skin, is shown as a kneeling bowman: the sculptor is able to convey the calm and steady aim of a first-rate archer superbly controlled in the heat of battle. While the balance of one group of figures with another is so perfect as to become unnatural and dull, one can well understand when one examines the individual figures and sees the mastery of observation which gave them this vitality, strength and easy movement, why Aeginetan sculptors got so many commissions for statues at Olympia. Nor were the athletes of Aegina of merely average standard; Pindar wrote at least seven odes in their honour as victors.

Aegina's history is a success-story in many ways, but tragically illustrates the worst flaw in the Greek character—the inability of these proud, independent-spirited people to live peaceably alongside other Greeks equally endowed—or is the better word 'handicapped'?—by the same spirit.

Jealousy between rivals in trade was the source of the trouble. In the seventh and sixth centuries B.C., the merchants and seamen of Aegina had raised their island to a position of importance out of proportion to its size. By 500 B.C., next to that of Samos, their fleet was supreme in the Aegean. Part of their mercantile success was due to their sagacity in introducing a coinage everyone could trust. Their 'tortoises'—silver coins with the emblem of a sea-turtle on the obverse—were widely held as 'good money', and their regularized system of weights and measures was in general use. The Athenians hated their rivals. The immense fleet they mustered at Salamis against the Persians had in fact been built to oust the Aeginetans from their superior position as a naval power. Though Athenians and Aeginetans fought side by side at Salamis and Plataea, the old enmity, based on economic competition, continued. In 457 B.C. Athens overcame her rival by superior force, dismantled her walls, closed her famous mint, and forced her into the Athenian empire. Aeginetan hatred smouldered hotly. Early in the Peloponnesian War, Athens expelled the population from the island. Sparta gave them a new home at Thyrea. In 424 B.C. the Athenian, Nicias, captured the town and took the survivors to Athens. There, says Thucydides, 'the Athenians resolved to kill all the Aeginetans, because they had hated them for so long.'

Pericles had dubbed the island 'the eyesore of the Piraeus'.

A Chapter of Islands

It is, in fact, a lovely island, as Attalus I, king of Pergamum, and the Emperor Augustus thought when in their days they spent a winter in Aegina.

The town of HYDRA is all but invisible from the sea, because of the narrow entrance to the harbour between two high bluffs. As the ship turns to enter, the effect is of a curtain suddenly drawn to reveal the perfect stage-set of a Greek water-side town, with brightly coloured caiques and boats clustering at moorings or with sterns made fast to the harbour wall, and the white and blue and pink-washed houses rising in terraces up the hillsides, enveloping three sides of the harbour. It is strange that no traces of occupation in classical times have been found.

Many of the best houses in Hydra date from the end of the eighteenth century when the town was the headquarters of a large fleet of merchant ships, owned in the island. These ships were carriers of produce from other sources; for the island itself is not, and never was, a fertile one. The islanders lived by the sea alone, and won a great name as pirates as well as carriers.

By 1821 Hydra had 40,000 inhabitants and a burning spirit of attack against the Turks. Their fleet was converted for war purposes and it served well in the cause of Greek Independence.

Today this pleasant little town attracts Athenians who want respite from the crowds and noise of city life. There can be few more delightful waterfronts in the Aegean.

POROS is a pine-covered island separated by a very narrow channel from Troezen on the mainland. The waterfront town itself has not the charm of Hydra, but the position of Poros on the enclosed waters, surrounded by hills and mountains, gives it a lake-side character of its own. The island was occupied from the Mycenaean period; and in classical times had its temple of Poseidon in a sanctuary near the agora of the old city on the hill-top above the harbour. A Swedish excavation in 1894 brought to light the foundations of the temple and other buildings. When Demosthenes in 322 B.C. was charged with fraud and the death penalty was certain, he fled to Poseidon's temple for sanctuary. But his enemies pursued him there, and he committed suicide by sucking the poison he had placed in his hollowed pen.

A Chapter of Islands
II. KYTHERA

KYTHERA lies off Cape Malea, the south-eastern point of the Peloponnese. It is a wild mountainous piece of land where a livelihood is hard to come by, and a solution has long been found in emigration to Australia. Kythera grows sheep, and presumably her shepherds go to Australia in the hope of rearing larger flocks. They cannot *all* run cafés 'down under'.

It is difficult to see any logical reason why Aphrodite—'the Kytherean'—should have honoured this rugged little island by making her denouement here. One legend tells how she found the island somewhat small when she landed from her scallop shell, and so went on to the Peloponnese. Certainly, she had an important sanctuary at Kythera, the locality and precise position of which seems at last to have been established on the south-western slope of the Palaiokastro, the old acropolis of the town of Kythera. Some Doric columns and other architectural fragments incorporated into a church a quarter of a mile away, had misled Schliemann into supposing that the church was built over the foundation of the ancient temple, as was a common practice. But similar fragments of worked stone from columns and metopes, and two sculptured heads, one in marble and one in bronze, together with many classical sherds and coins, indicate that here was an important sanctuary, surely the temple of Aphrodite. Pausanias calls the sanctuary the most holy and the most ancient of all the sanctuaries of Aphrodite in Greece. He adds that the cult statue was of wood and armed for battle. We know that in Sparta too Aphrodite carried weapons. He also tells us that the Phoenicians taught her worship to the people of Kythera. That Aphrodite was akin to Astarte is, in fact, more than likely.

Kythera was Spartan territory under a Spartan governor; but Chilon, a Spartan ephor and one of the Seven Sages, is quoted by Herodotus as saying that 'the best thing would be for Kythera to be sunk in the sea'.

The harbour is a natural one between a low peninsula and a gaunt 800-foot cliff surmounted by a large castle built at the time of the Crusades. The very small town is close by and reflects the difficult living conditions in the island.

Excavation in 1963 of a Bronze Age site on the south-east of the island, first noticed in 1930, has shown it to be Minoan.

III. THE CYCLADES

The CYCLADES are a group of twenty-four islands in the middle of the southern Aegean. Delos is the centre of the circle and was the most important: it has a chapter to itself in this book. The Cyclades are rocky, rather barren, and in summer often windy. In ancient times they were covered with trees; but the inhabitants cooked with wood and made no effort to replant, while the ubiquitous goat has nullified any attempts at natural re-afforestation. But the little waterfront towns, white and clean, are extremely pleasant places; and, in the valleys, there is still enough soil to grow vines, tomatoes, figs and vegetables; and the olive-tree seems able to extract its precious oil from the sun, the ever-fresh air and the dryest rock! On tiny terraced fields the barley grows, and there are always fish in the sea and fishermen to catch them.

MYKONOS

The town and harbour of MYKONOS are typically 'Cyclades': brightly coloured caiques ride at anchor, with their sterns made fast to the quay; the entire population, apparently, takes the air and the ouzo on the wide waterfront in the late afternoon; the houses are all flat-roofed and scrupulously whitewashed, and their balconies are full of flowers and spread cascades of colour into the narrow streets—often so narrow that outstretched arms may touch both sides at once. Steps and outside staircases, arches and arcades add variety. The innumerable churches—over 300 in this island—seem clean and cared-for, and though many are only used for public worship once a year, the lighted candles are a sign of private prayers: the skyline is fretted with the pattern of their domes and bell-towers, with the sails of windmills on the higher ground. To wander through these streets and feel the welcome and dignity of the island homes is a great delight.

Mykonos Museum—a modern, long, white building across the harbour—contains little beyond the vases from the tombs of Delos transferred to the island of Rheneia. These are in great numbers, but nearly all fragmentary.

A Chapter of Islands

PAROS

PAROS played little part in history. Nicetas, an emissary to the Saracens, put in here in A.D. 902 and found only one solitary hermit living in the island. Besides showing us the typical desolation of the Aegean when Saracen raids had made life impossible, Nicetas gives us valuable evidence about the date of the great church, still the island's chief monument. It was old when he saw it 'supported on every side by marble columns'. Tradition, corroborated by architectural study, says that the main church dates from the Justinian era—the sixth century A.D. It is, in fact, a complex of two or three buildings, constructed in close succession. The original building is the small church of St. Nicholas on the north side, with its Roman Doric columns, and this may date from the time of Constantine the Great; then the great Church of the Assumption was added, and the baptistery on the south. The church is known as 'The Church of Our Lady of the Hundred Gates' (Panagia Hekatontapiliani). Behind the altar is the Bishop's throne, in the centre of a two-tiered semicircle of stone seats for the elders.

Fragments of a sixth-century B.C. temple were used in the construction of a medieval fortress on the ancient Greek acropolis, the high point in the modern town of Paroekia, close to the waterfront. Drums of Doric columns, slabs of white marble and triglyphs are built into the walls. Various sanctuaries—of Apollo, of Aphrodite, and of Asclepius—have been found in the island.

The 'Parian Chronicle' was discovered in 1627 during the occupation by the Venetians. It is a marble slab inscribed with the dates of archons, and recording events, religious, literary, political and military 'from the time of the first king of Athens until the present'—which turns out to be 264 B.C. Part of the 'Chronicle' is in the Ashmolean Museum at Oxford.

In the classical period Paros made a major contribution to Greek sculpture in the provision of a marble of exceptionally fine quality and admirably suitable for the sculptor's hand.

Archilochus, elegiac poet and satirist, took part in the Parian colonization of Thasos, in the seventh century B.C., and was honoured as a hero in Paros after his death. Recently an archaic Aeolic capital has been found which had been converted in the fourth century B.C. to support a marble relief slab. The inscription on it shows that it was the funerary monument of the poet himself.

MELOS

MELOS was as round as the apple after which it is named until a volcano erupted to blow out a segment on its north-western side to give it the largest harbour in the Aegean. The same volcano provided its Neolithic inhabitants with an invaluable volcanic glass, called obsidian, which, taking a cutting edge, was an export from Melos to many parts of Greece, Asia Minor and Egypt for nearly 3,000 years. Obsidian was used for razors, arrow-heads, and all forms of cutting tools. When finally bronze could be forged and tempered to a sharp and durable edge, the wealth of Melos declined.

Excavations at Phylakopi show that, before 2000 B.C., Melos had a house-building style similar to that of other Cycladic islands—one small oblong room, sometimes two, the second opening out of the first. But, with the rise of Cretan sea-power, stretching out to dominate, Melian houses at old Phylakopi show the Minoan fashion of using columns and pillars. Rooms can now become larger; and Minoan-type frescoes appear. So do drains. Of this Minoan period, about 100 yards of thick walling survives. The top layer of the town is Mycenaean, for here, as in many other places in the Aegean, the Mycenaeans were the inheritors of the Minoan trading interests.

Melian art reached a high standard in many epochs. Of the Middle Minoan III period, the Bird vase, found in the treasury of the Palace of Knossos is a notable example; from the Mycenaean period comes one of the very first representations of men in early vase painting—four fishermen, each with one monstrous eye, walk in single file, each holding a pair of fine fish by the tail (oddly, the arms have no hands)—a striking vase, to be matched with the Warrior vase from Mycenae; the three-foot-high amphorae, which once marked graves in Delos, form a class of the Geometric period as fine as any found elsewhere in quality of manufacture and in their painted decoration with bold spirals and the confident use of human figures; a group of sculptured kouroi of the sixth century; the Melian moulded reliefs of the fifth century (used as wall decoration, or for the sides of wooden

A Chapter of Islands

chests); the impressive Asclepius of the fourth (now in the British Museum): all these bear witness to a long-lasting and high artistic achievement in this small island.

But the most familiar of all Greek statues—the Venus of Milo —came of course from Melos. The discovery in 1820 of this beautiful goddess was to set many hearts beating, but none more deliciously than that of the peasant who found her behind his terrace wall when he was repairing it on his steep hillside. He realized the worth of such beauty, delightedly exchanging her in the village for three trusses of hay *and* three cream cheeses. At this moment she was entire and perfect as she had come to life in 100 B.C. But, alas, she fell on her nose and lost her arms on the sharp corners from the grotto behind the terrace wall to the harbour below. The man who had generously thrown in the cheeses for the peasant, had sold her to the French naval officer whose ship happened to be in the harbour. He had no money on him and arranged to fetch it from the French Ambassador at Constantinople. When he swiftly returned with it, he found she had been sold a second time to a Turkish naval officer whose brig was lying in harbour with hatches open to receive her. A team of Turks was already hard at work with ropes and bars, and Venus was truly 'in the cart' when the French team appeared with mingled admiration and battle in their eyes. The rival sailors fought for the lovely lady and blood was drawn; but cash in the end prevailed and Venus moved to Paris.

In 426 B.C. the Athenian general Nicias attacked the island, but failed in his attempt to force Melos into the Athenian Empire. The second attempt to achieve this is one of the darkest spots in the history of Athens. Thucydides, instead of briefly recounting what was a small episode in a great war, goes out of his way, in the long dialogue he puts into the mouths of the Athenian envoys and the dignified Melian leaders, to show up the utter degradation of the Athenian national character at this time. To the Athenians 'might was right'; and Thucydides makes them say so. A typical passage in shortened form:

ATHENIANS: Do not let us waste time thinking about right and wrong. Right means nothing except between equals. We all know that the strong do what they can, and the weak suffer what they must. We want

202

MELIANS: How in our interests to be your slaves?

ATHENIANS: You will avert destruction: we are the most powerful state in Greece, and you have only one city to lose. Be sensible.

MELIANS: But if we remain neutral, why must you regard us as enemies?

ATHENIANS: Because everyone will say we are afraid of you, if we do not bring you to our side.

At the end of this debate, the Melians conferred and then gave their fateful answer to the tyrant state which once had been the 'Eye of Greece', the 'School of Hellas':

'Our resolution, men of Athens, is unchanged. Our city has been free for 700 years. We will not in a moment surrender it. We trust the good fortune which, under the gods, has hitherto preserved us: we will hope for human help—from Sparta: we shall endeavour to survive.'

There followed a long siege with a terrible end. All the grown men of Melos were put to death, the women and children sold for slaves, and 500 colonists were sent to occupy this cemetery of Athenian honour.

Plaka is a typical white-washed flat-roofed Cycladean town, on a pleasant curving bay inside the huge natural harbour. One of several churches is medieval, with a richly patterned façade and a pebble mosaic courtyard. Inland, one may see the meagre ruins of the theatre; perhaps enjoy picking obsidian fragments out of a cutting through which the road runs nearby; and certainly find delight in the wide view over the stage to the sea and the many mountains beyond.

A mile or more away from the theatre, cut into the hillside, there are Christian catacombs containing a number of sarcophagi in several small chambers.

TINOS

The name of TINOS is as familiar to Greeks as that of Lourdes is to Roman Catholics, and for the same reason. Many thousands of invalids make the journey to Tinos from all parts in the hope of a miraculous cure at the church of Panaghia Evangelistria.

The healing sanctity of the place was borne in upon the minds of pious Greeks in 1822, when a buried ikon of the Madonna was discovered in a grotto which is now the crypt of a church built over it.

The large, white church stands at the top of the water-side town. The approach is up a long, straight street, lined with stalls, on which are set out such a display of souvenirs, that the humblest Greek of ancient times who ever carried home a common water-jar from the fountain-house, would turn away from these products of the industrial era in astonishment.

The courtyards of the church are laid out with cypress trees and flowering shrubs, the surface covered with pebble-mosaic. The healing festivals are held each year on March 25 and August 15; and the continuity with the practice in the sanctuaries of the healing god Asclepius in ancient Greece can be seen in two modern features of these festivals. At Epidaurus, the sick slept in rows together in the temple precincts in the expectation that, while they slept, the god would visit them in the form of a snake, and heal. 'Incubation', as this sleeping on holy ground was called, survives in a modern form at Tinos, but without the snake. For at festival time, many hundreds of people sleep in the courtyards of the church, covering every square yard of them. The same continuity is perhaps also seen in the large collection of jewellery, paintings, furniture and other costly gifts made by pilgrims, and now on view in rooms off the courtyard, reminiscent as they are of the votive offerings made by the worshippers in many ancient Greek sanctuaries. This honoured church of Panaghia Evangelistria, with its power to elicit so much faith even in this materialistic age, is the high light of Tinos.

There are traces of the Venetian occupation which began in 1207 and lasted 500 years. The castle and city of that period were not on the waterfront, where surprise piratical attack would be easy, but up in the mountain, at Exoburgo, an hour's walk away. The larger survival of the Venetian period is the concentration in Tinos of many Roman Catholics.

In classical times Tinos played a curious part in the Persian invasion under Xerxes. The ships of the Tinians and their crews had evidently been pressed into the Persian fleet by the latter's overwhelming superiority. But in the hours before the decisive battle of Salamis, when the huge Persian fleet was making its dispositions to trap the smaller Greek fleet inside the Bay of Eleusis, a Tinian ship bravely contrived to desert to the Greeks and tell them of the Persian plans.

SYROS

At my first visit to SYROS, I arrived late on a pitch-dark evening. After three hours we were to sail for Athens. I had been below but went on deck at the sound of brass bands. For a moment I thought we had already reached the Piraeus, for the harbour was fantastically crowded with ships. In parallel lines, six ships lay close together with their sterns made fast to the quay: three were warships and three passenger ships. We worked our way in, and we were seven. All were festooned from masthead to bow and stern with necklaces of light-bulbs; several were making music in careless rivalry. The population of island and ships, in one dense and happy crowd, sauntered the length of the waterfront or sat sipping their drinks at the countless café tables. Beyond the bright lights by the water, the lights of the houses of the town, built all the way to the tops of two steep hills, pierced the black velvet night. It looked to me, who did not know that the city entirely covered two conical hills, as if the stars of heaven had come down to shine at a new angle on the world. It was an astonishing spectacle; and the contrast with the normal dock-side scene so absolute that an almost visible spirit of gaiety swiftly drew us all ashore.

A century ago, Syros was the chief port of the Aegean because of its central position in the open sea with a deep and sheltered harbour. The big sailing ships could always be sure of a wind and, with the sea all round them, need never be embayed. It was also, of course, on the main routes north and south, and between Greece and Asia Minor. When steam supplanted sail, the shipping interests wisely built up docking and repair facilities, which are now a considerable source of prosperity to the island. Spinning mills, cotton weaving sheds and tanneries all help towards maintaining Syros' leading position in the Cyclades.

SANTORIN

SANTORIN—Thera in ancient times—at the southerly point of the Cyclades, is unique among Greek islands. The ship enters an almost land-locked bay ten miles across, formed by the crescent shape of Thera and the smaller island, Therasia, lying between the horns. Of trees or vegetation on the shore there is no trace, for the bay is bordered by a vast wall of cliffs up to 1,000 feet high. Red, black, green-grey and white, they look savaged and torn as if they had just emerged from the elemental volcanic cataclysm which formed them. The ship is sailing inside the flooded crater of a huge volcano. In the eruption the crater split open and let in uncountable megatons of cold sea-water—cubic miles of it—to fall upon the magma—the mass of molten incandescent rock in the cavernous deeps below the cone. In the resultant explosion of super-heated steam and gases 80 square kilometres of Thera were blown sky-high. This sudden release of unimaginably vast destructive forces on a small island would create major earthquakes on the surrounding sea-bed and they in turn would raise tidal waves—tsunamis. The Krakatoa explosion of 1883 was smaller, destroying one third of the land-area which Thera lost, yet the tsunami, 100 ft. high, in the Sunda Strait drowned villages up to 60 miles away and caused the majority of the 36,000 deaths.

When did Thera explode and on what coasts did the tidal wave expend its dreadful energy? Professor Marinatos believes he has the answers to these questions.

In excavations on Thera begun in 1967 and now using mining and tunnelling techniques, Professor Marinatos and his team have found *under* 150 feet of volcanic ash Minoan buildings, one house with a complete groundfloor wall, windows and door intact, part of an upper floor, and many pithoi and decorated vases of the style current in Crete about 1500 B.C. It has long been known that in the region of 1500 B.C. Minoan Crete suffered a catastrophic loss of power and that towns, harbours and palaces on the north coast had been destroyed or badly damaged, but the cause had not been known, nor the reason why this time the Minoans failed to re-build. Destructive earthquakes had occurred before. In 1965, during an oceanic survey, cores from the sea-bed stretching south-east from Thera almost to Egypt were found to consist of Thera ash, in places a metre thick. Similar fall-out of ash has been traced in the recent excavations in and near Kata Zakro in the north-east of Crete. These facts point to a date of *c.* 1500 B.C. for the eruption of Thera, and to the north and north-east coastal regions of Crete, with their vital harbours, towns and agricultural areas as chief victims of the overwhelming tidal waves and earthquakes and the fall-out of Thera ash, so damaging to agriculture.

The story of this sudden shattering blow to Europe's first great civilization — Minoan Crete — would be told, re-told and embroidered in the telling in the thousand years or so which had passed when Solon, an ancester of Plato, heard it through interpreters from priests in Egypt, and, generations later, Plato (in his Timaeus and Critias) handed on the family's story. In the long chain of story-telling the geographical position of the almost Utopian lost civilization was lost too—until perhaps today. For Professor Marinatos believes that it was in fact the disaster to Minoan Crete of which the Egyptian priests told Solon. A fascinating, reasoned and detailed argument to support this is set out in Mr. J. V. Luce's recent book *The End of Atlantis: New Light on an Old Legend.*

Several times in history the volcano has resuscitated itself from the submerging sea and coughed up islands of ash. At the moment there are three of these 'Burnt Islands' in the centre of the bay. But the arrangement cannot be regarded as definitive. The last outburst from the underworld was in 1956 and though no new volcanic cones appeared on this occasion, an earthquake destroyed very many houses and killed fifty-five people. Eusebius, Justin, Strabo, Plutarch and Pliny (inaccurately) refer to these upheavals of volcanic islands. The newest island is 'Little Burnt Island' (nearest to the landing point of Phira) and appeared in 1711. These ash islands are the tops of submarine mountains 1,500 feet high.

It is hard to understand why this volcanic cone—which is what the island is—was once named Kalliste, 'fairest of islands', unless it was from a motive of propitiation. The Greeks called the stormy Black Sea the 'Euxine', the friendly sea, in the hope that it might live up to its more friendly name. Perching high on the lip of the crater are the brave rebuilt white houses of the modern town of PHIRA. The approach from the landing at the foot of the high precipice is up an interminable zigzag path. Some travellers who choose a mule for the journey end it on their own legs, for the mules are apt at wiping their riders off against the walls.

The Romans naturally added a theatre and baths, and perhaps a temple of Mithras; finally the Byzantines occupied the site and left walls and fortifications and churches behind them.

The population today is 15,000, almost the same as it was a hundred years ago. They make a heady wine from the grapes which the volcanic soil abundantly produces; and this, with tomatoes and the minerals deposited by the volcano, with a little contributed by the tourist trade, provides a scanty livelihood. Cyrene, however, offers none to-day: the mother has outlived the daughter.

CHAPTER XX

Islands off the Asia Minor Coast: Lesbos. Samos. Patmos. Cos

LESBOS

Lesbos, in the north-eastern corner of the Aegean, close to the Asia Minor coast, is a beautiful island, mountainous, and well covered still with trees; fertile, too, and blessed with a mild climate. It has a population of over 100,000. In its greatest days in the seventh and sixth centuries B.C., the chief city, Mitylene (also spelt Mytilene), traded as far as Naucratis in Egypt where it helped to administer the Hellenium, the shrine and enclave built by the Greek traders in the 'treaty port' concession area granted by Amasis, king of Egypt.

Lesbos was the island 'where burning Sappho loved and sung'. It is interesting that she was the first poet to write that poetry can ensure immortality. For many people Lesbos stands for Sappho only. But there were other great lyric poets of the brilliant seventh century in Lesbos whose gifts were evoked by the beauty of this island: Terpander, said to have invented the seven-string lyre; Arion, the writer of choral lyrics; and Alcaeus, contemporary of Sappho and a political revolutionary whose poetry tells of war and wine. One of the Seven Sages, Pittacus, was governor of Mitylene and famous as statesman, warrior and philosopher.

After the Persian wars, Lesbos was the richest of the East Greek islands and an autonomous member of the Confederacy of Delos. Later, in 428 B.C., at the instigation of the oligarchs in

Mitylene, Lesbos tried to break away from what was now an Athenian Empire. The Athenians, however, secured the capitulation of Mitylene, and the awful decision was taken by the Assembly at Athens to kill every male in the city and sell the women and children into slavery. A trireme was dispatched with these orders for the Athenian commander of the city. Next day, after further discussion and a brilliant speech by Diodotus, who wisely based his argument not on pity but on the true interests of Athens, the Assembly countermanded their decision, and a second trireme set off. The ship with the death sentence aboard rowed slowly: in the ship that could save the lives of all in the city, the rowers rowed for those lives and arrived in time to halt the execution about to begin.

Osbert Lancaster rated the modern town of Mitylene as among the ugliest he ever saw anywhere. Perhaps he flew in, and did not see the wonderful, almost circular, harbour with gaily painted caiques in scores making the waterfront a feast of colour and interest. The Museum is small, as are the remains of classical buildings in the island. Some early Aeolian volute capitals show the beginnings of the Ionic order.

Mitylene was in Turkish occupation for nearly 450 years until 1912; architectural traces of the Turkish period are to be seen in the wooden balconies and fretted gable ends, especially in village houses.

SAMOS

SAMOS, mountainous, wooded, and with fertile plains on the south side, is a large island, separated from Asia Minor by a channel a mile and a half wide, and dominated by the bold promontory of Mount Mycale on the Asiatic shore. Vathy, the capital, is a typical waterfront town on a long arm of the sea on the north side; its excellent Museum contains archaic sculpture and a large collection of bronze figurines from the great sanctuary of Hera. This is close to the southern shore, three miles from Tigani, the site of the ancient capital. Hera was worshipped in Samos from earliest times, and recent German excavations in her sanctuary have brought to light foundations of Mycenaean buildings. Egyptian bronze statuettes found there are no surprise, for Samos was known to have been a great naval power, with overseas trade second only to that of Miletus.

AT PHILIPPI: A BEAUTIFUL BYZANTINE CAPITAL OF THE SIXTH-
CENTURY CHURCH

*In design and workmanship the equal of the capitals in Santa Sophia, built in
the same century.*

AT EPHESUS: THE THEATRE AND THE COLONNADED ARCADIAN WAY

*It was in this theatre that the riot, led by Demetrius the silversmith against St
Paul, flared up, to be extinguished finally by a very competent Town-Clerk
As the sea receded, the life of Ephesus ebbed away. The harbour water-front
was once at the end of the Arcadian Way: the beach is now six miles distant*

The great days of Samos were those of Polycrates, the tyrant, in the second half of the sixth century B.C. Like many tyrants throughout history, he was a builder. In 530 B.C., he began to rebuild and greatly enlarge the temple of Hera, the fourth on the site, and made it the largest in the Greek world, 379 feet long, with a double row of Ionic columns in the peristyle at the sides and a triple row at the ends, the porch having five columns in two rows. Polycrates was in alliance with Egypt and had probably admired her many-columned temples. A solitary column, on an unusual Ionic base turned on a lathe, stands in the now marshy ground, a pathetic survivor of the forest of columns in that great enterprise. But the huge platform of the temple and many column drums can still be seen.

Two other monuments of Polycrates are largely intact. A most ambitious water tunnel, over 1,000 yards long, ran through the mountain from the water source, and under the fortification walls into the old city, now Tigani: and the harbour mole which he built was said to be 120 feet deep to its foundations, on which the modern mole at Tigani now rests. Herodotus calls these three constructions undertaken by Polycrates the greatest works to be seen in any Greek land.

In the classical period Samos was distinguished, on the one hand, by its refusal to accept Athenian domination, even at the cost of war; and, on the other, by the everlasting civil strife between oligarchs and democrats in the island, with Persia always at hand to step in to her own advantage.

Samos played a notably courageous part in the Greek War of Independence in 1821, and though she did not become part of Greece again till 1912, she was given by the Turks a special status under a Christian 'prince' of the island, and a parliament of her own.

Samos is, as it always was, much more than 'just another island'. Moreover, Samian wine is good—when it is 'dry'.

PATMOS

'I, John, your brother in the tribulation and the sovereignty and the endurance which is ours in Jesus—I was on the island called Patmos because I had borne my testimony to Jesus. It was on the Lord's day, and I was caught up by the Spirit. I heard a

loud voice, like the sound of a trumpet. I turned and saw . . .'
and his vision he wrote down and we have it in 'The Revelation
of John', at the end of the New Testament. That is why Patmos
is the most familiar island name of all. St. John had probably
been 'relegated' to the island (as Roman justice called a temporary sentence of exile without loss of property) by the
magistrates of Ephesus about the year A.D. 95.

Half-way up the southern hill over the deep bay which almost
cuts the island in two, is a very small church built to include a
cave; it is the church of a monastery. The cave is the traditional
place in which John lived and wrote the Apocalypse. It has been
a place of pilgrimage for nearly a thousand years. Certainly at
some period the cave was lived in, for convenient ledges and
'lockers' have been cut in the rock and a flat, sloping surface on
which one might write. But we cannot know whether this is the
authentic cave; only that piety has long hallowed it and that
words heard by John in his vision seem to have a double power
when pondered in this place.

The earthquake which damaged Santorini so severely in 1956,
also did damage in Patmos. Santorini's volcano, if active in
John's time and glowing red in the night sky to the south, may
have given his unconscious mind some of the vivid imagery of
'Revelation'.

On the highest point of the hill is the monastery of St. John
the Theologian. It looks like a fortress, and it had to be exactly
that in the lawless days when in 1088 the Emperor Alexius
gave the island to a monk, Christodoulos, for the foundation of
a monastery. It is full of interest, for it has never been sacked as
have so many monasteries. The Library has a fourth-century
Gospel of St. Mark, written in gold and silver, and over seven
hundred manuscript books of the pre-printing centuries. Visitors
are welcomed by the monks and they will find that this monastery
is very much alive.

Cos

Cos, like Patmos and Rhodes, is one of the group called by the
Greeks 'the Dodecanese'—the twelve islands. It is close to the
south-west corner of Asia Minor, and lay on the trade route
from Egypt and Syria to the north. It was considered one of the

most beautiful of the islands in antiquity, and that can be well understood. The waterfront today, with the walls of a Genoese castle at one end, shady trees and public gardens, and boat-building yards to add interest, is all that even a Greek waterfront should be. Near to it are the ruins of the Roman town, and one of the largest trees in Europe. This is a plane-tree, the trunk forty-six feet in circumference; ancient columns and a Roman altar support the aged sagging limbs. The credulous are asked to believe that under this tree Hippocrates passed his 'surgery hours'. What is true is that Cos was the home of Hippocrates (*floruit* 410 B.C.), a very famous physician, teacher and personality. It is not known how much, if any, of the medical treatises which have come down under his name, were written by him: for though he has the great name of founder of scientific medicine, the written works are inconsistent and unscientific, showing quite contrary views towards diseases and treatment. Best known of these writings is the 'Hippocratic Oath', to the ethical standards of which doctors of many nations and races have ever since it was written felt bound to be loyal. Some clauses have a special contemporary interest: 'I will give no deadly medicine to anyone if asked, nor suggest it: nor will I aid a woman to produce abortion. . . . Into whatever houses I enter, I will go there for the benefit of the sick, and will abstain from every act of corruption, and above all from seduction. . . . Whatever in my professional practice—or even not in connection with it—I see or hear in the lives of men which ought not to be spoken of abroad, I will not divulge, deeming that on such matters we should be silent.' (Translation: Dr. Charles Singer.)

The Asklepieion, the curative centre of the healing god Asclepius, was established at Cos by colonists from Epidaurus on a superb site on three terraces above the city. The Italians, who seized Cos from the Turks in 1912, completed an earlier excavation and made some reconstruction. The retaining walls of the terraces are high, and the staircases from one terrace to another positively magnificent. The temple of Asclepius was on the top level, overlooking the whole splendid sanctuary: on the middle level, the great altar was flanked by two smaller temples: and on the lowest level, a colonnade led to the hydropathic establishment, as at Pergamum. Asclepius believed in the curative value of bathing and of a peaceful and beautiful environment.

CHAPTER XXI

Two Islands in the North: Samothrace. Thasos

SAMOTHRACE

'Are we going to be able to go ashore?' It is the inevitable question as one's ship approaches the island of Samothrace in the far north of the Aegean, for there is now no harbour. If the wind is in the south, there will be smooth water under the lee of the magnificent mountain, Phengari, which rises 5,000 feet straight up from the sea, and we shall be able to go ashore in the caiques waiting for us, and land on the pebbly beach close to the ancient city and sanctuary. There must have been a harbour of some sort in ancient times, for Samothrace was once a frequented place. It lay on the sea route which joined Europe and Asia Minor, virtually an extension of the Roman Via Egnatia, the quickest line of communication between Rome and her Eastern Provinces. This route was taken by St. Paul when he sailed from Troas in north-western Asia Minor to bring Christianity to Europe and landed at Neapolis, the European landward terminus of the road.

We can well believe those who report that from the peak of Mount Phengari, an immense panorama is visible, Mount Athos and Chalcidice, Thasos, the coast of Thrace, Lemnos, Imbros, the Dardanelles and Mount Ida. Homer placed Zeus on Mount Ida and Poseidon on the peak of Samothrace to watch the siege of Troy. Seen in the distance from the decks of ships, Samothrace was a valuable navigational aid, and on one side or the other her mountain mass would offer shelter.

214

Two Islands in the North: Samothrace. Thasos

But there were others than seamen who came to Samothrace: such as Lysander of Sparta, and the rulers of Egypt and Antioch in Hellenistic times, King Ptolemy and his queen Arsinoe, Prince Philip of Macedon, and many a great man of the Roman period; Varro for instance, and Piso, Caesar's father-in-law, we know came here. Romans had a special interest in Samothrace, for they, who claimed descent from the Trojans, wished to be associated with the place from which came Dardanus, the founder of Troy. Like tens of thousands of ordinary folk from everywhere, they all had come to be initiated into the Mysteries of the Great Gods. The sanctuary excavated by the American archaeologist, the late Professor Lehmann, is of fascinating interest, and the whole site exceptionally easy to follow. It lies on a low hill, astride a watercourse, overlooking the sea and dominated by the rugged mountain above, and with trees about it. Here the ancient stones speak of man's old and perennial effort to seek divine help 'amid the changes and chances of this fleeting world'.

When Greek colonists arrived in the seventh century B.C. from the East Aegean (Pausanias says, from Samos—hence the name), they found that the indigenous people worshipped a fertility goddess whom they called 'Mother of the Rocks'. She had a subordinate male, Kadmilos, and was assisted by twin divinities of fertility, known as the Kabeiroi. Typically, the Greeks took over and developed the sanctuary on their own lines. The mother goddess became Demeter; Kadmilos, the former consort, they said was Hermes; and the twin Kabeiroi, who had also been worshipped as saviours of seamen, became the Dioscuri who already in the Greek mind had that function.

After elaborate initiation ceremonies which evidently took place at night, judging from the great number of lamps which were found, and included feasting—so many were the plates— the initiate might hope for good fortune and especially for 'happy landings' after sea voyages. It is not certain whether the good hope of the initiate extended, as at Eleusis, to happiness in a future life; but in one interesting respect the Mysteries of Samothrace may have gone beyond those of Eleusis. The evidence is thought by Lehmann to show that a better moral life, beginning perhaps with 'confession', was one of the gifts of a blood-baptism in the optional second and final initiation. A better moral life was not in Greece one of the objectives of religious observance. That the holiness of God requires an answering effort to holiness in man is the vastly important contribution of the Jewish Faith.

The first building, nearest the sea, is the Anaktoron, a hall of initiation, dating from about 500 B.C. Some of the walls still stand to a height of ten feet, and traces of the plan can still be seen—the hearth, the lustration area, the benches for spectators, and the inner sanctum for the display to the initiate of the sacred symbols.

Next to the Anaktoron is the largest circular building known in the Greek world, the gift of Queen Arsinoe in 281 B.C. This building was constructed over the remains of the earliest rock altar, and part of a cyclopean wall of the Bronze Age can still be seen inside the circle of the Hellenistic building.

Further towards the south is the Temenos, an enclosed courtyard, perhaps the scene of the feasting. Adjacent to it is the Hieron, built over an older building. There the final ceremony took place for those who were prepared to go the whole way—a way which included a descent to a cell under a sacrificial altar and a baptism of bull's blood.

Between the Hieron and the watercourse was the Great Altar, and adjacent to it the Hall of the votive offerings.

The theatre is just across the watercourse and, in fact, the stage buildings must have bridged it. Only the shape of the cavea remains. But on the hill above the theatre there was a fountain which played into an ornamental pool; and, in the centre of it, on the bow of her marble ship stood Victory, winged, and proudly breasting the breeze. She is, of course, the grand Victory of Samothrace, now in the Louvre. How wonderful she must have looked, silhouetted against the blue sky in that position above the crowded theatre.

The Emperor Hadrian was the last of the royal visitors to Samothrace. The sanctuary faded in importance as Christianity spread, and it was closed towards the end of the fourth century A.D. But it must be recognized that for more than a thousand years initiates, men and women, slave and free—there was only one qualification and that was desire for communion with the great gods—journeyed to far Samothrace and came away with confidence and hope.

THASOS

A dark mountain range in the background, pine woods climbing up to the rocks, the high tree-clad arms of a sheltered bay, neat white houses on a long waterfront shaded by tall plane-trees, a galaxy of brightly painted caiques in the harbour and, in the distance across the sea to the north, the coast of Thrace and its buildings sharp in the clear light but miniature—this is Thasos, one of the loveliest and remotest of all Greek islands. But its long distance from the main centres of Hellenic life in the south did not prevent its growth to a position of great commercial wealth and importance.

A colony of adventurers from Paros, under Telesikles, arrived at the beginning of the seventh century B.C. An oracle of Apollo at Delphi, which may be the only genuine foundation-oracle to survive, runs in the usual hexameters:

> *Telesikles, I bid you announce to the people of Paros:*
> *'Found now a city far-seen, in the Isle of Mists. I command so.'*

A follow-up contingent came to Thasos twenty years later, led by the founder's son, the poet Archilochus.

The island is indeed 'far-seen', and its 4,000-feet-high mountain-range a comforting landmark for seamen sailing the course from Asia Minor by way of Tenedos, Imbros, Samothrace and Thasos to Northern Greece. Thasos had the harbours where one could go alongside in safety however hard it blew. The present twin harbours have their moles built on foundations of the sixth century B.C. The construction of these harbours was throughout the history of the island to put money into the State's coffers. For Thasos was not only a boon on the regular east-west line of sea communication, but an equal service on the Greece-to-the-Black-Sea run.

From the earliest days of the Greek polis, the gold of Mount Pangaeum on the mainland close by was the big factor in the island's prosperity. We also hear of gold-mines in the island itself, though modern geologists doubt the possibility. The gold was at best not easy to get, but if the Thracian inhabitants of the gold-bearing regions on the mainland sometimes combined in overwhelming numbers to throw out the adventurers, and gold-washing with fleeces pegged to the bottom of mountain streams had to be abandoned, it was only a temporary withdrawal, for the miners were safe behind the walls of their acropolis in Thasos. This was built on one of the twin summits, joined by a long and narrow ridge, of a hill 450 feet high which rose steeply above a narrow coastal strip and almost enfolded, as it certainly sheltered, the city and twin harbours.

On the acropolis stood the Temple of Athena—now under the ruins of a Genoese castle—and half-way along the ridge was the Temple of Apollo, silhouetted against the sky-line for every eye that looked up from the waterfront. By the end of the sixth century or the beginning of the fifth, the city on its landward side was entirely enclosed by a 4,000-yard-long wall; considerable stretches survive. Ten gateways have been traced; and ten towers strengthened it. The Gate of Silenus on the south-west is the best preserved. Such a large fortified area provided also for the farming element of the population in times of danger. For the land too was a substantial source of wealth. The mountains were clothed with pine forest, perfect material for ship-construction, and soil and climate gave Thasian wine a bouquet appreciated far and wide. Amphorae bearing the Thasian mark have been found as far away as Susa, Egypt, Magna Graecia and the Adriatic coast. Inscriptions in the Agora show a rigorous control over this precious export.

Thasos is called 'a rampart of Hellenism' against the barbarians of Thrace and the North, but it always had a mixed population. Inscriptions and lists of officials repeatedly bear names of Thracian origin; a sanctuary of Archonda indicates the survival of local worship; the sanctuary of Herakles has produced evidence that the Asiatic Herakles, introduced to the island by the pre-Greek gold seekers, the Phoenicians, was still not completely hellenized in Classical times. Moreover, the great variety of sanctuaries in itself suggests an unusually mixed city population. In addition to the temples of Athena and Apollo, Pan had a simple sanctuary, Artemis a most elaborate one; Poseidon and Dionysus, Aphrodite, Zeus too, all had their centres of worship. It was a real achievement to have unified diversity in so successful a polis.

In the Persian wars, Thasos submitted without a blow and, giving a feast to the army of Xerxes which cost 400 talents of silver, incurred the contempt and hatred of Athens. This was mitigated after Salamis by a Thasian contribution of thirty ships to the Confederacy of Delos. But finding that Athens purposed to cut her trade with Egypt and the East, Thasos seceded from her Athenian alliance, and war broke out with Athens. The outcome was disaster. She lost her fleet, her walls, her gold-mines. The long story of later rise and fall cannot be told here, but the French excavations prove a great building programme in the fourth century B.C.

Polygnotus, a foremost Greek painter, but a 'primitive' who did not know 'shading', came from Thasos. He loved to paint historic scenes where great men performed greatly. We know of his work at Delphi in a club-room—the Lesche of the Cnidians—and again in the Agora and on the Acropolis at Athens. Another Thasian of different gifts was Theagenes, who as a nine-year-old schoolboy carried off a full-size bronze statue from the agora. Pausanias was much impressed and gives a long account of his later athletic successes. He appears to have broken many records for events based on exceptional physical strength; the pancration and the boxing prizes at Olympia, Nemea and at the Isthmian games were just a few of the 1,400 prizes he carried off! After he was safely dead and buried, an enemy whipped the bronze statue of the hero set up in the agora at Thasos. It fell and killed him. Obedient to some law, the brazen homicide was duly exiled by being thrown into the sea. Famine followed in Thasos. The Oracle at Delphi advised the recall of all exiles. Dangerous men trooped back to their old homes, but the famine continued. A second appeal to Delphi produced the answer, 'You have forgotten Theagenes.' Fishermen eventually recovered the statue: it was replaced in the agora, and there was food for all.

The walls and ramparts were splendidly rebuilt and remain among the finest of the ancient monuments: the theatre, halfway up the hill to the east of the harbours, was reconstructed, and the sanctuary of Poseidon near the northern harbour completed. The agora (behind the Museum) became an impressive public place, a large colonnaded rectangle with sacred enclosure and altar of Zeus Agoraios, protector of civil concord, built towards the centre; and a sanctuary of Artemis stretching out from the stoa on its eastern side; the sanctuary of Herakles (whose cult Theagenes appears to have done much to stimulate) was provided with a large new building of five parallel rooms opening on a new colonnade. Excavation by the French School continues in the ruins of the fourth-century city.

The chief pleasure of a visit to Thasos is likely to be the beauty of the setting, the climb up the path through the pines to the shaded theatre, the walk on the ridge from the Genoese castle and the fine views both east and west (the agora lay-out is well seen from the platform of the Temple of Apollo) and the descent by an ancient stairway with the marble walls on our right to the pleasant waterfront.

The Museum shows that Thasos had contacts with all the chief vase-producing centres from its foundation onwards, Ionia, the Cyclades, Rhodes, Corinth and Attica. There are painted terracotta architectural fragments from early temples of the sixth century. The chief pride of the Museum is the colossal kouros. This great marble Apollo of the sixth century B.C., carrying a ram on his shoulder, as shepherds in Greece and Turkey may still be seen to do, confronts one impressively on entering the Museum. It was found embedded in the fortification walls of the acropolis. In early Christian art, the Good Shepherd is shown in just this attitude.

CHAPTER XXII

With Alexander the Great at Pella, and St. Paul at Philippi

PELLA

It is strange enough that the site of a large sanctuary like that at Olympia should have been lost and remained undetected for over a thousand years, but even odder that Pella should have disappeared off the map. For not only was it the largest city of Macedonia but the first capital of all Greece when Philip II of Macedon had forced unwilling unity upon it; and it was the main base from which Alexander the Great set out with his army to conquer and Hellenize half the known world. A farmer, Basil Stergion, digging a cellar store-room under his house in 1957 and chancing to come upon a fine marble Ionic capital, put Pella on the map again. Basil's village is no longer called 'Holy Apostles'; it has reverted to Palaia Pella. For the farmer told the village policeman of his marble find; the policeman, obeying the sensible rule, told District headquarters. They reported to the Prefect; he cheered the Military Governor of Northern Greece with the news, and in no time the Curator of Antiquities at Salonika, Mr. Photios Petsas, ephor of the Archaeological District, had his nose to the ground, and in it. The Central Authority arrived in the person of Dr. Marinatos, and all Greece was thrilled at the certain discovery of ancient Pella.

Large Greek houses, Greek pottery, objects of bronze, gold coins, some splendid pebble mosaics, Greek in design, Greek in subject, a wide road, Greek Ionic columns of a portico . . . all were Greek, and that was the cause of the general delight. For archaeology in Macedonia, in the far north of Greece, has important political undertones. There can hardly be any part of the earth's surface about which more prolonged and bloody argument has raged as to whom it should properly belong. Macedonia has changed hands a score of times. Had there been a United Nations in the last century, the Macedonian problem might have driven them even crazier than has the Congo to-day. Every schoolboy knows that 'Macedonia became the tilting-ground for the Slav comitadji and the Muslim bashi-bouzouck'! After the second Balkan War, half Macedonia came to Greece. In World War I the Bulgarians hoped to get all Macedonia, and half a million British troops with those of France, Greece, Serbia, Italy and Russia protected Salonika and Macedonia. In World War II, the Bulgars were back in occupation—for a time. But still today there is propaganda inflaming passion and claiming that Macedonia is not and never was Greek. And now archaeology is proving that Macedonia *was* Greek, that the culture and art, architecture and the way of life was surely Greek and can be seen to have been Greek—at least in the time of Philip II and the astonishing Alexander the Great. We can be sure that the excavation at Pella will continue.

The village of Pella lies on the high point of a low hill, probably the acropolis, which slopes steadily down to a level plain of great extent, in summer a wide sea of wheat. Even the non-geological traveller realizes that the great plain was once covered with water. So it was in Alexander's day, and navigable too. Pella was an important port, and it is now twenty-three miles from the sea, for the old lake and navigable river are silted up. Pella was destroyed by the Romans in 168 B.C., but it would have died a natural death in any case, the slow death that has come to many an ancient port by silting. Ephesus and Miletus, for instance, died this death; their life depended on sea-borne trade, and the sea deserted them.

King Archelaos (400 B.C.) was the first to choose Pella as a palace site and he had great ideas: he chose Zeuxis to decorate his palace, and this painter, Polygnotus and Apelles have come down as the three greatest artists of Greece. So lavishly did Archelaos spend on the appearance of the palace and so little on his own, that the wit remarked that people came from all over the world to see the owner's house but none to see the owner. Nevertheless the court was a centre for men of learning and philosophy: Euripides saw his plays produced at Pella, and Aristotle was there as tutor to the young Alexander.

Trial trenches have been dug, establishing the size of the city as between three and four square kilometres. Inside the perimeter, scores of further trial trenches have laid bare foundations: none were negative. Some walls are six feet thick. Given time and money, the archaeologists will recover a great site. Where excavation is completed—close to the road and Museum shed— the evidence of a well-ordered city is clear in the thirty-foot-wide cambered road, the drainage system, the fresh water supply which includes settlement tanks, and in the construction of the big houses with fine Greek pebble-mosaic floors and Ionic colonnades.

Three mosaics from one house are of special interest, for we have not elsewhere found many of this technique in which pebbles are used. The Romans developed the art of mosaic, using coloured marble tesserae; but the invention of mosaic is Greek, and even with the difficult material of pebbles the effect is surprisingly good. Dionysos rides his bounding panther: a griffin attacks a running deer: and two men with sword and spear hunt a lion. Some 300 coins have been found. Are we as careless of our coins as the ancients so conveniently were? Roof tiles at Pella, stamped with the name of the city or that of Lysimachus, one of Alexander's 'Successors' are, exceptionally in Greece, as much as three feet long. Evidently some of the buildings to be found are of very great size.

At Pella was formed the idea to unify all Greece, and from Pella went out the power to bring it about—diplomatic and military power. A unified Greece would remove for ever the menace of the barbarian Persian. Philip II would have led the army to conquest in the east; but he was assassinated, and Alexander stepped into his shoes. He found even these large shoes too small for his extraordinary ambitions. He had come from a unified Greece; he could and did defeat all armies that confronted him wherever battle had been joined: why not a world at unity under a god? Had he himself not been hailed as son of Zeus Ammon by the god's oracle in the distant oasis of Siwa?

With Alexander the Great at Pella, and St. Paul at Philippi

Today in lonely, deeply-rural Pella, with the prairie-like wheatfields all about the still restricted areas of excavation, instead of the intense satisfaction in the finds which warms the patriotic Greek, the foreign visitor, though sympathetic with the Greek national spirit, is likely to feel aware of the transience of human glory more sharply than is comfortable. Alexander's achievement, reaching to India and boundless in its vision of a Hellenic world at peace, was colossal: and are these wheatfields all that's left?

'No, no!' cries the Greek chorus, 'Alexander laid the foundations of Hellenism in vast tracts of the east on which Christianity in due course could build. The early Church could never have developed among barbarians. Pella, like Jerusalem, Athens and Rome, is fundamentally important in the history of civilization, and lives on in its grand achievement.'

So there is plenty to think about at Pella beyond the actual mosaic floors and porticoes, roads and drains; and the future is pregnant with possibilities.

Philippi

Philippi as a place-name is familiar to all for the two decisive actions which took place there: the first, the decisive battle in the Civil War in 42 B.C. in which Roman Republicanism died with Brutus and Cassius, and from which Octavian was well set —after one more battle—to mount the throne of Empire as Augustus; and the second, a century later, the arrival of the Apostle Paul on the mainland of Europe and the establishment in Philippi of Europe's first Christian church.

As the road from Cavalla, the port which St. Paul knew as Neapolis, climbs to the watershed, the old Roman road comes into view, the Via Egnatia which ran across the whole peninsula from Durazzo (Dyrrachium) on the Adriatic to the Aegean at Neapolis. When the plain beyond is reached, the old and the new roads run together for several miles in the familiar straightness of the Roman surveyors. Eight miles from the sea, the eye picks out the obvious acropolis of Philippi, a rocky mass, 1,000 feet high, surmounted by towers. The traveller in Greece or Asia Minor soon becomes accustomed to spotting likely-looking hills for an acropolis and he is usually right in his guess. The Via

Egnatia and the modern road on top of it runs through the old city, part having been built on the lower slopes of the hill and part on the plain at its foot.

The first Greeks at Philippi were gold-miners from Thasos, living under shanty-town conditions. When they were in danger from the local Thracians who from time to time forcibly objected to this Greek intrusion, the Greeks would retire to the safety of Thasos. Later, Philip II of Macedon, father of Alexander the Great, in his efforts to control the wild mountaineers, decided to build a proper fortified city and to change the name of the locality, Crenides, to his own. The line of these walls, complicated by later Byzantine building, can in parts be followed. But most of the remains on the site are not those of the Hellenistic city but date from the Roman and Byzantine periods.

The agora or forum is a large rectangular court surrounded by a colonnade, with the ground plan of a library building on its east side, and traces of the tribunal half-way along the long north (or road) side.

Cut into the hillside and close to the north-eastern walls was the theatre of the Hellenistic period. The rock-cut grave reliefs of the earlier Greek period, which are numerous on the lower slopes of the hill, are perhaps of greater interest in this quarter of the site.

The Roman latrines of the palaestra (to the west of the once domed Byzantine church south of the Forum) are worth an inspection. One will return from them convinced, with Burke, that 'custom reconciles us to everything'.

The great battle of 42 B.C. took place on the plain: the two low hills, on and around which the rivals centred their armies, are visible to the right as one looks from the road over the forum and the large area of the excavations. Of this battle Appian gives a full and fascinating account in his fourth book of the Civil Wars. Brutus and Cassius had fortified their camp on good rising ground with easy communications to the sea and an excellent food supply behind them. They had marshes to protect their left flank as they faced the army of Octavian and Antony to the west. This army's supply position was however precarious: food could only be obtained from distant Amphipolis and that by a circuitous and difficult mountain route. Octavian was obliged to force the fight. Secretly, hidden by the tall reeds of the marsh, and silently by the exercise of the utmost care, his army engineers built a causeway across the marsh and so out-flanked the unsuspecting Republicans in a sudden assault. A general engagement followed and with a most curious result. Each army captured the other's camp: half of each army was victorious, half defeated. Cassius was dead. Neither army dared renew the fight. The pause lasted for twenty days. Then, in desperation, the hungry army of Octavian and Antony violently attacked—less for a great cause than to capture Brutus' food supplies. They wasted no time on the usual barrage of javelins and arrows: this was an affair of the sword in the hands of starving men. The soldiers of Brutus gave way and were scat-tered. 'I am of no more use to my country, if this is how my army feels,' said Brutus: and at his order a friend thrust his sword into his side. Only his rival Antony now stood between Octavian and supreme power over the Roman world. The battle of Actium was to remove that obstacle. So the empty plain of Philippi is still full charged with significance.

It is not necessary here to describe the coming of St. Paul to Philippi in obedience to the vision he saw at Troas, for the whole story is vividly written in the Acts, Chapter XVI, by the doctor, Luke, who travelled with him. But for those who would like literally to walk in the footsteps of the Apostle, Philippi pro-vides an opportunity. They may walk down the main road to the west—the Via Egnatia—till they come to the river bridge a mile away and marked by a line of trees. Here is the place, Luke tells us, where Paul met the women, and in particular Lydia, who were to be of such a help in the foundation of the Church at Philippi. 'On the Sabbath we went out of the city by a riverside, where prayer was wont to be made: and we sat down and spake unto the women which resorted thither. . . .' The road-bridge is modern, but the paved Roman road here made a short swing away from the straight, presumably to reach a shallower stretch of water suitable to ford. Nearby is a pleasant wood and the river waters tumble over the stones with a quiet garrulity. In the background rises the peak of the Acropolis.

When we read St. Paul's letter 'To the Philippians' written from his prison in Rome and note the tone of it, we will not be surprised that this Church, so firmly and happily established, should—later in its growth—have raised such splendid churches as those of which we see the remains. Three are known. The first, on a terrace below the Acropolis, on the edge of the main road and on the side towards the hill, is thought to be the oldest. It was on the basilica plan, with an apsidal east-end where the Elders of the Church sat behind the altar. The French archaeologists who excavated here found evidence of destruction by earthquake. It is likely that its place was taken on the plain by a new large church of which the massive piers of the fallen main dome are the largest standing ruin on the site. The carefully cut Byzantine capitals are very similar to those of Santa Sophia and equally beautiful. It is not yet clear where in the sequence a newly excavated and remarkable church should come. For the Greek Archaeological Service has recently uncovered an early Christian building, square on the outside and octagonal inside. The four corners inside were built with 'shells' or semi-domes: and the aisle is a circular one, colonnaded, with a gap to the east for the altar.

Recent Greek excavations have also laid open the foundations of buildings adjacent to, and north of, the octagonal church. After some hesitation, these have now been identified as a baptistery complex and, beyond this, a bath building with its hypocaust and usual arrangements.

Unless the imagination is alive, and eye and ear sensitive to the flash of the sun on fifty thousand spears, and the glitter and clash of sword on sword in ancient battle; or unless there is some inner response and a quickened beating of the heart at the sight of the place where, long ago by the riverside on a sabbath-day, the seed was planted that was to grow into a mustard-tree, a visit to Philippi is not to be specially recommended: it has no special quality of natural beauty and there are many sites of greater architectural interest.

CHAPTER XXIII

Ephesus: 'The First and Greatest Metropolis of Asia'

Ephesus is one of the most impressive of historic sites in the Aegean, and there is more left of the city than can be seen within a day. Every season the Austrian Institute of Archaeology extends the already large area of excavation, and where one year squads of Turkish women plant tobacco, the next year yet another large building is there to be added to the long list of market squares, public bath buildings—there are already four large and elaborate thermae—gymnasia, fountains, colonnades, temples, houses, shops, a library, a large theatre, odeum, city hall, an early church, and about 2,000 yards of marble-paved and colonnaded streets. The Turkish Government is well aware of the attractions of this wonderful site and, to encourage visitors, has built a fine new quay at Kusadasi, across the sea from Samos, and also made from it a good bitumenized road to Ephesus.

Much of the architectural ruins are of a late period—of the first four or five centuries A.D.; for though the city was founded by colonists from Athens about 1100 B.C., probably in the steep valley where the Austrians are working, there have been changes of site forced upon the population for various reasons, to be explained as the city's history is told in outline.

Ephesus was chosen by the colonists as an ideal site for two distinct reasons. It was on the sea at the mouth of a river, the Cayster, and would be, if a defensible city were built there, an excellent outlet for the goods of the interior and for those brought by camel caravan from the more distant East. It would, equally, be a convenient port of entry for Greek and Western goods. An old tradition gives an elaborate account of how the colonists were divinely guided by the actions of a goat to settle at this place. This is hard on the colonists who obviously were sagacious men with a good understanding of their requirements. Not only had they there a promising port in a favourable locality for trade and in Mount Pion, a high, detached hill, an excellent acropolis; with another mountain range (Coressus) running down to the sea immediately to the south, on the spine of which they could build their walls, with the river to the north as the northern defence line; but also the place was already known as a magnet for pilgrims to the sanctuary of a great Anatolian goddess of fertility. All that was needed was development and exploitation. In the typical Greek manner the local deity was assimilated: she was obviously Artemis, queen of the beasts and giver of fertility to man and all animals. Her temple was a mile away by the river at the foot of another hill, but one could not interfere with that: the place had its inviolate sanctity. So the first city grew in the steep valley between Pion and Coressus with its fine acropolis on Mount Pion.

In the sixth century B.C., however, Croesus, King of Lydia, decided to take the city, and did so. He disapproved of its site and had it rebuilt near the temple. He was a wise conqueror and contributed handsomely to the rebuilding of the temple on a great scale. Some of his sculptured drums are now in the British Museum, brought by the kind offices of the Royal Navy, for whose seamen in the last century the handling and transport overland into their ships of vast blocks of ancient marble was deemed on several occasions a proper exercise in the use of rope, block and tackle and, accordingly, beyond criticism as a misuse of public funds!

But Croesus had chosen the site badly, for it was damp and unhealthily near marsh-land. His temple stood, however, and its size and beauty were widely admired. Herodotus, after seeing the temples of Egypt, was somewhat scornful of the small-scale buildings of the Greeks. 'Lump the whole lot together,' he wrote, 'and you would hardly notice them by the side of Egypt's buildings.' But he did exclude the Artemision from this comparison: that, he admitted, *was* a building. On the night of the birth of Alexander the Great, the temple was burnt down by the deliberate act of a maniac who hoped thereby to ensure that his name would be for ever remembered. Unhappily it is. Far be it from me to further his wicked plan by the mention of his name here. Alexander the Great offered to rebuild the house of the goddess if he could have his name recorded on the temple's façade. The wisdom, as well as the diplomatic finesse, of the priests' answer is to be admired. They wanted the new temple to be the pride of all men in Asia Minor, and they knew that people value most highly, not what has been provided free, but what they themselves have paid for—a truth of human nature which we are re-learning today. 'Sire,' they replied, 'we are obliged to refuse your offer: protocol does not admit the building of a temple for one deity by another.'

The new temple was on the same plan as the old, but of a greater height than had ever been seen before. The stylobate was fourteen steps high instead of the usual three, and the columns, according to Pliny, fifty-eight feet. The Parthenon columns are thirty-four feet high. The temple was one of the 'Seven Wonders', and the sanctuary was filled with sculpture, much of it the work of Praxiteles. Kings, governments and individuals banked there, for no enemy would touch the temple of Artemis, such was the sanctity of the goddess whom 'all Asia and the world worship'. From coins and statuettes her general appearance had been known as a many-breasted fertility goddess, with animals sculptured on her, as it were peeping out of the panels on her dress. But the recent Austrian excavation of the City Hall has produced two more than life-size statues of her. These are important finds which evidently show us in detail what the cult statue—probably fifty feet high—was like. The goddess has the amiable face and apple cheeks of the country girl and wears a pleasant smile and a friendly expression. She is glad to be confronted by her worshippers, and she has something to give. But at this point her charms come to an end unless it be agreed that in two of the statues her dress falls attractively over her feet, revealing well-manicured toes. For on her head she wears a head-dress one-third her own height—in three storeys; there is, literally, an architectural *motif*, and the top storey is her own temple façade. Her hair is populated with pairs of horned beasts. Her undergarment is deeply embroidered at the neck

with four winged figures. These are framed by a thick necklet—
or it may be a soft edging to a breastplate—elaborately carved
with centaur, scorpion, deer, lions and other creatures. Below,
some twenty-four eggs, large and small, are attached to the
goddess. These were once thought to be breasts; but these
statues, with so much detail preserved, mercifully show that they
are not. From the waist down, animals—in threes—are carved in
high relief. The goddess is the very emblem of fertility, for all life.

The Artemision, however, has gone for ever. Justinian took
some of its magnificent columns to adorn the church of Santa
Sophia at Constantinople, and stones from it were used in the
enlarged church, on the hill above the temple, which he built to
do honour to the tomb of St. John. The Turks, building a large,
marble-walled mosque at the foot of the hill, used the remains of
the temple as a quarry; and the meandering, marsh-making river
completed the process of liquidation. Even the site was unknown, so that it took Mr. Wood of the British Museum six
years of hard work to find it in 1869. With a squadron of traction
engines driving pumps and exuding mud and water for weeks,
he finally came to the foundations, thirty feet below the ground
level. From that excavation, and from a later one by Professor
Hogarth of Oxford (who found that there had been three temples
in succession before that of Croesus), 3,000 votive offerings
were taken—pieces of jewellery, statuettes of gold, silver and
ivory, and little models of animals and of priestesses.

The making and selling of these objects for pilgrims to devote
to the goddess was the livelihood of Demetrius and his fellow-
silversmiths. It seemed an outrage that Paul, the apostle, should
be diverting honour from Great Artemis, and trade from him
and his friends, by so successfully preaching the Gospel. In
Acts xix, the riot of protest in the theatre is vividly described,
ending with the speech of the Town Clerk, firm, wise, and
anxious that the episode should not come to the notice of the
Roman authorities. The account in Acts was being read to the
members of the Hellenic Travellers' Club who were sitting in
the theatre and visualizing the riot. The lecturer was trying to
make the scene live and was using gestures and a voice unsuited
no doubt to a cathedral but perhaps permissible in the theatre of
Ephesus. A Turkish policeman, observing the performance of
the speaker and the rapt attention of the audience, leaped to a

conclusion and the call of duty. He went to those in charge of the visitors to enforce the law. Luckily, an interpreter was there. 'Stop that man from speaking! Political speeches are not allowed!' It was a little difficult to convince the policeman that the speaker was reading from one of our holy books, about an event 1,900 years ago.

To listen in church to the story of the riot is one thing, but it is entirely another to have the story from Acts xix read in the theatre, in the heart of the city, where the riot took place. The familiar words take on a new value and for many people the apostle himself is seen with a new stature when the scale of his achievement in Ephesus is borne in upon the mind. For even in ruin and in only partial excavation, the city is immensely impressive in size and in magnificence, and the message of the marble-paved streets, the massive buildings, the columns and statues, vaults and arches is of luxury, power and pride. And one man, 'this Paul' shook it to the core. Truth and the Sword of the Spirit were his weapons.

The riot of Demetrius took place, not in the city where Croesus had re-sited it, but in the city built on the original site once again by Lysimachus, one of Alexander's successors. Town planning, first invented by Hippodamus of Miletus, was now fashionable, and Lysimachus determined to lay out a new city on town-planning principles. He did it in the grand manner. From the waterfront a straight marble-paved, colonnaded road ran up, past the Harbour thermae and a great complex of courtyards and public buildings, towards Mount Pion and the huge theatre, to seat 20,000 people and built with monumental grandeur into its flank. On the right, as one drew near the theatre, was the central agora, or forum, and above it on a terrace of Mount Coressus, the temple of Isis for the use of the merchants from Egypt. At the theatre, another paved and colonnaded road crossed, going north and south: north to the gymnasium and the stadium and more baths, south to the fine Library of Celsus and the most elaborate of the baths; there it turned and ran east up the steep valley, which proves to be the main road of the city. All these buildings were not raised at once. But the evidence is that, while the lay-out of the city is Hellenistic, most of the bigger buildings belong to Imperial and Byzantine times, often on the foundations of the old.

Ephesus: 'The First and Greatest Metropolis of Asia'

The newly-excavated valley road runs from the Library of Celsus half a mile uphill to the Magnesian Gate. It was colonnaded nearly all the way, and numerous statues were set up in convenient open spaces. To erect a statue of a man the city wished to honour had become a normal method of public recognition. A typical statue base reads, 'The Council and People of Ephesus honoured Alexander, son of Alexander, the doctor.' Among the more imposing of the public buildings in this Street of the Curetes are the Baths of Scholasticia, a rich Christian who presented this additional amenity to the city in the second century A.D., the temple of Hadrian, perhaps too rich in its sculptural decoration, a fine fountain-house, the town-hall with its 'Siamese-twin' Corinthian columns, and an odeum or small music hall. There are, in addition, a number of shops, a six-storied Roman house, warehouses, the remains of a monumental gateway, and the newly-found platform of a Temple of Domitian.

The Twin Churches of St. Mary, an early Christian construction close to the harbour thermae, are of great interest, for here was held the famous Council of Ephesus, attended by 243 bishops in A.D. 431, at which Mary was proclaimed Theotokos—Bearer of God. In the beautiful baptistery of the Twin Churches, which was panelled in marble and domed, the deep baptismal pool is still to be seen.

There is an old house in the hills a few miles away, on the higher slopes of Coressus, which is reputed—but on no firm evidence—to have been the home of Mary, the Mother of Our Lord, when she came to the Ephesus region in her old age in the care of St. John. The house has been restored and is a place of pious pilgrimage.

Another site connected with early Christianity is the legendary Cave of the Seven Sleepers, on the north-east side of Mount Pion. The story goes that seven Christian children fled to the depths of the cave from the Decian Persecution in A.D. 250, and the entrance was walled up by order of the Roman authorities. In the time of Theodosius II (A.D. 425) a child went to buy bread and paid for it with a Decian gold coin. He was seized by the baker who hoped to force the child to reveal a treasure hoard. What in fact was revealed was that all seven children were still alive in the cave, having slept for nearly two centuries.

At this time Ephesus, once the third greatest city in the

Eastern Mediterranean after Alexandria and Antioch, was shrinking in size and wealth, for her harbour, the source of her wealth, was silting up, and the big merchantmen could no longer load their eastern cargoes and sail away with them to the west: a fatal blow to the city now that the second source of wealth—the temple and worship of Artemis—had also come to an end with the advance of Christianity.

CHAPTER XXIV

Pergamum: The City of the Attalids

The Acropolis of Pergamum when its buildings were all standing must have looked uniquely grand. We would have to go back to about A.D. 100 to see it in its perfection, planned and laid out to look its best from the city 1,000 feet below. No architect could be presented with a more convenient natural site on which to create an architectural sensation. The thousand-foot-high hill, long and narrow at the summit, lay on a north-south axis, with the city, which he was to impress, at the base of it on the west side. The hill, in its full length, would be a back-cloth to the city for everyone coming to Pergamum from the sea. To make things easier for the architect, the summit of the hill was tilted down from east to west, so that his buildings on the eastern side would be visible from the west, rising, as they would, above the level of the western roof-tops. He now constructed several terraces, at different levels on the hill-top; and, making the entrance at the southern end, between two towers, he placed the Palace at the high point on the eastern side. The barracks for the household guard, and the arsenal, were disposed at the northern limit of the hill-top. On an intermediate terrace a later architect built a large temple of Trajan in the handsome Corinthian order, near the edge on the city side. The first design, however, included also the Library in the centre, overlooking a big open square. This was colonnaded on two sides only, so as to leave the view from below open to the temple of Athena in the square. But this hill was a fortress and must have walls. These would normally shut in the buildings inside and ruin the effect from the city. Therefore, on the city side, the walls are built not *up* from the ground at the summit, but *down* the steep side of the hill and the view of the buildings suffers not at all.

So far the architect has made a magnificent summit; but the bare western side too could be planned to add to the effect. In the centre of the side, in a slight hollow of the hill, the huge theatre was built. The usual semicircle of the cavea or auditorium was not possible, so the curvature in the tiers of seats was reduced and the number of tiers increased. They look like a frozen cascade. The foot of the theatre and the orchestra and stage are perhaps only one-third of the way down the hillside. A long terrace, supported on arches, was built boldly across the face of the hill, to give access to the seating more conveniently for the citizens, and to provide room for the stage itself. But it would spoil the balanced effect if this terrace were to end at the stage, half-way across the face of the acropolis; so it was continued an equal distance beyond. For this extension there had to be some logical reason: it was provided by a temple of Juno, built at its end, raised high on a stepped platform. Above it, on the summit, was the much larger temple of Trajan. The stage of the theatre was a sore problem, for it would occupy all the width of the terrace and cut off access to Juno's temple. The solution was the unique one, in a large theatre, of making the stage (a wooden one) portable. The post holes remain.

A great altar of Zeus was required. The position chosen at the south end of the acropolis, balanced Juno's temple to the north. The altar, a structure forty feet high, colonnaded on three sides, its base decorated with the famous frieze of the tempestuous battle between gods and giants, was built on another terrace eighty feet below the summit. It need hardly be said that the fourth side of the altar was open on the city side so that the citizens could see the smoke and fires of sacrifice rising continually to Zeus. The city was not forgetting Zeus: he would remember them. The theme of the battle of gods and giants, expressing the triumph of civilization, with the help of the gods, over barbarism, of law, order and efficiency over chaos was no bad choice in Pergamum to illustrate the achievement of the Attalid rulers who, within a short period of rule, had thrown back the Gauls and made their city one of the great powers controlling large areas of Asia Minor. Much of this handsome frieze is in the Pergamene Museum in Berlin. All that is left of the great altar is a quadrilateral mound, within which are foundations perhaps of an earlier building; around it a few stunted pine-trees struggle to survive where once the sacrificial fires of Zeus smoked in such grandeur.

Little is left but foundations on the acropolis itself, enough for us to see in imagination that the builders of Pergamum used their architectural skill with impressive results.

The modern road to the summit of the acropolis climbs in one complete well-graded sweep round the entire hill. On the west one can see across the valley the remains of a large amphitheatre which lies on the far side of the river: and, as the road passes the northern end of the acropolis, a few surviving arches of the aqueduct come into view below. This brought water from a source more than 1,000 feet high in the mountains twenty or more miles away to the north. The height of the source, coupled with the use of metal pipes, enabled water to be forced to the summit of the acropolis.

The history of Pergamum begins in 282 B.C., and is the 'success story' of the Attalid kings who made the city not only one of the most powerful bulwarks of Hellenism against barbarism and the inroads of the Galatians, but also one of the most beautiful and cultured cities in the Mediterranean world. The beginning of all this success, however, was a thieving betrayal of trust. Alexander's successor, Lysimachus, had entrusted part of his treasure—9,000 talents—for safe keeping in his fortress at Pergamum to Philetaerus, one of his generals. This rascal then changed sides and went over to Seleucus, another of the Successors, who gratefully recognized him as dynast of Pergamum. Philetaerus paid an answering tribute by putting the portrait of Seleucus on his coinage. He was, indeed, a diplomatic manipulator, gaining favour with his neighbours by loans and gifts and services. He built up an efficient army and began that careful exploitation of the country's natural resources which was to mark the work of all his successors. The arsenal on the acropolis and the barrack buildings with a fortress wall enclosing the summit of the acropolis were his work. In the many magazines of this arsenal were found large quantities of what look for all the world like the standard cannon-balls of the seventeenth and eighteenth centuries, but made of stone. After the initial shock

Pergamum: The City of the Attalids

of surprise, one realizes that these are ammunition for the ballistae, the artillery of the pre-gunpowder era. The stone ballistae-balls went up to 100 lbs. in weight. They are probably Byzantine, for the Byzantines, in their day, occupied the fortress.

Eumenes I continued this policy of development, construction, and daring in the face of enemies. These Attalids looked far, worked hard and lived dangerously. Eumenes made an alliance with Egypt, broke with the powerful Seleucids and, facing Antiochus I in battle near Sardis in 262 B.C., defeated him, thereby extending his frontiers. This was also a great building period in Pergamum itself.

Attalus I succeeded, took the title of King, and, refusing to buy off the barbarian Galatian hordes, the plundering menace of Asia Minor, beat them in battle. The sculpture 'The Dying Gaul' was part of the triumphal monument. Attalus emerged as one of the great Hellenistic monarchs. But he had to face danger on two flanks, from King Philip V of Macedon and from Antiochus; and so he allied himself to Rome for the second Macedonian War, which dealt with the one flank; and his efficient army dealt with Antiochus on the other, and gained further large territories.

Pergamum was now a wealthy and powerful state; and its ruler had time to be a patron of the arts, literature and philosophy, to gain prestige and pleasure with his chariots and horses at Olympia and other Greek racing-centres, and to enjoy what history has declared to be a conspicuously happy domestic life with an exceptionally fine wife, Queen Apollonis.

The city was a royal capital indeed; and though great numbers of prisoner-of-war slaves were used for the constructional, industrial, and agricultural enterprises in which the Attalids themselves engaged (Attalus III wrote a textbook of agricultural science), it seems likely that such progressive rulers who were efficient, scientific and thoroughly 'up-to-date' would have avoided the economic waste which cruelty to their slaves would have involved. More than most, these Attalids deserve the title of 'Philosopher-Kings'. The end of the Dynasty came when Attalus III, having no son in any case, decided that the day of kings was over in a world fast becoming Roman, and bequeathed his highly prosperous kingdom to Rome in 133 B.C.

In the town of Bergama, as one passes through the narrow and very crowded streets, the eye snatches glimpses of ancient foundations, column drums used as plant-pot bases in little back yards, or marble blocks, cut for the walls of a temple, still serving but in a humbler way as a doorstep to a house of sun-baked brick. There is a very large brick building of the basilica type in the town, near the foot of the acropolis which, in its gaunt, roofless, ruined magnificence, offers a subject that Piranesi missed. This huge building, which perhaps began as the Central Hall of Justice, was turned into a Christian Church.

The *ASKLEPIEION*: *Sanctuary of Asclepius*

In a sheltered hollow of the low hills to the west, a mile or more out of the town of Bergama, there are the substantial remains of a once famous Asklepieion. The springs which flow in the folds of these hills are radio-active, and this presumably explains the foundation of the sanctuary in this place in the early part of the fourth century B.C., before the town of Pergamum existed. The god of health must have been found to be active in those waters.

Epidaurus was the first and the senior-ranking centre of Asclepius; and because results at Epidaurus were good, and treatment apparently more successful than local doctors could normally provide, Asklepieia, based on the Epidaurus principle, began to be founded in many of the big centres of population, even as far away as Rome. To keep the connection between the original sanctuary and the new daughter-hospitals, one or two of the sacred snakes of Epidaurus, who were thought to represent the god, were customarily packed up and sent to the new foundation. The Pergamum sanctuary was one of the early daughter sanctuaries; but it gained its highest reputation in Imperial Roman times, and its most elaborate buildings probably date from that period.

Galen (A.D. 129–199) was the great name in the medical world at Pergamum, as Hippocrates was at Cos; and since his attitude to medical science was combined with a strong religious feeling, his works were very acceptable in the Christian Middle Ages. The title 'Asclepiad' denotes, unexpectedly, a secular doctor, not a priest of Asclepius. But there was a close connection between the secular doctors in, for example, Cos and the sanctuary of Asclepius there: and it is thought that this famous Asklepieion of Cos was in fact founded by followers of the great

Pergamum: The City of the Attalids

Hippocrates, an Asclepiad of Cos. So it is likely that Galen of Pergamum was at least an honorary visiting physician and surgeon in the Asklepieion of Pergamum. He began his practice as a patcher-up of gladiators; for these highly trained slaves were not expendable. Nevertheless, the sport inevitably gave him an endless supply of fine bodies for the anatomical dissection and research which was his speciality. His books were standard works for fifteen centuries. Galen ended his career in Rome as the most famous doctor in the world and court physician to the Roman Emperor, Marcus Aurelius.

In the Asklepieion at Pergamum, as at Cos and Epidaurus, the environment, physical and psychological, was admirable: one might say that it combined the values of a Lourdes, a Harrogate or Bath, and a modern hospital. The place was built to be beautiful, to give the patients light, fresh air, and hydropathic treatment, and to provide some diversion to turn their thoughts away from their ailments; and all this in a religious atmosphere under the guidance of a god whose benevolence and gentleness to suffering men and women is shown in the face of his statues.

The plan of the Asklepieion at Pergamum is, basically, a large, colonnaded level quadrangle, entered by a once fine propylaea. The most important and largest building, dominating the whole quadrangle, was a circular, and obviously domed, temple of Zeus and Asclepius, roughly contemporary with the Pantheon at Rome. Only the marble foundation platform is left, but this clearly shows the plan. On three sides of the quadrangle, deep porticoes, with monolithic columns of the Ionic, Corinthian and composite Orders, provided air and shelter and, in summer, excellent dormitory quarters. At one angle was the Library, at another the fine theatre, at the third the marble-lined, forty-seater latrine, at the fourth a remarkable hydropathic establishment of which only the undercroft survives, with its many vaulted chambers and some baths and considerable evidences of plumbing. The approach to this curious building was, and is, an underground, vaulted passage, leading from a sacred spring in the centre of the quadrangle. Towards the centre of the quadrangle there are foundations of other buildings, probably those of an earlier temple and of incubation-rooms where, as the climax of treatment, the patients slept, hoping to be visited in a dream by the god Asclepius, or by his representative, a sacred snake.

We may well be sceptical about the healing properties in the lick of a snake in the dark. But it is not possible for us to measure the faith of those fortunate enough, as they thought, to be the objects of attention by these representatives of Asclepius. We know, however, quite certainly that a patient's faith and trust in what is being done for him can be of high importance in certain kinds of illness, and will be a factor not ignored by the good physician today. The eye of the most scientific of doctors has a wide-angle lens. In any case, the treatment of ailments was not confined to the use of snakes and the evoking of faith. The writings of Hippocrates and of Galen are proof enough of that, if the long life of the many Asklepieia is not, in itself, evidence that they served humanity well.

CHAPTER XXV

Rhodes

If the statement of Geology that Rhodes emerged from the sea through volcanic upheavals at the end of the Tertiary period leaves us unshaken, we can hardly remain unmoved by the fact that Greek mythology *knew* that the island rose out of the sea. Pindar tells how the Sun, to whom by accident, in the casting of lots to allocate lands to the gods, no land had been assigned,

> '. . . *averred that he had seen*
> *beneath the hoary foam*
> *a goodly land uprising from the deep*
> *that gave men promise of a fruitful home*
> *with kindly pastures for their browsing sheep.'*
>   (Translation by C. J. BILLSON.)

Helios was very satisfied to possess this new island, and he certainly shines upon it bountifully. The worship of Helios was the chief cult in classical times and, in annual celebration, a four-horse chariot team was sacrificed by being thrown into the sea. This was, of course, to provide Helios with a new team for his daily course through the heavens. Tradition, as Pindar records, said that Rhodes was blessed by Zeus with a shower of gold in return for the praiseworthy efforts of the sons of Helios to be the first to sacrifice to Athena at her birth, full-grown, from the head of Zeus. Helios was in a good position to give early information of the coming happy event, and told his sons to get busy. In their haste they forgot to take fire to the altar, and, in consequence, Athena was ever after worshipped at Lindos with a fireless sacrifice. The historian observes that this fireless sacrifice only proves that the original goddess at Lindos was not Athena at all, but a Minoan earth-goddess who naturally preferred the first-fruits fresh! Anyway, the Rhodians believed that Athena was pleased with the sacrifice and gave them her gifts of craftsmanship in return. Pindar puts it like this:

> *'With craft beyond compare*
> *their hands made things so fair*
> *that forms of beauty seemed to live and move*
> *by all their roads and glory held them dear.*
>
> (C. J. Billson.)

All of which underlines the historical fact that Rhodes has been much favoured, has a fine climate, produced a people with skill of hand, with brains and taste, was in the third century by far the richest of all Greek city-states, and had Schools of rhetoric, philosophy, painting and sculpture of international reputation, and more than its share of poets and writers. She had, too, a navy which kept the seas open for the wide trade the island enjoyed: for the island's proximity to Asia Minor and its position at the eastern entrance to the Aegean had from the beginning been advantageous to her trading interests. The pottery made in the island was widely exported and shows strong oriental influences in the designs of heraldic animals and the filling up of empty spaces with rosettes and geometric patterns, exactly as in oriental carpets and textiles.

The position of Rhodes at the entrance to the Aegean Sea and lying on the route to Syria and Egypt made it inevitable that first the Minoans and then the Mycenaeans had settlements in the island for trading purposes. From the arrival of Dorian colonists, about the tenth century B.C., till the closing years of the Peloponnesian war, there had been three cities, Lindos on the south coast, Ialysos, near the present city of Rhodes, and Kamiros on the northern coast; and the two on the sea did not have good harbours. The population was growing fast and opportunity, too. For Rhodes saw that, given a good harbour at the north-eastern point of the island from which ships could sail either the northern or southern routes on leaving Rhodes, she could advance her maritime position, especially as a defeated Athens would lose much trade. So, about 412 B.C., opportunist

Rhodes changed sides, and built the city of Rhodes with two fine harbours; and peopled it with the population of Ialysos, with additions from Lindos and Kamiros. Her prosperity increased at once; but there followed internal dissension—oligarchs versus democrats (so often the bane of Greek political life), as the city fell first under Sparta, next under a revived Athens, then under the dynasty of Mausolus, till the Persians seized it, and finally Alexander the Great captured it. That was the end of the real troubles for 300 years. Rhodes became a leading power, and her coinage and system of maritime law and her political sagacity won her wide respect. But sagacity did not undermine courage, and she resisted siege by Demetrius Poliorcetes in 304 B.C., and fought vigorously against Pergamene and Pontic kings, and any others—pirates included—who dared to interfere with her trade routes. This was her greatest day of civilized prosperity.

Rhodes sided with Rome in the Macedonian wars, stood a siege by Mithridates in 88 B.C. (the year in which he utterly destroyed Delos) but was reduced to ruin in a struggle against Julius Caesar. For Rhodes had sided with Caesar's rival, Pompey. The crippling war with Caesar was followed by an earthquake; and Rhodes played no notable part under Byzantine or Saracen rule.

As the ship approaches the town of Rhodes, the range of medieval walls and bastions and turreted gateways which dominate the view, with the massive palace of the Governor rising high above all, takes the mind straight to the central point of interest in Rhodes as we see it today—to the Knights of the Order of St. John of Jerusalem, who built this fortress in the fourteenth century as a stronghold of Christendom against the Mussulman. In 1291 the last Christian forces were driven from the Holy Land, and, determined to hold at least an advance post, the Knights came to Rhodes. The solidity of the walls and the quality and severe beauty of their buildings show that they had every intention of staying. During this period, the Order was organized by nationalities into eight Langues, or Tongues— those of Auvergne, Provence, France, Aragon, Castile, Italy, Germany and England. In the 'street of the Knights' we shall see many of the headquarters—auberges—built for these Langues, decorated with their carved coats of arms.

Rhodes

In the two hundred years of the occupation of the island by the Knights, trade revived; but its protection on the seas from molestation by pirates or Turks, and the piratical and high-handed acts of the Knights themselves, brought on a headlong collision with the new leaders of Islam, the Turks. Their earlier assaults in 1444 and 1480 were repulsed, but in 1522 Sultan Suleiman I laid siege to the fortress with vast forces: the Knights resisted with traditional and incredible courage. Suleiman lost 90,000 of his 200,000 men, but in the end he succeeded. Yet it was such a victory that the Knights were allowed to sail away with heads high—to found, after a short time, a new stronghold in Malta. To sit, in the evening, in the public gardens while with 'Son et Lumière' the tremendous fortress before one's eyes is flooded with light and with the sounds of battle and the exhortations, commands and the judgments of the Grand Master in the crisis of treason, is a stirring experience indeed.

The remains of ancient Rhodes in the city and on the hill above, though it was an exceptionally beautiful city in its time, are not now of great size or of special interest; but the Museum has a very good collection of Rhodian and Attic vases, and there is a collection of sculpture well worth a visit. It is housed in the noble Infirmary of the Knights.

The city has three distinct characters. First, there is the old Turkish quarter, with the minarets of its mosques still fretting the sky-line, and the carved wooden balconies of Istanbul and Asia Minor, and the shops and workshops open to the streets, recalling the long Turkish occupation which lasted until 1912, when the Italians captured the island. Then, the immensely impressive fortifications and towers of the fourteenth, fifteenth and sixteenth centuries, and the numerous handsome buildings of the Knights (all built of the same warm brown stone which has a texture responsive to the light and adds an interest to every wall) make the Old City one of the most beautiful of all medieval cities. Mussolini spent prodigally on the restoration and did it well, though there is an element of excess in the mag-nificence of the rebuilt Governor's palace—which is a film producer's dream of a castle. As for modern Rhodes, the tree-lined streets, the cascades of bougainvillaea and beds of hibiscus, good shops—the best, after Athens, in Greece, it is said—the clean, broad waterfront, the old harbour wall, adorned with its medieval windmills and crowned with a castle, and the distant rampart of the blue mountains of Asia Minor ten miles across the sea, and, last, good hotels and bathing on sandy beaches— all conspire to make Rhodes a peaceful and lovely place, 'the fairest flower of all'.

LINDOS: Here on a steep peninsula rock, nearly 400 feet high, was the Greek acropolis and the small fourth-century B.C. Doric temple of Athena Lindia, superbly placed on the edge of a perpendicular cliff above the sea. Her sanctuary is entered through a noble propylaea and up a broad flight of stairs. The old fortification walls were rebuilt by the Knights of St. John and given an added splendour. Their church and the Governor's quarters survive. At the foot of the last steep and narrow stairs to the inner entrance to the Castle, the Danish archaeologists, to whom we owe the excavation of this wonderful site, discovered a relief of the stern half of a trireme, carved in the rock in the second century B.C. Though lack of space here forbids a proper description of Lindos, the visitor will agree that the beauty of the place and the sight of the golden stones of Athena's temple seen against the blue sea are infinitely rewarding as the sensational climax to the thirty-five-mile journey from Rhodes.

PHILERIMOS: Seven or eight miles from Rhodes on the north-western side, is the site of the old city of Ialysos. It was built over the whole of a flat-topped, almost vertical-sided, hill 900 feet above the plain. So the modern Italian road which zig-zags up the side of it through the woods, is a triumph of Italian engineering, and a source of vertigo. One goes to Philerimos, not to see ancient ruins, though there are the foundations of a temple of Zeus and Athena, and an unusual Doric fountain-house, 150 feet down the steps on the far side; nor, perhaps, primarily to see the curious combination of Byzantine chapels in the reconstructed church, and the charming modern monastery; but, rather, to walk the woods on the top of the world, or so it seems, with a glorious view over plain and hills to the mountains of Rhodes and the sea.

KAMIROS: Kamiros, too, is certainly to be visited. In a setting of great natural beauty of trees and sea and hills, are the considerable ruins of a Hellenistic city, excavated by the Italians. Like Lindos and Ialysos, Kamiros dates from Minoan and Mycenaean times when there were trading-posts there; but while pottery, jewellery and figurines of these periods were found in several large cemeteries in the hillsides of the inland valleys, nothing earlier than the Geometric period has been found at Kamiros itself. On the lower of two terraces above the sea are the agora, small public baths, and a temple of Apollo; and all the way up the hollow of the hill runs the steep well-drained main street with houses to right and left. On the higher terrace was a colonnaded portico, 200 yards long, forming a magnificent sky-line; and behind this, the temple of Athena. The Italians erected six of the Doric columns of the portico and the architrave above, using some of the original drums and stones, and strengthening the whole with ferro-concrete. After a life of thirty years, this structure was thrown down in a gale in 1962. If some fancied they heard sounds of ironic laughter from Greek architects in the Elysian fields, is it surprising?

CHAPTER XXVI

Turkish Interlude: From the Beaches of Gallipoli to Istanbul

Gallipoli is the name of that fifty-mile-long peninsula which stretches down from Europe towards the south, on the west side of the Sea of Marmara and, running roughly parallel with the coast of Asia, offers entry to the Sea of Marmara, to Istanbul and the Black Sea by the famous narrow strait, the Dardanelles, or Hellespont as it was once called. Despite its swift current, this stretch of narrow waters which separate Europe from Asia has been the scene of many a clash between East and West. Great armies have crossed here, those of Xerxes advancing westwards to his ultimate defeat at the hands of the Greeks, those of Alexander the Great advancing East to conquest. On both shores of the strait armies have fought historic battles.

It is the older generation on a British ship entering the narrows that is sure to turn its first and longest gaze to port, to the beaches and hills of Gallipoli. There is likely to be a group of men and women in their sixties, one or two men especially lean and tanned by Australian or New Zealand sun, who clearly have a deep—a personal—concern with all this peaceful landscape. They are remembering 1915 and one of the bloodiest and costliest campaigns ever fought in the history of war. The Turks, both old and young, cannot forget it, for soon visible when the ship enters the Narrows close to the town of Chanak, the most effective of all war memorials has been set up starkly in huge white letters on a hillside. It is merely a date, 18.3.15, and every Turkish child would ask 'What date?' and the answer is 'The date when the British Fleet was turned from the attack.' The attacking fleet had lost three battleships in that one day by mines, and the decision had indeed been taken at Cabinet level to risk no further loss in an attempt to force the Narrows. Instead an army was to be landed in the face of the enemy.

The southern end of the Gallipoli Peninsula is marked by three towers. One is the lighthouse but the others, one on each arm of Morto Bay, are war memorials. The white obelisk, at Cape Helles, is the British memorial to 20,000 men 'missing' in the Gallipoli campaign in 1915: and the almost overwhelmingly heavy tower, is the Turkish memorial.

Close under the Turkish memorial, in the sheltered waters of Morto Bay (the bay at the entrance to the strait on the port side), the British right flanking attack was successfully made at first light on April 25th, and de Tott's battery on the cliff-top was captured. But at the other arm of the bay just below the old Turkish fort and village, V Beach, the sea was red—literally, as the seaplane reported—with poured-out life and courage. It was here that the famous *River Clyde* was run ashore, in the hope of aiding a landing. The Turks were dug in on the low cliffs and hills and directed their machine-gun fire on the ship's gangways and the lighters and the men wading ashore, from a range of one hundred yards. Our casualties were dreadful, but the landing was eventually effected.

The equally famous beaches at Suvla Bay, and at Anzac Cove where in a sense the young nations of Australia and New Zealand came of age in the eyes of an admiring world, are on the west side of the peninsula and not visible from the Dardanelles channel.

The large war cemetery on rising ground above the centre of the sandy sweep of Morto Bay is French. It is generally forgotten that the French fought at Gallipoli: they had landed on the Asiatic shore at Achilles' tomb to cause a diversion, did so successfully, and then re-embarked to join the forces fighting in the peninsula.

The Imperial War Graves Commission, as every traveller knows, has created oases of peace, dignity and beauty in many a desert place. But none of the thirty-three British and Commonwealth war cemeteries on Gallipoli are easily visible from the ship. Where, however, there are tight clusters of pine trees, standing high amid the rough scrub of this sparsely populated, poorly watered peninsula, these are likely to be sheltering a British cemetery. The long lines of headstones lie in lawns of tended grass where beds of English roses, flowering shrubs and hedges of rosemary bring a sense of home affection, untouched by time's erosion.

The Gallipoli campaign was a ghastly British failure in the military sense; but in a different way it was a signal triumph of the spirit in both opposing armies. Each army came to feel admiration for the tenacity and fighting spirit of the other. Heat, clouds of flies and the dysentery they spread, lack of water, shortages of ammunition and sheer exhaustion were added burdens; and the frequent confusion and muddles in a terrain of ravines and scrub, cliffs and hills which with inadequate signal-systems the staffs were often unable to sort out, would turn great battles into a series of private struggles between small groups of each army. It was a fight to the death of tens of thousands on both sides. In those few rugged square miles, the British and Anzac casualties were 50,000 greater than those of far larger British and Canadian armies in all their fighting from the Normandy beaches to the Rhine. Both the Turks and the British lost, in killed and wounded, half the total numbers they put into the peninsula. It is not military success which hallows this ground, but the endurance and self-sacrifice of so many in the name of duty for their countries. At the end of a memorial service held off Gallipoli on a Turkish ship chartered by the Hellenic Travellers Club, and attended by the Turkish captain, he was seen to shake hands with the English chaplain, adding the words, 'What your men and ours killed on Gallipoli was enmity between us.'

It is with relief that we turn our eyes to starboard, searching the hills that border the three-miles-wide plain to pick out the hill of Troy—at the Aegean end of the long line of hills—and think of 'Far-off things and battles long ago'. On the west of the strait, opposite the town of Chanak where one lands for the journey to Troy, is a fine medieval Turkish castle, towers and walls intact. This is close to the site of the Greek city of Sestos, while Abydos was opposite on the eastern shore. This is the Narrows, where Xerxes made his double bridge of boats, covered with planks and earth and fitted with wooden walls so that his horses and elephants might not see the water and refuse. At this point, too, we think of Leander's perilous swim to Hero's warm candlelight, and of the less rewarding swim of Byron and his friend, immortalized in his ingenious rhyme:

> *'he could, perhaps, have passed the Hellespont,*
> *as once (a feat on which ourselves we prided)*
> *Leander, Mr. Ekenhead and I did.'*

ISTANBUL

To THE CITY—*eis ten polin*—such is the Greek origin of the word Istanbul, and the key to our understanding of its importance and place in history. The Greeks called the city Byzantium when it was founded in the seventh century B.C. as a colony from Megara near Athens. But it eventually rose, as the deep springhead of Byzantine culture, to be the pride and centre of the whole Eastern Mediterranean. For a full thousand years after the lights had dimmed or gone out in so many of the old intellectual centres of the Western world, in Byzantium the Greek fire blazed with a many-coloured flame. Two great structures are witness, the one to the aspiring spirit of the City, the other to the determination of its rulers and people to maintain it at all costs. The first, the splendid Church of the Holy Wisdom, Santa Sophia, built in five years from A.D. 532–537: the second the vast fortifications, amongst the finest in the world.

'New Rome' succeeded Byzantium in A.D. 330 when Constantine transferred the capital of the Roman world to this superb site, but the name soon gave way to that of Constantinople. Here was the secure base for the ascendant Christian Empire of the East. The hordes from Persia and Arabia, the invaders of the West, Bulgars and Slavs and Goths, were kept at bay through the centuries till at last in 1453 the Turks broke through.

The seaward approach to Istanbul can be a rare experience of pleasure. The first impression is of domes and minarets beyond count, with three huge buildings dominating a unique and romantic sky-line: Santa Sophia and the Mosques of Sultan Ahmet and of Suleiman. Santa Sophia can easily be identified by its yellow-wash colour and by the heavy buttresses to the dome, added after many centuries when it showed signs of cracking.

On the Asiatic shore, well down towards the Sea of Marmara, the long low building with towers at its ends is the barracks building where Florence Nightingale made her famous hospital. This is in the region of Chalcedon, founded before Byzantium and called by a Persian general 'the city of the blind' because its founders had not seen the obvious and splendid site for a city then vacant on the opposite, the European, shore.

Kinglake in *Eothen*, after his travels in the Levant in 1834, sang the praises of Stamboul's position:

'Nowhere else does the sea come so home to a city. You are accustomed to the gondolas that glide among the palaces of St. Mark, but here, at Stamboul, it is a hundred-and-twenty-gun ship that meets you in the street. Venice strains out from the steadfast land, and in old times would send forth the Chief of the State to woo and wed the reluctant sea; but the stormy bride of the Doge is the bowing slave of the Sultan—she comes to his feet with the treasures of the world—she bears him from palace to palace . . . —she lifts his armed navies to the very gates of his garden—she watches the walls of his Serail—she stifles the intrigues of his Ministers—she quiets the scandals of his Court —she extinguishes his rivals, and hushes his naughty wives all one by one.'

This last service of the sea refers to one of the less endearing habits of a Sultan in his technique for the liquidation of unwanted members of his harem: the dark night; the weighted sack; and the sea so conveniently close to the Seraglio.

In Istanbul one literally breathes the dust of the ages. After all, 2500 years of continuous occupation by people hemmed in by walls in one small peninsula is bound to tell. Ruthless and successful efforts are being made to modernize the city, destroy the dense, if picturesque, areas of old wooden houses and, by cutting boulevards of immense width straight through and across the city, to let in light and air and transport too. Characteristic sights are men in immense numbers in the streets, few women: mosques beyond count, built of the finest materials most intricately worked, their domes and minarets, semi-circles and vertical tangents making so often a striking shape on the sky-line, and in such large numbers that they form a pattern of great beauty: crowded wooden houses and narrow streets, dark and worn: yellow bulldozers, squadrons of them, cutting their way through decay and preparing sites for an ambitious future: men with their backs bent double carrying even wardrobes on them: the muezzin calling the faithful to midday prayer and getting a response: the construction of fine university buildings: pavement 'factories' such as the coppersmiths, who occupy the whole length of a street near the Bazaar: in short the old traditional life rubbing shoulders with the new at every turn, so that it is hard to be sure in which century one lives.

The number of ancient monuments is small, apart from the large collection of sculpture, classical, Hellenistic and Roman, in the Archaeological Museum. For the Hellenist the most interesting of the monuments is the serpentine column brought from Delphi by the Emperor Constantine. It stands in the Hippodrome made on a grand scale by the Emperor Septimius Severus in A.D. 196 and adorned by Constantine and his successors with trophies from Greece and Egypt. The Greek bronze serpentine column is made of three intertwining snakes on whose heads rested the legs of a golden tripod. This was a thankoffering to the gods and a memorial of victory over the Persians at the decisive battle of Plataea in 479 B.C. British officers returning from the Crimean War dug the pit in the ground which reaches the original level of the Hippodrome and exposes the base of the memorial, with the names of thirty-one Greek city-states who resisted the invader, cut into it. A similar pit dug at the same time opens to view the sculptured base of the obelisk of Theodosius. This pink granite obelisk is a magnificent Egyptian work, dating from 1600 B.C., covered with clear-cut hieroglyphics which tell the proud story of Thotmes III and 'his conquest of the entire world'. Sculptured on the base some two thousand years later, Theodosius and his Empress receive ambassadors, watch a chariot race (the obelisk is shown in this scene), give away the prizes, and sit, looking regal. The other obelisk is ugly, but like much of the treasure and beauty of the city, it suffered at the hands of the Crusaders in their cruel sacking of the Christian city in A.D. 1204 when they pulled off the bronze plates which covered it and which told the story in bas-relief of the victories of the Emperor Basil.

Near the Hippodrome on the main road westward is the column of Constantine. It is made of porphyry and held together

by bronze rings. It was Constantine's own memorial of his re-
foundation of the city and the scene for centuries of an annual
national thanksgiving service. But it has sorely suffered in the
flames which so often burnt up areas of a city largely made up of
wooden houses.

The mosaics of Justinian's palace are a comparatively recent
find of first importance made by Professor Talbot Rice. Most of
this palace is under the Mosque of Sultan Ahmet and can never
be excavated, but on the lower ground to the south-east, behind
the Mosque as seen from the Hippodrome, a large area of
mosaic shows, in complete realism, first-class observation by a
lover of animal life who also found pleasure in country scenes
and the activities of the domestic staff.

The underground cisterns are monumental works indeed.
They held the water brought in by the aqueduct of Valens
(A.D. 378), a typical Roman-style aqueduct, under which the
main boulevard from the Ataturk Bridge passes. There are
several of these enormous underground cisterns: the easiest of
access (150 yards north-west from the entrance to Santa Sophia,
isolated on the road-side, is a small brick kiosk where one
descends) and the most beautiful is the Yerebatan Sarayi, or
Sunken Palace of Justinian's day. It gets its palatial name from
the 336 huge columns with richly carved capitals which rise out
of this great underground lake, and have supported the roof and
the houses and the streets above for fourteen centuries.

The Fortification Walls: The great circuit of walls was first built
in the early fifth century A.D. when Constantine's city extended
its boundaries. The walls ran for twelve miles, along the Sea of
Marmara, round the point where the Seraglio enjoys a lovely
view up the Bosphorus, along the waterfront of the Golden
Horn—the arm of the sea which runs in on the north of the old
city and divides it from Galata and Pera and the newer suburbs
to the north—and then turns to run down the neck of the peninsula to the Golden Gate near its southern end on the sea. A moat
and a double wall strengthened by towers made this fortification
a formidable barrier indeed for a thousand years. The landward
walls still stand. Cracked they may be and often leaning at
perilous angles; yet this enormous construction speaks volumes
of the wealth and the spirit to maintain THE CITY with the art and
architecture, knowledge, law and religion, and the capacity for

organization and for empire which flourished behind the protection of these walls.

Santa Sophia—The Church of the Holy Wisdom—Justinian's
great church, dedicated to The Holy Wisdom in A.D. *532*, is for
many people the big experience of a visit to Istanbul. From
outside it is much less impressive than the seventeenth-century
'Blue Mosque'; but the ugly, heavy buttresses which support
the dome were put there after the building's first 1,000 years
of existence—in 1574. Within was once a heaven of colour.
The Empire had been scoured for the finest marbles and the
noblest monolithic columns left from classical days—the eight
columns of green marble came from the Temple of Artemis
at Ephesus, the red marble columns from the Temple of the Sun
at Heliopolis. Above the levels of the marble facing, mosaics
told the story of Man's Redemption by the Son of God. Only a
few of these splendid mosaics survive, recovered from under the
plaster with which the Moslem covered them. But there may be
more to be brought again to light.

The envoys of the Prince of Kiev, as we can read in a medieval
Russian chronicle, went to Byzantium and were present at a
service of the Holy Eucharist. They reported to the Prince, 'We
did not know whether we were on earth or in heaven: for there
is no such splendour to be found anywhere upon earth. Describe
it we cannot: we know only that it is there that God dwells
among men.'

Today the glorious church which, after 1453, became a
mosque, is a museum; the colours are gone under a coating of
dust. Yet, though the music and movements and voices of
worship fill it no more, the mind and spirit will still find inspiration in the vast achievement of this building, the leaping out
into space of its arches and pendentives, its dome floating, it
seems, in the heights above, and the manifest devotion of its
builders to their art and to the Glory of God.

The Kahrie Cami: The Kahrie Museum, once the Church of the
Chora (i.e. in the country), or St. Saviour, was the chapel of a
monastery outside Constantine's landward walls, but the enlarge-
ment of the city brought the monastery inside the new fortifications. The church, then in parts a thousand years old, was
restored by Theodore the Logothete in 1381 at his own cost,
and given by this lover of art the finest possible decoration of

mosaic and fresco. Much of this work has been recovered from the layers of plaster and whitewash of the mosque period (i.e. after the capture of the city by the Turks in A.D. 1453) by the American professors, Whittemore and Underwood: and we can see mosaics in bright colour with all the dignity and power of Byzantine tradition in them but freed from the rigidity of the earlier phases. The inner and the outer narthex glow in gold and colour with the episodes of the Gospel story. The tall blue figures in the nave still call to worship; and the vigour and the message of the Resurrection fresco in the apse of the mortuary chapel parallel with the nave are not easily forgotten. The young athletic Prince of Life is seen risen up on Easter morning and through their heavy gravestones pulling up to new life with him a man and a woman—figures that represent us all.

The Suleymaniye Mosque: This is the work of the famous architect Sinan, expressing the splendour of an Empire which earned the Emperor his title 'the Magnificent'. It was built in 1557 and is now undergoing redecoration and repair. With Santa Sophia, the two mosques of Sultan Ahmet and Suleiman are surely properly accounted as among the greatest achievements of man in the art of building. Their architects have raised thousands of tons of stone into the air and enfolded vast volumes of space with an apparent defiance of the laws of gravity and with an ease and grace which are astonishing.

The Mosque of Sultan Ahmet—the Blue Mosque—is a high-water mark of Turkish seventeenth-century architecture. Its dome in width, and in height too, is very like that of Santa Sophia, which of course is a thousand years older. The great dome and the four semi-domes, supported by four enormous fluted columns, are evidence of rare vision, skill and mathematical genius on the part of the architect Sedefkar Mehmet Aga. Seen from the outside, this mosque makes an almost uniquely exciting picture and composition—the towering mass of dome on dome climbing to the point of the golden crescent, all within the vertical frame of the six tall slender minarets shooting their pinnacles to the sky.

The history of THE CITY in the long Byzantine period to A.D. 1453 recalls Shelley's lines on 'Life'. For the City's life was indeed 'like a dome of many-coloured glass'. There was radiance of an eternal quality in its art and architecture, in its expression of the Christian faith in worship and in liturgy, in intellectual precision, in its great Justinian Code of Law, and in its powers of organization and administration, for thereby the broad beams of its light stretched out over huge areas of the Mediterranean; but there was also in its old history many a blot of violence, intrigue, cruelty and bloodshed to 'stain the white radiance'.

Once again there is teeming life in the old city. Do we not see it in the crowds of serious-looking men on the Galata bridge, in the streets, packing the ferries, swarming in the Bazaar? We see, too, signs of the great determination of Government and people to sweep away the old slums and hovels and to renew ancient glories. The Turks of today are planning progress on a great scale and their allies in N.A.T.O. wish them good success with their vast projects, and all the more warmly because of THE CITY's place in history.

CHAPTER XXVII

Byzantine Greece

In a book about Greece and its ancient sites, a chapter on Byzantine Greece could hardly be omitted, for two reasons. First, the Hellenic traveller cannot move round Greece or Asia Minor, whether in town or country, without continually coming across the remains of Byzantine buildings, castles and, especially, churches of which the mosaics are the high point of interest. If they are of the early Byzantine period, which begins when the Roman Emperor Constantine in the city of Byzantium proclaimed Christianity as the State religion and, in A.D. 330, inaugurated the city as the new capital of the Empire, then these churches are likely to be found on the ancient sites themselves. This is so at Philippi where three early churches have been excavated. So, also, at Priene, Thasos, and Delos, at Ephesus, at Corinth and Corcyra, and at Olympia, where the workshop of Pheidias was converted and enlarged to be a church; and at Athens, where the temple of Hephaestus (the 'Theseum') was given a new barrel-vaulted roof and became the Church of St. George; and at many other sites. Moreover, the church buildings of the Orthodox Church in Greece are all derived in their architecture from the great churches built in Constantinople, as Byzantium, after a short period as 'New Rome', was called.

The second reason why the Hellenist comes to find an interest in Byzantine civilization is that, when the lights went out in Greece itself, through its long subservience to Rome, followed by the frequent incursions of barbarians from the north, the Greek fire was kept alight in the centre of the Byzantine world.

For, behind the walls of Constantine and Theodosius, a brilliant intellectual, philosophical, artistic and literary life developed, and spread from that stronghold of Christianity and culture over the whole eastern part of the Mediterranean and, at some periods, to much of the west as well. If the invaders, Avars and Slavs, Saracens, Bulgars, and Turks had not been repeatedly beaten back in the centuries before the final victory of the Turks in 1453, Europe and its life and values, whether of matters spiritual or material, would be wholly different.

When, in the fourth century, the house chapels and the little chapels built over the tombs of saints and martyrs became too small for their growing numbers, the Christians naturally turned to the large hall of the period, the basilica, as the model for their own building to hold a large congregation. The basilica was a long, rectangular building, with a narthex or vestibule, entered by three doors at one end and with a vaulted apse at the other.

The nave had two long rows of columns, from which sprang arches supporting the clerestory walls, pierced with windows. Sometimes there were four side aisles instead of two—four rows of columns. To make this standard basilica suitable for the services of worship, an altar was placed under a canopy supported by four columns on the chord of the apse, in the centre of which was the Bishop's cathedra, or throne, flanked by the seats of the clergy and elders curving round on either side. Some sort of screen, solid in the lower part, seems to have been regarded as essential between the altar and the nave at an early date. The baptistery was a distinct small building, opening out of the basilica at one side, and it was provided with a deep, stepped pool in the centre. The catechumen, the convert being instructed, at his baptism walked down the steps till he was submerged— symbolically dead by drowning to the old life, and then rose again up the steps on the further side to the new life of a son or daughter of God. The baptistery of the Twin Churches of St. Mary at Ephesus is likely to be the most beautiful seen by the Hellenic traveller. The ambo was also an essential part of the church. This was a stone pulpit, with steps up to the balustraded platform from which the Scriptures were read, litanies taken, and sermons given. Sometimes the basilican church was built over the tomb of a saint in such a way that the tomb would be in a small underground chapel below the altar. The churches were decorated with a vast array of mosaics, telling the story of our Redemption. Generally, the approach to a basilican church was through an imposing façade on the street, into an open atrium, or colonnaded courtyard, from which the narthex was entered. This plan is seen at Nikopolis and at Ephesus.

But the Eastern fondness for the dome was to predominate from the sixth century, and some basilican churches were 'improved' by the addition of domes, probably after earthquakes had necessitated some reconstruction. This happened, for instance, in one of the two basilican churches at Philippi, and the piers of the dome still stand on the plain. It was perhaps the immense effect of splendour produced in the great domed church of the Holy Wisdom at Constantinople which was decisive in changing the course of Byzantine church architecture. The classical tradition of the column, with the Roman contribution of the brick and the vault was not abandoned, but fused with the dome from the East. The dome was peculiarly suitable to the doctrine and theology of the Eastern Church. The worshipper, entering a Byzantine domed church, finds his eyes lifted up to the heights of the dome, bright with the light of the numerous windows at its circumference, and there at once he is confronted by the tremendous mosaic of the Pantocrator, the Almighty, whose gaze is directed straight at him and into him. Christianity is a religion revealed from on high. The Pantocrator, looking down from the heavens in the dome, reveals himself to the worshipper. He is surrounded at a lower level of the dome by the figures of the Old Testament prophets, and, at another level, of his apostles, till in due course, in the various parts of the wall surfaces of the building, the Gospel is visually proclaimed: the birth, the ministry of Our Lord, his miracles, the Cross, the Resurrection, and the glorious Ascension. In our Gothic churches, the eye begins at the base of the piers and pillars and rises from the ground to enjoy the verticality of the soaring shafts till they curve over space, like rockets arching over at the end of their flight, to reach the apex of the vault. This architecture suits our Western idea: our earth-bound natural selves begin humbly at the human level and go on, aspiring to reach the heights by effort, using reason as well as revelation and with the Grace of God to help us upward. The

Byzantine dome leads at once to the highest point . . . 'in the beginning, God'.

In Salonika, we can see both the earlier basilican and the later dome construction. The church of Hagia Paraskevi of the fifth century is the earliest intact basilican church in Greece. Till the fire in 1917 which destroyed an important section of the city, the basilican church of St. Demetrius, in honour of the martyr saint, was one of the finest in the Christian world. It too was founded in the fifth century and rebuilt larger in the seventh. Two of its magnificent eighth-century mosaics survived the fire. The church has now been rebuilt, and very splendid it is. There are important Byzantine mosaics also in the abandoned church of St. George. This is an oddity, a vast rotunda built soon after the arch of Galerius on the Via Egnatia as a mausoleum for Imperial personages, but soon converted to be a church. In the cathedral church of the Holy Wisdom, of the seventh century, we see the transitional stage of a basilica which has a dome, while in the church of the Twelve Apostles, the single dome has blossomed into five domes. This church of the fourteenth century is built on the cross-in-square plan, a very frequent type. The main dome is at the crossing, where the arms of the cross join the upright of it; four smaller domes cover the nave, transepts and sanctuary.

The church at Daphni, near Athens, dates from the end of the eleventh century, and is one of the great buildings of Byzantine Art. The power of the Pantocrator in the dome, with his piercing gaze, is awe-full and can never be forgotten. The mosaics, on a gold background, are nearly complete, and are a classic example of the Byzantine purpose to glorify God with their art, and to bring all people into closest touch with the history and the events of His revelation in Christ Jesus.

There is another church, of the twelfth century, off the beaten track some distance from Delphi, which is important in the study of Byzantine art. 'Truly this is the finest church I saw in all Greece next to Santa Sophia in Constantinople, notwithstanding it is very old and hath suffered much by earthquake and time.' So wrote a Caroline divine, doubtless of Irish ancestry. But he was right in this, that at the monastery of Osios Loukas, where more of the original decoration survives than in any other church in Greece, one can gain a better idea of the appearance of a

Byzantine church of the twelfth century than anywhere else in the world.

Athens shrank to be of little importance in the Byzantine period, and the few churches which survive are extremely small. The 'Little Metropolis', adjacent to the modern cathedral, was built about 1220 from fragments of ancient materials, bits and pieces of bas-reliefs, triglyphs, stelai and marble blocks, whatever came to hand. On the edge of the Agora, there is the small eleventh-century church of the Holy Apostles, with a cluster of little domes—the scale being so small as to make the tiles of the roof and domes seem inordinately large. But if these and the other small Athenian churches are not fair examples of Byzantine Art, then the beautifully arranged Byzantine Museum in Athens is a fine place in which to see examples of it.

At MISTRA, three miles from Sparta, on a steep 2,000-feet-high conical hill, separated by a ravine from the mountains which rise beyond, are the ruins of a Byzantine city. The hill is crowned by the battlemented walls of a fortress, which never seems any nearer as one climbs the tortuous paths between banks of flowers in spring, past churches, ruined houses, through gateways in outer walls, past the Governor's palace and yet another church, constantly stopping to regain breath lost not only by the climb but through admiration for the great panorama below. At one's feet lies the finest valley of Greece, Sparta's stronghold; and the mass of mountains in endless range, six miles across the valley floor, walls in this great domain.

At Mistra, the last hour of the long Byzantine day saw a brilliant evening light. The greater part of the Peloponnese (the Morea) had been lost to the Franks, but by 1349, the Byzantines had recovered it and for a hundred years, till the Turkish domination in 1460, Mistra was the capital, in effect, of the Byzantine Empire. For it was the centre of its culture and here, in the Metropolitan Church, the last Emperor, Constantine XI, was crowned. In the oldest of Mistra's many churches, the basilica of St. Demetrius (the Metropolis, or Cathedral), a marble floor slab, carved with the imperial, double-headed eagle, marks the place of the coronation. Recently an effort has been made to render all the six decaying medieval Byzantine churches of Mistra weatherproof, for they all contain frescoes, many of which are of a high order—the Last Judgment, for example, in the narthex of the Metropolis—and important in the sequence of skill and style which leads to El Greco of Byzantine Crete and the great developments of Renaissance Art. The Brontochion Monastery, with its two churches to the north of the Metropolis, was a bright filament in the intellectual light of Mistra in the fifteenth century.

The Peribleptos, of the mid-fourteenth century, with a single dome, is partly hollowed out of the rock. It contains some of the best preserved frescoes. Above this church is the Pantanassa (A.D. 1430). This church of the Queen of All still lives, and from the little low line of cells on the flowered terrace a kindly nun is likely to emerge to guard her beloved church and interest the visitor in it too. Pantanassa has the best of the frescoes.

The Venetians occupied the city at the end of the seventeenth century when its population was many times greater than that of Athens. But in 1779 it was destroyed by Albanians. Fortunately Mistra is too beautiful a place for unhappy ghosts; but perhaps they would not be so unhappy, for they had so bravely kept the lamp burning in the face of storms, political and economic, and the pressures of the enemy, which were soon, at Constantinople, to break the last defences of the Byzantine Age.

CHAPTER XXVIII

The Orthodox Church in Greece

Kalabata Cathedral, rebuilt in 1309, lies at the foot of a prodigious vertical rock cliff where the Pindus range walls off the plain of Thessaly on the western side. On the Saturday before Easter, the church was crowded all day, not for public worship but for private devotions. A party of some sixty visitors to Greece went to see a medieval church: they stayed a long time, seeing a living one. Round the interior of the building there was a stone ledge, and the older and weaker—the grandparents in their best black—had gone to the wall. Many of them had small children on their knees, and each child held a lighted candle. It looked a living parable; the past handing the torch to the future. A long, slow queue filled the nave—men and women, boys and girls. The queue was moving towards a high table; two arches of flowers sprang from the corners of the table and joined in the centre to honour a silver crucifix resting among flower petals. As each individual came forward, he (or she) made his devotions, and then expressed penitence by kneeling down and crawling on hands and knees under the table and the crucifix, through and round, to crawl again from one side to the other, in this way making the sign of the Cross in humblest fashion below the crucifix. At the four corners of the table, four soldiers stood with arms reversed, guarding the symbols of the national faith. This ceremony, with these sentinels officially on duty, is performed throughout Greece wherever it is possible. Greece is still a Christian nation in a sense in which England can no longer be said to be. For the majority of Greeks are not only believers, but worshippers. They go to church and they know the doctrines of their Church.

Doctrine is, and has been for centuries, taught by the liturgies which are varied to suit all the great festivals in the Church's year; and it is taught visually too by the vast array of mosaic and fresco decoration which in many churches covers the entire wall surface with the whole ordered story of our Redemption. A convention built up in early Byzantine times still seems to be an effective aid to worship. For it was felt that, as the shadow is close to the substance which creates it, so the picture in mosaic or fresco of the saint, or the scene of one of Our Lord's miracles, is in close relationship to the saint, or the reality of the event in the pictured miracle. And so the worshipper, gazing at the image, is effectively close to the holy one it represents; and one does not need therefore to travel across the sea or back into the distant past to be in the near presence of Our Lord in Galilee, or at the foot of the Cross on the green hill. The Cross is not 'far away without a city wall': it is close to him who worships. In the mosaic or fresco, the saint or the holy one looks always full face into the eyes of the worshipper; or, if the frescoed figure is shown as talking to some other figure in the scene, then the convention requires that he be shown in three-quarter full face, and the worshipper may still feel that the link is unbroken and that he is looking into the eyes of the holy one. Only the wicked, Judas or the devil, are in profile.

A Greek church has a tall screen, the ikonostasis, which shuts off the altar and sanctuary from view. No one normally is allowed to enter the sanctuary, except the priest. It would be a major mistake for a visitor to do so. This screen is adorned with ikons, often of silver. In many churches little silver votives are offered at the ikon, the intention being to put a prayer in a visual form. There may be a little image of a sailor or a soldier son, for whose safety the visual prayer is made; or of a limb, a hand, a heart, a body, because a prayer is intended for health or recovery from illness. Eventually, the silver votives will be melted down to add more silver adornment to the ikon of Our Lord, the Bearer of God, or the patron saint.

One does not ask 'What branch of the Church is the Orthodox?' For the Greek would answer, 'We are the original trunk: it is the Roman Catholic Church which is the broken-off branch, and the other Christian Churches are twigs of that broken branch. The Pope is the chief protestant.' The breach between

East and West in Christianity no doubt began with the theological dispute as to whether it was from God alone, or from God and His Son (filioque) that the Holy Spirit proceeded; but the split tree was cleft asunder by the appalling error of the Fourth Crusade which, instead of fighting to save the Holy Places for Christendom, turned aside and attacked, captured and sacked Constantinople. As if the sacking of Santa Sophia and the plundering of the sacred relics and wealth of every church in Constantinople were not enough, the Crusaders proceeded to remove the Greek bishops also from their Eastern sees and to install Latins in their places.

The Orthodox Church in Greece traces its descent back to the first church in Europe, founded at Philippi by the Apostle Paul; and because it highly values its amazing continuity with the past, it is slow to make changes of any sort. Its liturgy has remained virtually unaltered since the sixth century: it is often too long and there are parts which the more progressive would like to see dropped, but the authorities fear that to drop anything at all from the old established and loved tradition might lead to 'throwing away the baby with the bath water'. 'You have taught this for fourteen hundred years, and now you say it is wrong. If that is wrong, how do we know that the rest isn't wrong also?' So it is an ultra-conservative Church.

Orthodox bishops must be unmarried and remain so; but parish priests, on the other hand, must be married before they can be ordained. They must be not less than thirty years old and, after ordination, must never shave again nor have a hair-cut. In the very rare event of a parish priest being consecrated as bishop, his wife would retire to a nunnery. It follows, therefore, that the bishop normally comes from the unmarried clergy, that is to say, from a monastery or from the ranks of those who began their service as deacons, were then picked out to serve on the staff of a bishop, and later became archimandrites—an office which, in relation to a bishop is not unlike that of chief-of-staff to a general.

The parish priest in rural Greece is not normally educated above the level of the peasant farmers over whom he is set as 'papas'. A bishop may consult with the village elders as to their choice of a man to be ordained as their priest. Where this is done, even though his education may be slight, the 'papas' has the confidence of the village and his advice in their troubles is respected and valued by the villagers. The village 'papas' is not allowed to preach because he is not trained to do so. Instead, he will read a circular sermon sent him by the bishop, or the bishop may himself come, or send 'a sacred herald'. This is a priest-monk, often a graduate theologian, trained to the work; or he may be a layman, a professional man who for love of his Lord and his fellow-men works for the additional qualification to enable him to preach. This is like our English lay-reader system. For the same reason that he may not preach, the country parish priest may not hear confession, nor give absolution. The parish priest's salary is very small, but he will probably add to it by farming his own patch as he did before ordination. He will receive a good increment, however, if he is able to spend a year or two years at one of the Theological Colleges recently organized to cope with the problems of an untrained parish priesthood.

The diaconate is not the first step to the priesthood as in the Anglican Church. The deacon plays an important part in the singing of the service, and in the training of the choir. During services, men stand on one side of the church, the women on the other. The congregation follows the singing of the Liturgy, but sings only softly; private devotions during the Liturgy are discouraged, because the Eucharist is a communion of Christians, all sharing in the act of worship, and it is the performance of a drama, so that the individual cannot properly dissociate himself. Between Easter and Whit-Sunday one does not kneel: one stands, head high, for 'Christ reigns' triumphantly, and we are His. 'Lift up your hearts and heads': an inspiriting idea and typical of the Eastern Church's intense and original and lasting joy in the Resurrection.

There used to be a great number of monasteries in Greece, Mount Athos being the chief centre with no less than 20,000 monks and priest-monks. There are now about 2,000—typical of the general decline of monasticism in Greece. At Mount Athos the absence now of monks from Russia accounts for some of the fall; but more largely reflects a new view in Greece that a devout Church *can* have too many monks. In the wars, especially the Communist war, a terrible destruction of churches and monasteries, mostly in the north of Greece, took place, and 363 priests and monks were killed, not in battle but by murder. The Communists thought that if they could eradicate the leaders of the Church, the people would abandon their national religion and follow them. One priest-monk, Papa George Skrekas, they crucified on Good Friday, 1947. Their dreadful policy hastened their defeat. But there was no money for any wide-scale rebuilding of monasteries; and, in any case, Christian Greece believes that in the difficult conditions of modern, materialistic life, this is the time to rally the Christian forces and get them in the field for open battle with materialism, and not to withdraw from the world. Money from the sale of some monastic lands now goes into the training of those un-trained clergy whose simple devotion has won the respect of a Christian nation.

Monasteries are often in remote places: but none are so inaccessible as those known as 'the Meteora'—'the places up in the air'—at the foot of the Pindus mountains in Thessaly. Here is the oddest rock formation possible. The mountains fall steeply into the plain in a horseshoe of cliff, but, detached from the cliffs sometimes at a distance of only a hundred feet, there stand twenty-four pinnacles of rock, many hundreds of feet high, and many of these pinnacles have smooth-sided vertical cliffs. Mr. Osbert Lancaster's inimitable description of these geological extravagances as like the 'decayed and irregular denture of some gigantic mammoth' is too accurate to omit. In the fourteenth century, in despair of finding peace in a world of battle, murder and sudden death, twenty-four monasteries were established on these incredible summits. Four of the monasteries are still 'alive', though each inhabited by only half a dozen monks. Originally, the only approach to a monastery was by ladders— whole strings of them—let down from above. Then a windlass and rope system was used. One recalls the question of a nervous traveller who, on arrival at the summit, asked when the rope was last renewed, and did not relish the simple answer, 'When it last broke, of course.' Today, steps have been cut in the rocks and wooden bridges thrown across gaps. But it is still a vastly exciting business to walk the rickety and creaking floors, canti-levered in places over space. The visit to the Great Meteoron and its friendly monks is strongly recommended.

A hundred Hellenic travellers were looking round a church

and many of them at a particular ikon on the ikonostasis. A young man, evidently, from his bag of tools, an electrician, entered. Without a trace of embarrassment, he made his way through the crowd to the ikon, knelt before it, rose and kissed it, stood intent in his gaze upon it for a moment, and went on his way to the next job. The cynics and the sceptics perhaps felt a shot of envy at a faith so natural, so sure and so typical of Greece to-day.

CHAPTER XXIX

Outlines of Greek Architecture

The mental picture formed at the sound of the words 'Greek Architecture' is likely to be that of a temple or part of a temple, and of a Doric one at that. Nor would this be unfair to the fact that we are in a position to study the remains of a great variety of ancient Greek buildings. For, though no city in classical times was deemed complete without its agora (or 'city-centre' round which stood the public buildings, colonnaded shops, lawcourt and so on), its theatre, gymnasium, stadium, fountain-houses, monuments to its heroes and, of course, its defensible acropolis, it was commonly the temple of the city's patron god or goddess which was given the dominant position and the highest honour. Often the chief temple stood also at the highest point of the acropolis, the defended heart of the city and the nucleus round which the city grew in safety, itself enclosed by a wider circuit of fortification walls.

It is true that in Mycenaean Greece, a thousand years before the Classical period, the chief building of a citadel was the king's palace. This is seen at Mycenae, Tiryns and Pylos. In these palace-complexes the central feature is the megaron, a large rectangular room with the long walls prolonged to form the sides of an open porch with its roof supported by columns. A single large doorway gives access to the megaron. In the centre is a large hearth, the focus of the room: round it, in a square plan, are four columns supporting the roof: on the right a raised platform for the royal throne. At Pylos stairs survive, to indicate an upper storey for the private rooms and sleeping quarters. Both at Tiryns and Pylos there is a bathroom on the ground floor near the megaron: there may have been others on the upper floor.

There are forecourts to these megara, and pillared gateways. The latter feature was copied from the Minoan palaces of Crete and continued right through Greek history. The Propylaea of the Acropolis at Athens, or of twenty other sites, derives from the Minoan portico as seen at Phaestos. Clustered round the typical megaron and its forecourt were archive-rooms, offices, store-rooms for wine and oil and wheat, oil-press rooms, workshops, potteries, shrines, corridors, armouries—the whole forming an irregular complex of buildings, quite unlike the later development of precise, clear-cut design which is the hallmark of building in the Classical period. This irregularity is due to the influence of the Minoan palaces at Knossos, Mallia and Phaestos upon the Mycenaeans of the mainland, who learnt so much artistically from that earlier and foreign culture, itself indebted to the culture and palace builders of Anatolia.

But the megaron is Greek. The king's megaron was indeed a great room, but essentially only the ordinary man's house, built large. In some of the houses of ordinary men, as at Priene, this same megaron is found. And when religious shrines ceased to be mere house-chapels in a corner of the palace complex, as they were at Knossos for example, and the god was given a house of his own, his temple has the ground-plan of the porched megaron. In the full development there is a porch, or maybe a room, at the rear also; this is the opisthodomos, often used as a city treasury. Round the whole building runs a peristyle of columns. Thus the Greek temple is literally a god's house, and is intended, not for the assembly of worshippers, but to provide a great room to contain the statue of the god.

The early temple builders found that sun-baked brick, strengthened by horizontal and vertical timbers at intervals, was a suitable material even for large buildings, if set on a stone footing. This construction (orthostates of stone on a stone podium) had been used at Knossos and Phaestos and Mallia, and it was adopted for the temple of Hera at Olympia a thousand years later.

The columns of the early temples were wooden. Later, when marble began to be used for temples and other buildings of importance, constructional features appropriate to the use of timber were copied as decoration in the new material. This is undoubtedly true in the rock-cut and stone tombs of Lycia, where the mason used the forms of the carpenter. The triglyph—the three-fold stone slab set above the column and also above the space between columns in the Doric Order—may conceivably be derived from a decorative pattern found in Minoan art and architecture. But it seems much more likely, in view of the six stone pegs or guttae always seen below it, that the triglyph was a protective slab of wood or terracotta, in its original form, to keep the weather off the ends of the ceiling rafters, and that the guttae imitate in stone the tre-nails or wooden pegs which kept the triglyph in position. Again, the fluting of the stone Doric column may be reminiscent of the grooves which the long strokes of the adze would make as the woodworker cut away the bark and sap-wood of his tree trunk before erecting it to be the wooden column.

If the origins of the Doric Order are controversial, some holding that Egypt is the source, this much is clear, that the Greeks, using an elementary formula of vertical and horizontal lines of stone, the latter lying inert, without stress, without mortar, upon the supporting verticals, so refined it with skill and taste, with strict rules of proportion, that the total effect is one of balance, symmetry and power. At the highest development, they added a series of optical corrections to ensure that the human eye, easily misled by effects of light and shade and ready to see a sagging in a horizontal line on which stand a series of verticals alternately light and dark, such as columns and their shadows, saw the whole as an apparent pattern of truly horizontal and vertical shapes. In fact, with the application of these optical corrections, the entire building is made up of subtly curving or inclined surfaces.

These refinements called for mathematical ability of a high order in the design, and equally for extreme skill on the part of the masons. Two of them may be readily seen in the Parthenon —the slight swell (entasis) of the columns which are neither straight-sided nor vertical, for straightness would cause the eye to see them as 'waisted' and if vertical, they would seem to be inclining outwards; and, as a second example, the upward curve of the steps of the platform (stylobate) which, without the curve, would seem to sag under the line of standing columns.

Marble was the perfect material for buildings in which sharp edges, clear-cut outline, precision and the beauty of uncluttered wall surfaces were desired, so that each part, functional and decorative (the sculptured metopes and pediment) might do its work.

In short, the Greek mind took the simple idea of the upright and the cross-bar—the child's building-block technique—and, in developing it to its zenith in the Parthenon, produced a masterpiece which still has much to say about those ingredients in a building that will make for serenity combined with power, repose with majesty.

The Doric Order continued in use in Hellenistic and Roman times: but it is easy to distinguish Greek from Roman Doric. The later architects dared a wider space between columns, allowing space for three triglyphs between them: they used a base for their columns, whereas a Greek Doric column rests directly on the stylobate: they economized often by omitting the fluting in the lower part of a column where damage could easily be done, and they reduced the size of the capital most meanly. All these Hellenistic and Roman 'improvements' are seen in Delos.

The Ionic Order came to mainland Greece almost certainly from Asia Minor and the islands, when the Doric Order was well established both there and in the colonies of Magna Graecia. Ionic columns have bases; the flutes have no sharp edges to them but are separated by a substantial fillet; the columns are more tall and slender; the capitals, with their beautiful spiral volutes, decorative; the architrave has lost its alternating triglyphs and metopes, and in Greece proper, has a frieze of plain or sculptured stone, in Asia Minor a string of dentils to suggest the beam-ends of the ceiling. If the feeling of the heavier, more austere Doric Order can be described as masculine, then the Ionic is certainly feminine, and very lovely and especially suitable for smaller buildings. At any rate so thought the Athenian Greeks: for the Erechtheum and the temple of Nike on the Acropolis of Athens show the Ionic Order at its best. In Ionian Asia Minor, the greatest temples, such as that of Artemis at Ephesus and of Apollo at Didyma, were Ionic.

The Corinthian Order came later. Its first appearances were in the temple at Bassae, and in the circular building (tholos) at

Epidaurus where one of the capitals, perfectly preserved, is to be seen in the Museum. It is decorative and graceful; and, enjoying the beauty of its sculptured acanthus leaves and their slender volutes, one may contrast its simplicity with the complications bestowed upon the Corinthian capital by later Hellenistic and Roman architects in their constant striving for splendour and magnificence.

Though the Greeks built in the most durable of all natural materials, two factors have worked against the survival of their best buildings. In the naming of part of the ruins of Delphi 'Marmaria'—Marble Quarry—history reveals one reason for the destruction of fine old buildings. There, for the taking, was a source of cheap marble already cut and squared. Where the ancient stones were not too big and heavy easily to be moved, a vast quantity has been re-used in many later centuries of building. As recently as the seventeenth century, the stones of the temple of Zeus at Agrigento were used for the construction of the city's harbour wall.

The second destructive factor was the need for lime and the comparative ease with which marble statues, carved cornices, capitals, and drums of columns—anything—could be burnt in a kiln and turned into cash. At one period there was a lime-kiln on most of the now famous classical sites, a kiln that devoured the greater part and left posterity the odds and ends.

Perhaps theatres have a special survival value; their stones were inclined to be large and of a shape useless in ordinary building. Many theatres, as a result, have survived in a tolerable condition, while of other buildings only foundations of rough stone may be found. That the Greeks preferred the rectangular, the triangular, the horizontal and the vertical in their building lines is suggested by the extreme rarity of any other shape, except in the construction of theatres. These were built into the natural hollows of hillsides. In Eretria, however, the necessary hillside for once was not there, and the builders excavated half of the cavea in the soil and built up the other half with the spoil from the excavation. But they kept to the usual semicircular shape because it had been found to help audibility.

The number of circular buildings, attractive to our eyes, was small: the tholoi at Epidaurus and at Delphi; the tholos in the Agora at Athens, used for the Executive on duty for the day;

AT MISTRA, NEAR
SPARTA: BYZANTINE
CHURCH OF
THE EVANGELISTRIA
(FOURTEENTH CENTURY)

PATMOS: AUTHORITY
THE MONASTERY OF
. JOHN THEOLOGOS
(THE DIVINE)

*monastery was founded
088 in honour of the
or of the Revelation, and
is in active life.*

AT EPIDAURUS PALAIA ON THE SARONIC GULF: A TYPICAL MODERN
ORTHODOX CHURCH IN A TYPICAL SETTING

*An oil-filling station for fishing-boats has since been installed on the water's edge
below the church. O tempora! O mores!*

AT THASOS IN THE ANCIENT HARBOUR

the 'folly' of the family of Philip of Macedon, actually within the sanctuary itself at Olympia; and, biggest of them all, the sacred building in the sanctuary at Samothrace, built at the cost of Arsinoe, wife of one of the Ptolemies of Egypt; finally, there is the Choregic Monument of Lysicrates at Athens. There is no special difficulty in their construction. The conclusion is that the Greeks liked their building lines to appear straight.

Governed, then, by this strong addiction to the horizontal, and limited by the size and length of timber available for roofing, the Greeks were not able to enclose a great spatial volume without erecting a forest of columns to support the roof. We see this in the huge Hall of Initiation, the Telesterion, at Eleusis, where, in the fourth century B.C., six rows of seven columns blocked the view for the spectators of the ceremony, standing on tiers of steps all round the hall.

The Greeks must have known the arch early in their story, for it had long been used in the East, with which they had contact through trade. They did in fact use both arch and vault, but only in unobtrusive positions such as in the roofs of tombs, in the tunnels under stadia; there is an occasional near-arch in a fortification gateway. It is to the Romans that we owe the development of the use of the arch and the vault, and even they, for a long time, submitted to the architectural convention that the use of a column of, say, the Doric Order, demanded the laying of a horizontal architrave upon it. Accordingly, they sprang their arches from two-thirds up columns engaged on masonry piers, and faithfully built the architrave above. It was an immense step forward in the history of man's building, when some daring architect first sprang his arches from the tops of columns and so, unconfined by the horizontal, could confine space itself in a series of huge arching curves. The Greeks would have been dumbfounded, could they have seen, for instance, the Baths of Diocletian and walked below thousands of tons of masonry and concrete 'floating' in space above their heads.

Yet, if one would enjoy the beauty of a perfect wall, the Propylaea at Athens provides that sight better than any other construction of any time in any place. And the whole earth, from Washington to Australia and from Russia to Peru, has honoured the architecture of Greece by copying it in the façades, at least, of important public buildings for several centuries past.

CHAPTER XXX

Outlines of Greek Sculpture

To me one of the most fascinating uses of the motion-picture is the showing, within a few minutes, of the life cycle of a flower. We see the seed in the earth and watch it shoot; through the soil into the light and air the delicate blade emerges; it rises in the sun, grows a strong stem, puts out its leaves and buds; we watch the unfolding of the tight-packed petals and want to cheer when the full glory of the blossom smiles for all the world; and then in awe we see the death of the flower itself, and the gift of the seed falling to beautify the future. In the museums of Greece we can follow, with equal fascination, the growth and development to full flower, and then the slow death of Greek sculpture—at its best one of Earth's loveliest things. But what of the seed? Here the parallel with the flower fails. The seed could not be expected to reproduce the same flower, for the soil and spiritual climate of the successors of Greece, the Romans, and, later, that of Renaissance Italy, were so different. Nor will the conditions ever be the same again. But Greek sculpture of the human figure is for some of us a standard in respect of certain qualities it eminently possessed and quietly displayed—the expression of an ideal, restraint and dignity and calm detachment, and the repose of complete self-confidence. Above all, Greek sculpture demonstrates a freshness and fearlessness—a trustingness—in a people's outlook on life which many moderns must envy, and which is illustrated by the wonderful Apollo of Olympia (the central figure in the west pediment of the temple of Zeus) and the Lemnian Athena by Pheidias, as we have it probably in Roman copies at Dresden and

Bologna. This young prince of a god, strong, serene, and transcendentally in command, brings order into a scene of chaos and savagery. And the Lemnian Athena, standing on the Acropolis at Athens long ago, the immortal guardian of her city, is no aloof and distant figure, but a woman as well as a goddess, calm and most dignified, of clear insight and great beauty. That the Greeks thought of Apollo and Athena in this way tells us volumes about themselves and their attitude to life; and to see the evidence before our eyes is an exhilaration.

Though in their sculpture the Greeks reached a high watermark, they did not introduce the art into Greece. There was already an indigenous sculpture in the Aegean lands and islands when they arrived from the north. In the National Museum at Athens (in the long gallery which runs alongside, and is entered from, the Mycenaean room opposite the main entrance door) there are several examples of Bronze Age sculpture from the Cycladic islands. These are all small, but intensely interesting for their impressionistic style. They would fetch high prices in London or New York—supposing their antiquity were concealed—as exciting pieces of modernist art: no attempt at detail, just an enjoyment of smooth, round surfaces, with a face indicated only by a nose or perhaps a horizontal slit. The 'Harpist' sitting on his chair (since 2400 B.C.) with his triangular harp resting on his leg, does make one wonder why modernism goes back to the Stone Age and then fancies itself as *avant garde*. Professor John Evans, recently excavating twenty feet below the level of the central court at Knossos, found a statuette in a pit beside a Neolithic house. It is carved of a stone like marble and is a male figure; the arms (which never had hands) are folded across the chest, the head and one leg are missing, but, as in the 'Harpist', the Neolithic sculptor clearly has felt pleasure in working and polishing his stone to present the curves of the body and its touchable, undulating surfaces. This is in fact real sculpture.

In the Mycenaean period between 1600 and 1100 B.C. the modelling of clay into votive offerings of human or animal shape was a universal practice and paved the way for sculpture proper. This we can see in the Lion Gate at Mycenae. These lions are well-modelled, muscular. They stand on either side of a central pillar, their front feet raised up on a pair of altars. The heads are missing; but the Lion Gate sculpture is still a noble and effective achievement. The solitary pillar almost certainly represents the near presence of deity. In primitive times a lone tree, or an especially tall tree, was revered, it seems, as holy; and this supposition is corroborated by the so-called statue of Apollo at Amyclae near Sparta. This 'statue' was a tall wooden post, wider at the top than the bottom, as in Minoan architecture, and plated with bronze, and provided at the top with a head and arms. The earliest Greek statues were often made of wood, mere tree trunks cut short, but with the features of the head carved roughly on them, and hands and feet indicated by incisions. The Greeks of the classical period venerated these ancient crudities, believing them to have fallen from heaven, and preserving them as both holy and precious. Indeed, one of the main objects of the great Panathenaic procession in which a new robe for Athena was ceremoniously paraded, set as a sail on the yard of a ship drawn on a great carriage, was to glorify the ancient xoanon—the rough, tree-trunk statue—kept in the Erechtheum.

When the Greeks set about sculpture in marble on a large scale, beginning in the eighth century B.C., the old techniques of wood carving are still discernible in the new material, some of the figures looking wooden and like tree-trunks in their excessive roundness, for example the Hera of Samos, while others, flat across both front and sides, are reminiscent of the alternative method of using a thick plank of wood.

Undoubtedly Egyptian sculpture strongly influenced the early Greek efforts in marble. For several thousand years Egyptian figures had stood upright, at attention (except that the left leg was a little forward); a line drawn vertically downwards through the nose and the centre of the chest would bisect the figure into two symmetrical halves. This standing figure the Greeks copied in great numbers. Some are gods, others men. They look identical. But the Greeks added nudity to what they had learnt from Egypt, for they admired the human form—at its best. And this proviso introduces an important point, true about Greek sculpture until its latest phases: it was not to be portrait sculpture. They would try to express the ideal. 'Gods are more beautiful than their statues, as statues are more beautiful than men,' said Aristotle. And there is another vital point. The

278

statues of the gods were not idols. St. Paul, speaking before the Areopagus Court at Athens, seems to imply that they were. But, having been brought up as a Jew to flee from any and every representation of God, he naturally would recoil from statues of gods. To the Greek, the statue was a medium of worship, not the object of it.

In the National Museum at Athens there is a whole series of the early nude male statues, sometimes known as 'Apollos', now called Kouroi, young men. In either case they would be votives, acts of worship. The hair of the earliest, as we see also in the Cleobis and Biton at Delphi and in the sixth-century kouros at Delos, is treated in the familiar Egyptian manner. The tall, thin kouros, more than life-size, from Melos (560 B.C.), also in the National Museum, is an arresting work of art, despite the lack of muscle detail and the incomplete separation of the lower arms and hands from the body: for the eye sees him as a living form, frail indeed, but not as a marble mass of bits and pieces, trunk and legs and arms joined together. The kouros, Kroisos from Anavyssos (520 B.C.), in a further gallery in the National Museum, standing calmly and with such cheerful confidence in front of the terracotta-pink wall that sets him off so well, is still a stationary figure, but he is magnificently alive. Archaic? Yes, in time. Inaccurate? Yes, his legs are much too heavy. But this is surely sculpture of a fresh morning glory and, by the side of it, the technical triumphs of contortion in the latest Hellenistic period leave us cold. The inscription on the base of the Kroisos statue is typically Greek and emotive in its simplicity:

> '*Stand and mourn by the tomb of dead Kroisos, whom*
> *furious Ares slew when he was fighting in the front line.*'

Parallel in development with the nude kouroi are the delightful female draped figures, now in the far left-hand gallery of the Acropolis Museum. Like all the sculpture of the sixth century B.C. and the period before the Persian War, they wear the 'archaic smile', the 'smile of courtesy to the onlooker', as Sir Maurice Bowra calls it. Or is it what Robert Louis Stevenson prayed for—the 'morning face' of young and cheerful contentment with life? There is still some colour left on the borders of chiton or peplos, for the Greeks picked out the detail of borders, sandals, lips, hair and so on, in colour and gave a wax finish to the flesh which would take off some of the sun's glare from the white marble. The morgue-like figures we see in a plaster-cast museum of Greek sculpture are not Greek in their effect. These korai, or maidens, of the Acropolis stand erect, with one arm and hand stretched out at the elbow and the other often holding up their dress. In the Museum they are set up in a semicircle and so face one central point. You look from one to another: they all seem interested in you, addressing you gaily and smilingly. You are transported back in time, and you are enjoying this Athenian party with as charming a group of young women as ever man could meet. To be more accurate, you are in touch with the ancient Greek sculptors who drew this beauty out of the rock by their vision and their skill, and you begin to know the Greeks as people.

The sixth-century horse and hound in the same gallery show how, early in their story, the Greek sculptors learnt to concentrate on essentials and give form and simple surface textures a chance to speak without the interruptions of excessive elaboration and decoration. The hound is the very essence of the hunting dog. The hound of Pella, found by a countrywoman working in her field and handed over by her some years ago to the local school where it reposed unknown, seems to be work of the same hand. The power of much of this original Archaic work is extraordinary when contrasted with that of Roman copies or of some of the originals of the Hellenistic period. That technical efficiency is not enough and that great work springs only from a great spirit behind the sculptor's tools is a truism we accept and forget; but it is unforgettably brought home to the mind in looking at Greek Archaic sculpture. In the first gallery on the left of the Acropolis Museum there is a pedimental group of a sixth-century temple on the Acropolis, destroyed by the Persians in 480 B.C. Two lions have overpowered a bull. For all his strength he has collapsed under their weight and wounding; his massive head has been borne down till his brow is pressed into the ground and the folds of the dewlap are deepened in the strain of the great, bent neck. Dilated nostrils show that he still resists: a back leg is dislocated and lies stretched flat behind him. Enormous power is displayed, defeated by a greater power, and we suffer with the bull in the fall of his majesty. But when Laocoon, of the first century B.C., with his two children, struggles in the deathly embrace of the snakes, in the Vatican Museum, and despair in his contorted face calls loudly to us, we do not answer. We are bored by Laocoon despite his anatomical excellence: the Archaic bull excites. When the spirit moves a people, it is able to inform and live on in the material works of art the people's representatives, its artists, create. This is a mystery; and one of the realities of life, both then and now.

In the period after the Persian wars, a swift development and a change took place. Movement, already splendidly achieved in sculpture in relief, for instance in the long frieze from the Siphnian Treasury (in the Museum at Delphi), is now attained in free-standing sculpture. There is movement and vitality and, even where the figure is a stationary one, there is the poise and balance of life about it, and an almost startling dignity. Gone is the 'archaic smile': Hellas faces its responsibilities as the victorious champion of Freedom, Law and Order in a difficult world. The transition from the old to the new is well seen in the sculptures, now in Munich, of the temple of Athena Aphaia in Aegina. Here the smile still lingers but the figures are taut with action. But in the calm dignity of the bronze charioteer at Delphi, alive and aloof and self-confident, there is a new power. Nowhere is this new mastery of a living sculpture better seen than in the superb bronze of Poseidon hurling his trident—or of Zeus his thunderbolt. This is the finest of all statues in the National Museum. It was found under the sea off Artemisium. He must have been an atheist who said this figure might be a hoplite hurling his javelin—the weapon is missing—for the head and bearded face is of a nobler than mortal breed. Myron is the chief exponent of sculpture's new swing into movement; and luckily Lucian describes a statue by Myron of which several Roman copies exist. This is the Discobolos: 'the discus-thrower is bent down into the position for the throw, turning his head towards the hand that holds the disc and all but kneeling on one knee as he seems about to straighten himself up at the throw.' The period when Myron astonished his contemporaries with his new daring postures is now known, and it is surprisingly soon after the days of rigidity; it begins in 476 B.C. In his Marsyas (the Roman copy is in the Lateran Museum at Rome), we see the characteristic contribution of Myron—the suggestion of movement in a difficult and contorted posture. Marsyas has clearly checked a forward move and started back in surprise. But Myron's interest in composition is new too. Marsyas was part of a group in which Athena offset his movement by her own. The Discobolos stood alone, but is beautifully self-sufficient; the eye moves easily round the circular composition, following the clear lead of the limbs, eager, when the athlete straightens up, to follow the discus into flight.

In the judgment of the Greeks, their greatest sculptor was Pheidias (*floruit* 450 B.C.). In the capacity of general supervisor, he was the chosen instrument of Pericles in the beautification of Athens and the Acropolis, and himself designed and made the colossal gold and ivory cult statue of Athena in the Parthenon. The Panathenaic frieze and the metopes of that temple, and the pedimental sculpture were also his responsibility in design, at least. He had already made a name with his colossal thirty-foot-high bronze Athena Promachos which stood on the Acropolis. This was the largest of all bronze statues made at that time in Greece. The beautiful Athena Lemnia, to which reference has been made earlier in this chapter, had also been completed when he received his new commission from Pericles. Whether he made the most famous of all Greek statues, the chryselephantine Zeus at Olympia, before or after the cult statue of Athena is not clear: the sources of information disagree. But that he died in disgrace, or even was executed, is, sad to say, agreed. He had faced a charge in Athens and some years later at Elis. The charge brought against him by the bitter enemies of Pericles, his friend, was of peculation in his handling of the gold he used in his work, and of sacrilege in putting his 'signature' on the cult statue; for he had put his own portrait, as an old bald-headed man, and that of Pericles, in the relief on the shield of Athena, among the contestants in a battle of Greeks and Amazons which was worked upon it. That the little figures were a minute part of a great mass of relief decoration in gold on the base of the statue, on both sides of the shield which Athena rested on edge by her side, on her sandals, her helmet and her aegis, mattered not at all. The charge is an example of that cruelty, springing from political bitterness, which was liable at all times to erupt in ancient Greece. The greatness of the mind and art of Pheidias seems to have lain in a spiritual awareness matched by such skill that he was able to express in his work—whether it was a colossal figure or otherwise—not just the traditional aspect of a god or goddess, but a new and nobler conception added to it, and so to incorporate his idea with sheer beauty of face and form as to make the ideal acceptable to the minds and hearts of the Greeks.

The influence of Pheidias' style lasted through generations of sculptors in most parts of Greece, and is seen most clearly in the treatment of drapery. Pheidias contrived all manner of variations in the arrangement of the folds and in the contrasting use of thick and thin materials. This became the Attic tradition. In the figures from the Parthenon pediments (now in the British Museum) which were designed by Pheidias, this interest in drapery is well illustrated. The three Fates sit and recline with easy grace, the light on their garments with the dark shadows of the folds creating a beautiful foil to the smooth, bare surfaces of the shoulders, neck and face. Stanley Casson has pointed out the interesting technical innovation which made possible what he calls 'these elaborate adventures in the carving of drapery'. Pheidias designed his sculpture by making clay models—always necessary in the process of casting bronze which was his usual medium—and in clay modelling it is easy to experiment with every kind of elaboration. He now required his assistants to copy the clay models in marble. This explains both the first-class composition of the Parthenon frieze, and the second-class sculpture of a few sections of it, carried out by the less skilled of the assistants.

Perhaps the most beautiful example of sculpture intended to be seen at close quarters and inspired by the new style of Pheidias, is the marble slab from the balustrade which once enclosed the forecourt of the little temple of Victory at the Propylaea on the Acropolis. Victory is shown tying up her sandal. The sculptor's consummate skill is revealed in the composition of the work, for the figure is self-contained and holds the eye always on itself, never directing it outside the frame; and, again, in the astonishing feat of so using mallet and chisel on a block of cold marble that through the transparent drapery the body is seen and all but felt to be soft and warm. (This relief is to be seen in the Acropolis Museum in the second room on the right.)

Meanwhile in Argos a different tradition was being developed.

There, another master, Polyclitus (*floruit* 425 B.C.), was setting
a fashion and laying down a canon of right proportions for the
sculpture of the nude athlete. In his choice of subject he was
following the Peloponnesian tradition and, in the opinion of the
ancient critics, he achieved a high point of technical perfection
and ideal proportion. These nude figures, though in slow forward movement, are the culmination of a developing process in
sculpture which began with the rigid standing statues of the
seventh, and even of the eighth, centuries, reminiscent of
Egyptian work. In his sculpture Polyclitus expressed, not the
face and form of the individual in whose name the statue was set
up, but the ideal athlete, the ideal man, in his physical aspect.
There are several Roman marble 'copies'—which do not agree
even in their proportions—of his bronze Doryphoros in which
he embodied his canon of correct proportions. There is a copy
in the British Museum of his Diadumenos, a powerful young
athlete in the games, putting a fillet on his head in readiness for
the wreath of victory. Though we have nothing but copies, and
Roman ones at that, of Polyclitus' work, it is clear that his ideal
athlete was as gentle as he was powerfully built, and there is no
vestige of that brute strength, and indeed, brutality, that was not
unknown when athletics at Olympia declined into the hands of
professionals. But Polyclitus worked by rule, according to his own
canon; and working by rule and by inspiration produce different
results. The Romans, naturally, thought the world of him.

Praxiteles (*floruit* 340 B.C.) can be judged by a surviving
original marble statue, in almost fresh condition, designed to be
seen at close quarters: this is the Hermes, in the Olympia
Museum. It is there so arranged as to be out of sight until one
enters the room and sees it suddenly in its splendid and glorious
isolation. It makes an extraordinary impact on the mind. One
has only to stand there, and watch and listen as people enter the
room and are confronted by this masterpiece, to realize that
even the most inspired photographer fails to do justice to a
marble statue. For everyone knows this Hermes in 'black and
white'; and yet astonishment and admiration at the actual sight
of it is universal. At that moment, the aching tragedy of waste
which in medieval times threw lovely marble statues in their
hundreds from the ancient sites into the lime-kilns and left the
world only the odds and ends, comes sadly home to one.

Outlines of Greek Sculpture

There is great beauty in this figure, perfection in its form, but it is a sensuous beauty, and I do not see the god in Hermes. Nor do I think that Praxiteles was particularly concerned that I should. But I thank heaven that the temple of Hera at Olympia, in which Hermes stood, had walls of sun-baked brick; for when the floods came which drowned (but ultimately preserved) Olympia in twenty feet of silt, Hermes fell softly into a bed of mud, and so was saved to show us what miracles of grace Praxiteles could create in stone. The most famous of the works of Praxiteles was the Aphrodite, made for her temple at Cnidos. He broke the convention that goddesses were represented clothed, and boldly made her nude. If Praxiteles could create such beauty in a Hermes, which was not considered in antiquity to be in any way outstanding, what marvel would an Aphrodite be? No wonder people in thousands made the journey to Cnidos to see the statue. There is a Roman copy in the Vatican Museum. The head of Aphrodite (or is it the head of Praxiteles' mistress, Phryne?), known as the 'Petworth' head is believed to be an original, and it is certainly not only characteristic of Praxiteles' work in the extraordinary softness of outline his hand could give to marble, but also one of the loveliest things Greek sculpture has given us. A very similar head is in the National Museum.

The output of Praxiteles was large, and he too set a new trend. He brings the gods and goddesses down to earth, leaving their heavenly attributes behind: grace and beauty and charm, for their own sakes, was his aim and his wonderful achievement.

Scopas (*floruit* 370 B.C.) is another master who made a unique contribution and, in doing so, prepared the way for the sculpture of the Hellenistic period, which likes to tell a dramatic story. For Scopas put emotional intensity, fire and passion, into his faces and figures. The eyes are deeply set in: on the brow he emphasizes that bony ridge which we all have, known as the 'bar of Michelangelo' (who also made use of it), to make the deep-set eyes expressive of emotion and a new forcefulness. This feature is useful in dating a sculptured head; for if it is there, the sculptor cannot antedate Scopas. Scopas designed the temple of Athena at Tegea as well as providing the sculpture which, according to Pausanias, excelled all others in the Peloponnese. Sculptural fragments, and especially some heads which have been excavated, indicate a theme of violent motion, the boar hunt of

Atalanta, and the intense expression on the faces is justified. Scopas was one of the team of sculptors employed in the decoration of the Mausoleum of Halicarnassos. The beautiful fragment of a young charioteer in full career, bending forward over the rail of the chariot and swept by the wind, shows the typical intensity Scopas gave to his figures. We see it again in his Maenad in Dresden. A funeral stele from the Ilissus (in the National Museum), as E. A. Gardner points out, concisely sums up the tradition and the technique which was in vogue after Scopas had shown the way—a way which would have been unacceptable in the fifth century. The dead man on the left, strong and splendidly made, is gazed at by his old and sorrowing father whose grief is wholly unconcealed. A little boy sits weeping at the feet of the great athlete; even the hunting dog's sorrow is shown. The deep-set eyes of son and father, and the whole air of emotional intensity, are in the manner of Scopas: so, too, is the dramatic story told us in this marble relief.

With Lysippus of Sicyon (*floruit* 328 B.C.) we reach the last phase of Classical, as opposed to Hellenistic, sculpture; and we are lucky to be able to see an original, or at least a contemporary copy in marble of a bronze original, in his athlete Agias at Delphi. This is a portrait and a fine one. The face, with the characteristic treatment of the eyes that we owe to Scopas, shows that Lysippus valued the new technique and was not afraid to use it; while the nude body of the athlete, in the general Peloponnesian tradition systematized by Polyclitus, is a marked improvement on it. The figure is lighter, but, so far from losing strength, gains agility as well; the head is markedly smaller. The Apoxyomenos, an athlete using a strigil, a Roman copy in the Vatican Museum, is useful to demonstrate the immensity of difference between a good contemporary Greek copy and a later, Roman one. Agias is a live personality, handsome and interesting: the Apoxyomenos is a mere male at his toilet. Alexander the Great chose Lysippus as chief sculptor of his portraits. It is held by E. A. Gardner that the head of Alexander in the British Museum may be an original. The deep eyes, especially deep at the inner corners and shaded at the outer by the heavy rolls of a beetling brow, together with an expression of the character and spirit of Alexander, place the head in a high class. Portraiture was now an accepted aim, and, after Lysippus' time, there was a large production of portraits, many of which are in the National Museum.

The marks of Hellenistic sculpture (since one must here reduce the vast range of it to a brief generalization) are technical precision, with the ability to contort the human form into the most complicated postures of battle, struggle, life and death; and an urge to tell a story, rather than present an idea or an ideal. Much of the work is clever and accurate; not much is inspiring. Some of it—exceptionally—is extremely beautiful. The Venus of Milo requires no champion. That she is for sale in cheap snow-white plaster copies in miniature at every souvenir stall may be her misfortune, for it makes us careless of her beauty, but is no condemnation of it. Let the doubter see her in the Louvre, and he will bless the unknown admirer who long ago hid her safely in a grotto concealed behind a terrace wall on the slopes below a village in the hills of Melos. Here she was safe from the lime-kilns, and unknown until in 1820 a peasant found her. (*See p.* 202).

The splendid Winged Victory of Samothrace (*c.* 306 B.C.), also in the Louvre, has already been mentioned with enthusiasm (page 216), though it may now be added that to compare her with the Victory of Paeonius (425 B.C.) in the Olympia Museum may be rewarding. For the latter is seen coming in so quietly and lightly to her landing, while the first stands firm and strong in great nobility and grandeur—though the critical eye may see cause for grave doubts as to her ability to become airborne at any time.

Mention must be made of one Hellenistic bronze which excites and pleases every visitor to the National Museum—the Boy Jockey. He, and fragments of his horse, were fished out of the sea: the horse is still being reconstructed in the workshop of the Museum. The jockey is a small boy of light build but wiry. He bends low over his mount which must be at full gallop, and uses his whip to aid his strong will to win. Tension and effort and speed, and exhilaration in all these, are wonderfully conveyed in a composition which wholly satisfies. Mere realism? Yes, there is realism; but there is also artistry of a high order in the choice of the right moment and the right posture in which to hold the galloping and delightful child, for his earnestness to do his best is pure joy to see.

CHAPTER XXXI

Sorting Out the Vases

Every museum in Greece has its collection of vases, and on most of the ancient sites sherds show up on the ground as common as daisies on an untended lawn. At Ephesus or Delos one could fill a wheelbarrow in ten minutes with fragments of roof-tiles and domestic pots lying on the surface of the fields adjacent to the excavated areas of the sites; and that is in fact what teams of Turkish women may be seen doing at Ephesus before the planting of the young tobacco plants. The reason for this superabundance is, of course, the long life of many cities—Troy for instance was inhabited for two and a half millennia—coupled with the virtual indestructibility of baked clay. But the vases in the museums come chiefly from tombs, for the Greeks both in their own homeland and in their colonies overseas always placed a variety of vases with the dead in their tombs. Cemeteries in Etruria, first discovered in 1828, have produced thousands of beautiful vases, many of them unbroken because these tombs are often cut out of rock. Air-photography has shown the existence of hundreds of unsuspected tombs now being examined. The technique is mechanically to bore a hole down through the roof of the tomb which the air-photograph has identified, and to lower through the hole a small camera and flash equipment, worked by remote control. The series of photographs so taken will show whether the tomb is unrifled and excavation worthwhile. These methods are producing a wealth of splendid vases in Etruria of the same types as those in the British Museum's large collection taken from the tombs at Vulci in about 1835.

The importance of Greek vases may be of several kinds, archaeological, historical and aesthetic. To the archaeologist engaged in the excavation of a site the position of pottery sherds in the various strata can be invaluable for dating other objects found in the same context since, by careful study, he can establish a pottery sequence covering the whole history of the site. That cheerful, chattering women at well-heads were apt to let pots come apart in their hands or slip through their fingers and drop to the bottom of the well has made the discovery of a well on an ancient site a rich source of dating evidence, for the pot that fell from her great-grandmother's hands, when she was young and careless, will be at a lower level in the sludge than the beautiful hydria (water-jar) young Leucippe let slip.

The historical value of vases is more obvious. The lines of trade can be followed by noting, for instance, that the pottery of Corinth with its distinctive decoration appears to be influenced by oriental textile patterns, as also is that of Rhodes. Similarly, the large volume of trade between Corinth and Sicily and Italy in the seventh and sixth centuries is shown by the quantities of Corinthian ware found there. Again, Corinthian ware does not appear in Magna Graecia after 520 B.C.: the pottery found is entirely Attic. Athens has become the ceramic centre of Greece, ousting the Corinthian trade. Thasian wine-jars, amphorae with handles stamped with the Thasos trade-mark, have been found in Sardis, Egypt, Sicily and a dozen other places, telling both of trading far and wide and of the excellence of Thasian wine. What may be gathered from literary evidence is solidly confirmed by the evidence of vases.

When we look at the sixth-, fifth- and fourth-century vases of Attica, we are able to see the equivalent of a compendious illustrated book on Greek mythology and social and domestic life. This is of immense interest in many fields. All the colourful and dramatic tales of gods and heroes are there: Achilles and Hector lunge in their last combat before Troy; Dionysus sails across the sea with a fruitful vine wreathed about the mast of his ship; Herakles dumps the Erymanthian boar upon his tormentor, Eurystheus, hiding in a huge wine-jar. We can view the changing scene of everyday life at home, in the street, in the gymnasium or workshop: the customs of marriage, of death and farewell; the armour of soldiers and the rigging of ships; chariots and harness; wrestling and boxing; drinking parties, the dance and musical instruments; drama and the theatre; races and sacrifices—the whole gamut of life in lively and delightful career.

Then there is real pleasure in the beauty of the shapes and forms and fabric of the vases made in such large variety. Some of these shapes will be copied so long as pottery continues, for the Greeks surely reached the perfection of shape attainable, in their best vases—the amphora, the hydria and the kylix—where shape and function are so happily matched. One type of big amphora was chosen, at an early—and ungainly—stage in its development to be the traditional prize in the Panathenaic games. Athena always appears on one side of the vase, and on the other the contest in which the winner had taken part.

The products of Attica swept the field from the sixth to the fourth century, and where a master painter was at work, there is a sureness of line and a delicate handling of the figures and the fall of drapery, combined with the confidence to paint a sweeping curve on a surface, itself curved, which must be the envy of many an artist today. Vase-making and painting is a minor art in the sense that the great majority of vases were for commercial sale for domestic use. But the best of them were, and are, proud possessions. 'To whatever he set his hand, he gave beauty.' This is true of the Greek potter and painter.

A brief outline is given here of some of the main classes of pottery which may be seen in Greek museums.

1. NEOLITHIC PERIOD: 3000–2500 B.C.

In Crete: Hand-made, rough, black pots with irregular patches of brown-red made by firing: decoration, if any, with incised zigzags and other linear patterns.

2. EARLY BRONZE AGE: 2500–2000 B.C.

In Crete: the Early Minoan period. Beautiful vases made of veined limestone and other stones, copying Egyptian technique (seen in the Heraklion Museum): pots with handles and long, up-raised beaked spouts, consciously bird-like and having eyes indicated: simple linear designs in red paint on the buff surfaces.

3. MIDDLE BRONZE AGE: 2000–1600 B.C.

In Crete: the Middle Minoan period—the Old Palaces: early Kamares style with polychrome decoration of light colour on

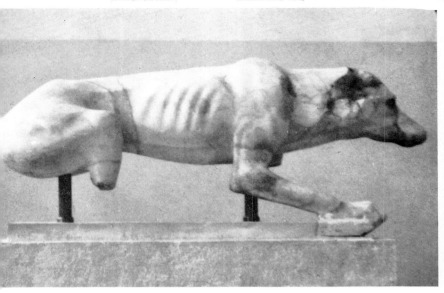

IN THE ACROPOLIS MUSEUM AT ATHENS: ARCHAIC HUNTING-DOG
(520–500 B.C.)
The early sculptor has brilliantly portrayed the intense concentration of a hound stealing up on his quarry.

AN EARLY SIXTH CENTURY METOPE FROM THE SICYONIAN TREASURY
AT DELPHI
With the minimum of distracting detail the sculptor has conveyed the boar's muscular power and energy under the taut hard hide.

ACANTHUS
The shapely leaves of acanthus supply the c[ ] decorative feature of capital of the Corinth[ ] Order.

ASPHODEL
A white flower with a pink tinge; disappointing as the chief flower of the Elysian fields.

dark background—red, orange, white on black. Some pots decorated in barbotine (small raised spots of clay applied to the surface). Crude designs of fish and other naturalistic subjects: spouts still beaked. In the full Kamares development, patterns are bold, large and well-drawn, continuous spirals, stylized plants, leaves, flowers: shapes of vases and composition of pattern of highest order, and fabric often of eggshell thinness: Between 1700 and 1600 B.C. the building of the New Palaces in Crete begins.

In Troy: Minyan ware, a new pottery style imitating metal vessels, is introduced: plain grey pots with incised linear decoration.

In Greece: the Middle Helladic period. Grey or yellow Minyan ware was in use over most parts of mainland Greece.

4. LATE BRONZE AGE 1600–1100 B.C.

In Crete: the Late Minoan I and II periods: 1600–1400 B.C.: The New Palaces. A change from light on dark decoration to dark on light: a fine naturalism in design: well-drawn palm-trees, spirals with emphatic 'eyes', grasses, olive branches, papyrus, lilies, and later on, octopuses and marine motifs. A tall beaked jug from Phaestos with shapely up-raised spout and entirely covered with a pattern of interlacing grasses—one of the most beautiful vases in the Heraklion Museum. Parallel with the above in Crete, but dated 1500 B.C. is a series of remarkable stone vases of black steatite, of which the Chieftain's cup, the Harvester vase and a conical-shaped vase are the best representatives: all come from Hagia Triada: they are carved with figures of men engaged in bull-jumping, boxing, and returning singing from the fields—not to be missed in the Heraklion Museum. In the Late Minoan II period, large, well-made amphorae of beautiful shapes with more stylized decoration found at Knossos: named by Sir Arthur Evans the 'Palace style'. Vases of a similar style found on mainland sites.

Late Minoan III period: 1400–1100 B.C.: After fall of Knossos, definite falling-off of style of decoration.

In Greece: the Late Helladic or Mycenaean period: 1600–1100 B.C. (The period 1600 to 1400 B.C. reveals increasing contact between the two great cultures, Minoan and Mycenaean, culminating in the last phase before the fall of Knossos in the use of a similar pottery style at Knossos and the Mycenaean sites on the mainland.)

Development of the Mycenaean style, showing at first a fusion of Minoan and Mycenaean skills: fine vase shapes and elegant, restrained representation of flower and plant forms but becoming rapidly more formal and stylized, sometimes reverting to simple linear patterns: designs appear in panels and, rarely, human figures introduced. These well-made vases (but with steadily deteriorating designs) become more or less uniform in Mycenaean centres in the mainland and were widely exported throughout the Mediterranean area—to Italy, Sicily, Egypt, Syria, Troy until the collapse of the Mycenaean empire, and the Dark Ages. The warrior vase (Nat. Mus. Ath.) is outstanding.

5. THE GEOMETRIC PERIOD 900–700 B.C.

The Attic School emerges as the most important. In the National Museum at Athens, the Dipylon vases, up to four feet in height, show this style in its noblest form. They were placed over graves: through holes in the base libations to the dead below could be poured. The decoration is in bands of every conceivable geometric pattern—swastikas, zigzags, cubes and dots, meanders, keys, etc.; some vases are decorated only with a fine ring pattern, closely spaced, in red on the light-coloured clay: others introduce human figures in their simplest form—almost a 'match-stick' drawing; some show the body of the dead man on a bier on a chariot drawn by horses; men carry the figure-of-eight shield; sometimes a row of birds forms a band of decoration. Though the drawing is primitive, the total effect of the Geometric style is masterly, and the texture of the design and the shape of the vases extraordinarily effective.

6. THE ORIENTALIZING PERIOD 700–575 B.C.

Corinth and Rhodes are the main centres and exporting widely. Both show the influence of Eastern patterns. The clay is of a characteristic greenish-grey colour: the decoration in bands, of animals well drawn and painted, sometimes in procession round the vase, at other times heraldically arranged. Among the many animals are lions, goats, deer and dogs; birds, too, are in procession. Some animals are imaginary creatures, winged and unlikely. The background is filled with rosettes, palmettes, lotus, almost any shape to fill the empty space. Rhodian vases of the period show Eastern influences of textiles and carpets in filling the background, and in arranging the animals in procession or heraldically; but their animal drawing is lively and the Rhodian artists were careful not to crowd their design, to do which appears an objective of the Corinthian painter. Wild goats are a favourite and delightful theme. The colours used on the light slip in both Corinthian and Rhodian ware are black and a purple-red, with a little white: incised lines, last used a thousand or more years previously, return, but for a new purpose—to emphasize lines and detail within the painted figure. Human beings at the close of the period become more common in vase decoration, and scenes from mythology begin to appear.

7. ATTIC BLACK-FIGURE PERIOD 600–490 B.C.
Leading potters and painters signing vases—
AMASIS—EXEKIAS—NICOSTHENES

In this period, Attic pottery wins a monopoly: it is the high point of the Greek Vase for many people though others may prefer the earlier phase of the next period. In the black-figure style, the subject is painted in black silhouette, with incised lines to give detail inside the figure. White is used for the face, arms and feet of women, and for the beards of old men. Purple, too, is used for detail such as hair and beards of younger men. The designs are often taken from mythology and the heroic legends. The red-buff colour of the clay is the background of one class of these black-figure vases. But the alternative is equally common: in this, the whole of the vase is painted black—a lustrous black which is itself a fine decoration—except for a panel on either side of the vase handles which is left red: on these panels the black silhouette is composed, and the designs fit their frames to perfection. Self-confidence, vigour, accuracy of necessary detail, a sureness of when to stop—'nothing in excess'—mark these black-figure vase paintings.

8. ATTIC RED-FIGURE PERIOD 525–400 B.C.
Leading potters and painters signing vases—
ANDOCIDES (BF and RF)*—EPICTETUS*
EUPHRONIOS—DOURIS—BRYGOS—MIDIAS

This period begins with a transition to a new style: a Kylix may have black figures on the outside, but in the inside a new type of decoration: on the red clay the figures were first outlined with a pointed tool, then a thin line of black paint was laid on outside this outline, leaving a red figure on which the details could then be painted in. Finally the whole vase outside the red figures was painted black. This technique allows a much greater freedom and expressiveness: it is true painting as opposed to the incision of detail in the old style. The figures can now show more of the contours of the living form, and the stiff archaic, but always dignified figures of the black-figure style give place to well-painted scenes, usually of ordinary domestic and social life, though the legends of gods and heroes are still popular. White and purple-red and very occasional touches of gold are used for detail.

Parallel with this red-figure style is a class of white-background vases, mostly lekythoi, used chiefly for sepulchral purposes. More colours are used, not lustrous, but matt—yellow, red, black and gold, as well as some green and blue. Towards the end of this red-figure period, the standard of composition falls off: figures are out of scale with the vase; they are too big, over-crowded and the decoration too ornate.

9. Period of Decline: Fourth Century

The painter forgets that it is a vase he is painting, and that the design must be composed to suit the shape. He is merely painting pictures on a curved surface, attempting elaborate scenes with far too many figures in them and raising above the base line those of his figures which he intends to be thought of as further away than others—a poor sort of perspective and never effective on a vase. The use of gold and white is overdone, and the total effect tends, in the majority of such vases, to look more like an over-all pattern than the picture intended.

10. Hellenistic Period

There is a complete change. Decoration in relief, either moulded or applied, is now the fashion, in imitation of metal work on bowls, jugs and other vessels. A black glaze is applied to the surface, sometimes fired to a reddish colour. This type of decoration is the forerunner of the Roman pottery style.

GLOSSARY OF TECHNICAL TERMS

ABACUS: the square stone slab which is the top element of the capital of a column, on which rests the horizontal beam of the architrave.

ACROPOLIS: the hill-top, fortified with walls and giving protection to the temple of the patron deity and, in early times, to the king's palace and the treasure, which was the nucleus of an early community living outside the walls but in a crisis sheltering inside them.

ACROTERION: the sculptured figure, tripod, disc or urn, of marble or terracotta, placed on the apex of the pediment of a Greek temple or other substantial building; sometimes also above the outer angles of the pediment triangle.

AGORA: conventionally the 'market-place' or 'city-centre': here were sited the shopping and commercial facilities and the main public buildings: the accepted open space where the citizens would gather.

ALTIS: the walled enclosure of the sanctuary of Zeus at Olympia.

AMBO: the raised pulpit in a Byzantine or Orthodox Christian Church.

AMPHICTIONY: an association of neighbouring city-states for joint supervision of some religious institution, such as the Delphic Oracle, or the temple of Poseidon in Calauria (of equal concern to the seamen of several cities on the Saronic Gulf).

AMPHORA: a two-handled vessel with a narrow neck, either of pottery or bronze, used domestically to hold wine or oil; often beautifully painted and provided with a proper foot: also the standard large two-handled wine or oil containers of commerce and export, coarse, unpainted and often with a pointed base for easy storage when worked into an earth floor.

ANAKTORON: strictly, the 'house of the king or queen': used at Eleusis for the original small house of Demeter of which the site at least was preserved inside all later enlargements of the Hall of Initiation.

Glossary of Technical Terms

ANNULI: the necking-rings cut into the lower part of the echinus in the Doric order: also grooves sometimes found cut into the top drum of a Doric column, concealing the joining of shaft and capital.

ANTA: the end of a wall of a building if it projects and is architecturally treated.

APSE: the semicircular recess in the short end wall of the long basilica or Roman law-court in which was the dais for the tribunal. When early Christians built churches on the basilica plan, the seats of the Elders were ranged round the apse to the east of the altar. cf. The early Christian Church at Delos.

ARCADE: a run of wall pierced by arches.

ARCHAIC PERIOD: from 700 B.C. to the end of the Persian Wars in the early fifth century B.C.

ARCHITRAVE: the lintel of stone or wood running horizontally over a doorway, or the whole horizontal beam-line of stones resting on the columns and their capitals.

ARCHON: strictly, 'one who rules': one of the chief magistrates of Athens, and in certain other city-states.

ARRIS: the sharp edge formed, for instance, at the meeting point of two flutes in the Doric column, a vulnerable feature of the Order, rectified in the Ionic by the substitution of a flat narrow fillet between the flutes.

ARTEMISION: a temple of Artemis, especially used of her temple at Ephesus: also of Cape Artemision, the northern point of the island of Euboea.

ASHLAR: applied to masonry, of squared hewn stone.

ATRIUM: literally, the 'place made black by the smoke' (of the altar) in a Roman house: the central feature of a Roman house, a small court open to the sky, colonnaded, four or more columns supporting the roof, and rooms opening on to the colonnade. Here stood the altar to the household gods and the death-masks of ancestors. There are many fine atria in the Roman houses of Delos, with mosaic designs on the tank-tops (impluvia) on to which fell rain through the openings above (compluvia).

BALLISTA: essentially, a colossal catapult: a war machine used in sieges by the Romans and made up of a framework in which twisted tendons, rope or leather thongs provided elasticity and force. When the twist was suddenly released, a stone of up to 100 lbs. in weight could be thrown a considerable distance to batter a wall.

BAPTISTERY: the place, usually a separate room entered from one of the aisles of an early Christian church, in which a pool of water provided with steps down into it, was used for the baptism of adult converts by immersion, e.g. in the Twin Churches of St. Mary at Ephesus, in the Church of the Hundred Windows at Paros, or at Philerimos in Rhodes.

BASILICA: see 'Apse'.

BAS-RELIEF: sculpture on the surface of a slab in low relief, e.g. the Parthenon frieze.

BEMA: the rostrum of a public speaker, e.g. in the agora at Corinth.

BOULEUTERION: a council chamber.

BOUSTROPHEDON: an archaic method of writing, found on some inscriptions, for instance in Gortyna in Crete, where the code of laws is written not in lines from left to right, but as an ox turns with the plough at the end of the furrow and having gone from left to right, returns from right to left.

CAIQUE: the small trading vessel, wooden, brightly painted and rigged for sail but usually today propelled by an engine, which adds colour and charm to every Greek waterfront **and** every passage in the Aegean Sea.

CAPITAL: the top element of a column above the drums or monolithic shaft: the three great Orders are the Doric, Ionic and Corinthian.

CARYATID: the sculptured figure of a woman acting in place of a column and supporting an architrave, e.g. in the porch of the archaic Siphnian Treasury at Delphi, or the Erechtheum at Athens (and St. Pancras' Church, London).

CATECHUMEN: in the early Church, one undergoing instruction prior to baptism.

CATHEDRA: the throne of a bishop in the early Church in the apse behind the high altar, e.g. at Paros, or—a unique survival in England—at Norwich Cathedral.

CAVEA: the auditorium of a theatre usually, in Greek practice, in the hollow of a hillside. The Romans, aided by their wealth and their development of the arch and vault, usually built up theatres on arches and vaults precisely where they wanted them.

Glossary of Technical Terms

CELLA: the great hall of a temple in which stood the generally colossal cult-statue of the deity.

CENTAURS: mythical Greek creatures, half-man, half-horse, living in Thessaly, of uncouth and libidinous habits, e.g. in the sculpture of the west pediment of the temple of Zeus at Olympia (Museum) they represent the forces of barbarism, lawlessness and uninhibited passion, despised by the Greek mind.

CHIMAERA: a fire-breathing monster with a lion's head and dragon's after-quarters with the mid-ship section of a goat: allegedly once a visitant to Lycia in Asia Minor: often used as a decorative design on vases of Rhodes and of Corinth whose trading connections with the East gave them familiarity with oriental decorative motifs.

CHITON: a garment of linen or wool worn next to the skin by women and by men. In the Ionian style the chiton was made of fine linen and fastened on the shoulders and down the upper arms to form sleeves; it was held at the waist by a girdle whence it fell in close folds to the feet. The Charioteer at Delphi wears a chiton. About 470 B.C., according to Thucydides, Athenian men gave up the Ionian chiton and adopted the more practical Dorian style, which was short, made of wool and fastened at the shoulders (sometimes on the left shoulder only, leaving the right bare). Spartan girls wore this garment.

Over the chiton women wore the himation, a cloak of wool, often coloured or with a coloured border, arranged in a variety of ways but frequently draped over the left shoulder and about the body, leaving the right arm free (e.g. the Korai in the Acropolis Museum, who wear Ionic chiton and himation).

The Dorian peplos is shown on Attic black-figure vases as worn by women over the chiton and appears to have been patterned or embroidered (see the *Peplos kore* in the Acropolis Museum). The peplos was rectangular in shape, of wool or linen, sleeveless, pinned on each shoulder and, in Classical times, very full, the material being twice as wide as the distance between the wearer's outstretched elbows. Spartan women wore this dress open down the right side; others sewed it up as far as the waist. The special feature of the peplos was the deep fold hanging free from neck to waist. Beneath the edge of this fold the garment was held in to the waist by a girdle

298

over which it was pulled and draped; below the waist the peplos fell in full wide folds to the feet (c.f. the Caryatids at the Erechtheum). Every four years the women of Athens presented to Athena a richly embroidered peplos which was carried as a sail on a ship as the central feature of the Panathenaic procession to the Acropolis, the rectangular shape of the peplos making this possible.

CHRYSELEPHANTINE: of a statue built up on a wooden core and covered with plates of gold—for the clothing—and of ivory—for the uncovered parts of the body. e.g. the Zeus at Olympia, and the cult-statue of Athena in the Parthenon.

CHTHONIAN: literally 'belonging to the earth' and used to describe a god or goddess of the earth, by which is meant the divine creative force, and source of fertility in the crops, the animals and in Man, thought in early times to be the gift of earth deities: also of underground deities connected with death. Belief in the Olympian gods, under the sky-god Zeus, succeeded the old belief in chthonian powers.

CLASSICAL PERIOD: from the Persian Wars to the unification of Greece under Philip II and the world empire of Alexander the Great.

COFFER: the marble ceilings of important Greek and Roman buildings were patterned and lightened by rows of sunk panels in their surface. e.g. the coffered ceilings of the Propylaea on the Acropolis at Athens.

COMPOSITE ORDER: of architecture: a combination of the Corinthian capital's rows of acanthus leaves with the volutes, slightly reduced in size, of the Ionic Order: a late development, seen at Pergamum and Ephesus and used, for instance, on the façade of Somerset House, London.

CORNICE: the upper part of the horizontal entablature in a Classical building which projects over the face of the building and throws off the rain.

CULT STATUE: the statue of a god or goddess: to house this in great dignity was the purpose of a temple. Often it was more than life-size, i.e. 'colossal'.

CYCLOPEAN: applied to a wall constructed, not of ashlar masonry however big the blocks, but of large boulders of a size which called for giants to handle them, and with interstices filled up with small stones. Early Mycenaean walls, at

Glossary of Technical Terms

Mycenae, Tiryns, and also here and there on the Acropolis at Athens, were Cyclopean.

DENTILS: the line of teeth-like blocks of stone, suggesting the rafter ends of a flat roof, under the cornice of a building of Ionic or Corinthian Order.

DEUS EX MACHINA: the sudden appearance, towards the end of a dramatic performance in the theatre, of a god, high up on the façade of the scene-building (perhaps achieved by the use of a crane or moving platform) who gave to mortals the solution of some humanly insoluble problem: this practice has given rise to the proverbial expression of unexpected aid on a big scale.

DIOLCHOS: literally, the 'drag(way) across', i.e. for the portage of ships across the Isthmus of Corinth: (see 'Corinth Canal' in text), invented by Periander in the seventh century B.C.: ships were hauled on a carriage running in grooves cut on a stone track across the Isthmus, thus avoiding the danger of the long haul round the southern promontories of the Peloponnese.

DORIC ORDER: the typical architectural Order of the best period in Greece, and the oldest and least complicated.

DROMOS: the long horizontal passage, bordered by stone walls, cut into a small hill and giving access to a tholos, or beehive tomb, in the hill in Mycenaean Greece.

ECCLESIA: the assembly of the whole male citizen body which gave its decisive vote on policies put before it by the Boule or Council at Athens: later, the Christian Church.

ECHINUS: the element of the Doric Order, convex in form and circular, between the column and the square abacus above: from Archaic to Roman times the size and curvature was gradually reduced till the convexity (as seen in profile) gave way to a straight line: a useful factor in dating a building in the Doric Order.

ENGAGED COLUMN: a half-column (divided longitudinally), standing out on the surface of a wall.

ENTABLATURE: a term to cover all the horizontal stone-work resting on a row of columns including the architrave (the lowest member), the frieze and the cornice at the top.

ENTASIS: the slight swelling of a column so that the eye sees it as straight-sided and freed of the optical illusion which in

Glossary of Technical Terms

bright light would give it the appearance of being slightly narrower half-way up its length.

EXEDRA: the curved marble wall, often used as a base for one or more statues, and provided with a marble bench which offered dignified and sheltered casual seating in public places.

FILLET: a flat and narrow moulding on the surface of a wall, or between the flutes of an Ionic or Corinthian column.

FLUTES: the vertical hollows cut into the sides of a column which emphasized its rotundity—a device necessary in the brilliant sunlight falling on white marble—and which took off glare from the marble by the easy gradations of light thereby reflected from it.

FOUNTAIN-HOUSE: a water supply for domestic purposes was centralized in public fountain-houses throughout a city where numbers of people could be supplied at one time: they could be highly decorative with a Doric or Ionic façade and lions-head water-spouts: the beautiful fountain-house of Peirene at Corinth, or that at Olympia, both given by Herodes Atticus, are examples of Roman date.

FRIEZE: a band of alternating triglyphs and metopes, the central element of a Doric entablature: also a continuous band of bas-relief sculpture on an Ionic entablature, e.g. the temple of Nike on the Acropolis at Athens. (Part of the Ionic frieze, incorporated in the Doric Parthenon, is still visible inside the colonnade on the west end.)

GEOMETRIC PERIOD: of the post-Mycenaean period when, with the Dorian invasions, the Iron Age was fully established throughout Greece and the country had settled again after a grim period of turmoil and population movement. A sub-Mycenaean, followed by a proto-Geometric period, are transitional to the Geometric period proper, which in Athens runs from about 900 B.C. to 700 B.C. The period is characterized by its well-shaped pottery, decorated with horizontal bands of geometric patterns, later incorporating animal and human figures.

GUTTAE: literally 'drops': referring to the six stone droplets below the marble or stone triglyph in the Doric Order and reminiscent of the wooden pegs which (in the earlier period of timber construction) kept in position a cover-plate of terra-cotta to protect timber rafter-ends from the weather.

Glossary of Technical Terms

GYMNASIUM: physical education loomed large in the Greek curriculum, and the gymnasia were provided with spacious courts for exercise and games and with good washing room: there were stone benches for the sedentary school periods, e.g. at Delos.

HELLADIC PERIOD: applied to the Bronze Age civilization of the Greek mainland: as Cycladic refers to that of the islands, Melos and others in the Cyclades. The period corresponds roughly with that of the Minoan civilization in Crete and, like it, is sub-divided into Early, Middle and Late periods. It was during the Late Helladic period that the Mycenaean civilization developed, first at Mycenae, then at other centres in Greece and spreading throughout the Aegean.

HELLENISTIC PERIOD: conventionally, from Alexander the Great to the time of Augustus and the Roman Empire, i.e. 300 B.C. to 30 B.C.

HELLANODIKAI: Judges and directors at the Olympic and Nemean Games.

HELOTS: the original inhabitants of Laconia and Messenia, enslaved by the Dorian Spartans after the conquest of these territories.

HERM: a square-section pillar, tapering out from ground level, about five or six feet high and surmounted by the sculptured head of Hermes, bearded in the fifth century B.C.: they were set up in cities in large numbers as boundary marks, and also outside houses and temples, and were treated as sacred, e.g. in Delos, at the entrance to the Sanctuary of Apollo.

HIERON: the 'sacred place', either of the buildings and the temple itself, or of the whole enclosure (temenos).

HIPPODROME: the course for horse and chariot racing, which had to be much larger than the stadium for athletics: at Delphi, in the Pythian Games, the chariot race was held on the plain below the sanctuary.

HOMERIC HYMNS: songs in praise of gods, e.g. the Hymn to Apollo: not composed by Homer or even belonging to his time, but carefully written in the Homeric epic style by a later poet or poets, perhaps of the seventh or sixth centuries.

HYDRIA: a large full-bodied Greek vase in which to carry water from the fountain-house: provided with three handles, a

Glossary of Technical Terms

vertical one at the back for easy pouring and for carriage when empty, and two horizontal ones at the sides for lifting when the jar is full.

ICONASTASIS: the tall continuous screen in an Orthodox church which cuts off the sanctuary with the altar from the nave and, usually, from the sight of the people until the central door is opened at the crisis of the Eucharist: ikons of Our Lord, the Holy Mother, the patron saint of the church and of others are set up on the iconastasis, as its name states, and are used as an avenue to worship.

IMPLUVIUM: the tank to receive the rain which fell through the open centre of a Roman house (the compluvium): at Delos the shallow impluvia, decorated with mosaic, are in fact only the tops of tanks cut deep in the rock below.

IONIC ORDER: of architecture: a development, perhaps originating in Aeolia in north-west Asia Minor: an Order more decorative and elaborate than the pure, austere and earlier Doric: its columns have bases, ornamented with a variety of mouldings, and are more slender, with deeper flutes and no sharp and vulnerable edges as in the Doric Order: the capital has a pair of spiral volutes extending out on either side, front and back, over a ring of egg-and-tongue moulding round the top of the column: there are no triglyphs.

KORE, KORAI, KOUROS, KOUROI: conventionally applied to the clothed female and the nude male sculptured figures of the Archaic, pre-Persian War, period: they stand erect with the weight distributed between the feet, of which the left is slightly forward, but no motion is suggested; on their faces the 'archaic smile'. The best of these beautiful korai, or maidens, are in the Acropolis Museum at Athens, and of the male figures in the National Museum, where the steady progress of the sculptor's art from the purely static figure to the dynamic is readily seen and enjoyed.

LABRYS: a double-axe, i.e. with two blades facing right and left: a religious symbol in the Minoan period, carved on pillars and found in great numbers in miniature as votives in sanctuaries, and in more than life-size form as religious furniture.

LABYRINTH: double-axes (see Labrys above) were numerous as religious symbols at Knossos in the Minoan palace: the palace was a most elaborate complex of rooms, passages and staircases: hence the 'place of the double-axes' gained its second and commoner meaning.

LAPITHS: a mythical people in Thessaly who, under King Pirithous, fought and conquered the Centaurs. This conflict was used frequently, as in the metopes of the Parthenon, to represent the triumph of civilization over barbarism, of Greeks over Persians.

MEGARON: the central feature of a Mycenaean house or palace: the great room containing a large central hearth.

MELTEMI: the strong north-east wind of the Aegean, apt to rise quickly in the summer months from June onwards.

METOPE: the plain panel, alternating with the decorated cover-plate for the roof beam-ends (the triglyph) in the Doric frieze. In Classical times a sculptured relief decorated the plain space, the series of metopes round the temple illustrating a single theme, e.g. Greeks versus Amazons, Lapiths versus Centaurs, or the Labours of Herakles (as seen in the Olympia Museum).

METROON: sanctuary of the Mother of the Gods.

MINOAN: referring to the Bronze Age civilization of Crete: Sir Arthur Evans adapted the name of the legendary King Minos of Crete to this civilization when he discovered and excavated the king's palace at Knossos.

MINYAN: the name of one of the Bronze Age peoples of mainland Greece: Orchomenos was a main centre of the Minyans and from Schliemann's discovery on this site was named the fine, smooth, grey-coloured pottery, made on the wheel, found widely from about 2000 B.C. from Thessaly and Macedonia to the Argolid and considerably at Troy.

MYCENAEAN: from Mycenae, the principal centre of the earliest Greek-speaking people in the late Bronze Age. This civilization, at first limited to mainland sites, spread throughout Greece and across the Aegean after the fall of the Minoan empire; it collapsed only after the capture of Troy by the Mycenaeans when their return to Greece was soon followed by the destruction of their fortress centres at the hands of the Dorians, another Greek-speaking people who entered through Northern Greece, armed with iron weapons, and tools.

NARTHEX: the long and comparatively narrow vestibule of an early Christian church which stretched along the whole width of the church at the west end: often adorned with mosaics or frescoes: three doors opened from the narthex into the church proper and, when open, enabled catechumens and penitents (whose place was in the narthex) at least to hear the service.

NIKE: goddess of victory, portrayed in Greek art as a winged figure descending to award victory. The earliest Nike statue was found in Delos. The most famous are the winged Victory of Paeonius (Olympia Museum) dated 425 B.C., and the Victory of Samothrace (Louvre) (about 320 B.C.).

(EARLY) NEOLITHIC PERIOD: Professor John Evans by his recent excavation to the rock, twenty-three feet below the Minoan levels of the Palace of Minos at Knossos, has put back the date of the earliest known human settlement in Greece to about 6100 B.C., a date derived from the 'radio carbon 14' test on burnt grain found on a primitive camp-site.

(MIDDLE) NEOLITHIC PERIOD: Belonging to a period 1,000 years later, at the top of fifteen feet of accumulated soil deposit, Professor Evans found another settlement whose people could spin and weave. A charcoal sample submitted to the same test gave a date 5050 B.C.

(LATE) NEOLITHIC PERIOD: Three other groups of Neolithic settlers have left traces of their homes, habits and craft in many parts of Greece and the Aegean:

(a) the seafarers, probably from the coasts of Asia Minor who settled in Cyprus, in Crete and its islets and in the Cyclades about 3000 B.C. The Minoans who arrived in Crete about 500 years later were probably akin to the earlier settlers.

(b) a group who preferred the climate of central and northern Greece to the hotter South and presumably came from the cooler upland hinterland of Asia Minor. They settled in numerous places in the plains of Thessaly and Boeotia, but, when branching out, sent their folk North and West, for instance to the cooler regions of Servia and Dodona. This group made good quality pottery and statuettes of its goddess, as did group (a), and built its small rectangular houses of sun-baked brick with stone foundations and with stone lower courses.

(c) a third group appear to have come from the far forest-covered North: to begin with they are hunters, unlike the

Glossary of Technical Terms

pastoral and agricultural groups (*a*) and (*b*). The stone axe is a common tool, to be expected of a people accustomed to forests. When they settled, they built houses with a porch with tree-trunk pillars on a plan which was to be used in Mycenaean and Classical times, and is known as the 'megaron'. But despite this advance in house design, their pottery is crude. They built walls round their villages, e.g. at Sesklo in Thessaly.

Professor N. G. L. Hammond, to whose new *History of Greece to 322 B.C.* this note is largely indebted, points out an interesting contrast between the first two groups and the third: the steatopygous figures, made by groups (*a*) and (*b*) represent belief in a goddess of fertility; while the phallus made in clay by the third group indicates a distinctly masculine view of the sources of life and power.

OBSIDIAN: a dark glass-like mineral rock produced by volcanic action, which takes and keeps a good cutting edge: found at Melos and exported widely over the Eastern Mediterranean area: a source of wealth to Melos in neolithic times until the smelting of metals ousted obsidian for cutting purposes.

ODEUM: a small building in form and plan like a theatre with semicircular seating. Some were roofed. Chiefly used for musical contests and concerts and other meetings. Pericles built an odeum at Athens, the roof of which was carried on many pillars, as Plutarch says. Herodes Atticus presented a large odeum to Athens which is used, with new seating, for Greek Drama festivals to-day. cf. a beautiful odeum at Ephesus.

OPISTHODOMOS: literally, 'the room at the back', i.e. of a Classical Greek temple: used often as a large safe deposit, when the porch would doubtless be fitted with a strong metal grille, as in the temple of Athena Aphaia in Aegina: usually no communication between the cella and the opisthodomos.

ORCHESTRA: the large circular space for the dancing of the chorus in a Greek theatre, with an altar of Dionysus in the centre: it is similar to the circular threshing-floor still seen commonly in rural Greece; for the threshing-floor, when the harvest was in and the grain stored, was the scene of the country dances and thanksgiving, the seed of Greek drama.

Glossary of Technical Terms

ORTHOSTATE: one of a line of large flat squared stones set up on edge, on a projecting base, which protected from rain-splash and other damage the lowest few feet of a wall made of sun-baked brick with timber beams for strengthening: used in all the major Minoan buildings and seen in the Temple of Hera at Olympia, built 1,000 years later; and still seen in rural buildings in Greece. In Classical times, and in stone or marble buildings, the lowest course continued to be of large stones and was two or three times greater in height than the other courses.

OSTRACISM: from 'ostrakon'—a potsherd used as a voting paper in democratic ancient Athens. The institution of ostracism is said to have been introduced by Cleisthenes as a device to eliminate a likely-looking tyrant before he gained excessive power: first used in 487 B.C. Voting was secret: each citizen scratched on a sherd the name of a citizen he wished to see banished (without loss of property and for ten years). Hundreds of ostraka were found in the Agora excavations. In fact, none of the leading citizens who suffered ostracism look to the historian to have been embryo tyrants. Ostracism was one of the least noble or ennobling of Greek institutions.

PALAIOCASTRO: a common place-name, meaning 'ancient forti-fication walls'.

PALAESTRA: a building smaller than a gymnasium, often built as a colonnade round a central court, for the training of boxers, wrestlers and pancratiasts.

PANCRATION: an 'all-in' contest in the athletic games in which no holds were barred: boxing and wrestling combined, and with only one rule which forbade biting or the gouging out of eyes.

PANTOCRATOR: literally, 'the Almighty', nearly always the subject of a mosaic or fresco dominating from its central position at the height of the dome (inside) every eye which looked upward—as is inevitable on entering a domed build-ing where most of the light comes from the windows of the dome. cf. the famous Pantocrator of Daphni.

PARIAN MARBLE: the marble quarries of the island of Paros produced a white, close-grained marble peculiarly suitable for sculpture: it was widely used by the leading sculptors.

PARODOS: the passage-way on either side of the scene building

Glossary of Technical Terms

and between it and the cavea, for the entry of actors and chorus to the orchestra in a Greek theatre.

PEDIMENT: in the Greek temple, the triangular space at the vertical ends of the ridge roof, and formed by the horizontal cornice and the raking cornices of the roof: pedimental sculpture in the round was fixed in this space, probably against a background painted blue or red.

PELASGIAN: the name in Greek literature for the pre-hellenic peoples who were in the country, chiefly in central and northern Greece, at the time of the immigration of the first true Greeks, about 2000 B.C. The Pelasgians were widely dispersed in these mass movements, and Herodotus mentions pockets of the Pelasgian language surviving to his own day in Chalcidice and near Cyzicus on the Sea of Marmara. The Athenians claimed a Pelasgian ancestry and in doing so believed that they were the autochthonous inhabitants of Attica. The name of their city and goddess is indeed pre-hellenic: more probably, a Pelasgian element survived and was absorbed when Attica was occupied by Greeks in the early immigration. The Dorian invasion had little effect on Athens, which was the only citadel of Mycenaean times to survive.

PENDENTIVE: the curving and overhanging triangles of stone or brickwork which transmit, to four piers below, that part of the weight of a dome which is not carried by the four arches which spring from those piers: in other words, the method of carrying a circular dome on four piers, square-in-plan.

PENTELIC MARBLE: named from its source on the mountain bordering the Attic plain on the north-east: eminently suitable for fine building both in ancient and modern times: all the finer Athenian buildings of Pericles are made of Pentelic marble: the particles of iron in it give it the famous golden tinge of colour.

PEPLOS: a woman's garment, made of wool, long and sleeveless, being fastened on each shoulder with a pin, and having a deep fold hanging free from neck to waist. In the Panathenaic festival every four years a new peplos embroidered by Athenian women was carried in procession to the Acropolis and presented to Athena. (For women's dress see also 'Chiton'.)

PERIBOLOS: the wall of a sanctuary or temenos.

PERISTYLE: the row, or occasionally rows, of columns round a temple.

PINAKOTHEKE: picture gallery, e.g. the north room of the Propylaea on the Acropolis at Athens.

PITHOS: a large earthenware vessel, from four to eight feet high, especially used in Minoan Crete to contain oil, grain, etc.

PODIUM: the top course of the stone foundations of a building if it projects slightly out from the line of the wall: more generally a base.

POLYGONAL: of a wall made of stones with many angles, each stone being shaped and laid to fit tightly with the corresponding angles of its neighbours: an expensive but effective device to reduce the effect of earthquake.

PROPHYLACTIC: literally, 'intended to guard against (evil)': used, for example, of the eyes painted on either side of the handles of a wine-cup.

PROPYLON, PROPYLAEA: the dignified entrance between columns to a sanctuary or an agora or major building within an enclosure: an idea from Minoan architecture adapted by the Mycenaeans and retained in the Classical period.

PROSKENION: the front of the low building which supported the stage in a developed Greek theatre.

PRYTANEUM: the town hall in which a fire was always kept burning on the altar of Hestia, a sign of the city's continuity with its past.

SERAGLIO: the complex of buildings and courtyards which made up the Palace of the Sultan at Istanbul.

SHERDS: fragments of broken pottery.

SIBYL: perhaps originally a single prophetess who wandered from centre to centre: but later we hear of a Sibyl at Delphi, Claros, Dodona, Cumae, etc.: that an early Sibyl was important at Delphi is proved by the preservation of an outcrop or rock, left unworked in its natural state, in the midst of an area of fine building and statues, just because in early times the Sibyl had given her utterances from that improvised platform.

STADIUM: a Greek running-track, providing for spectators by raised earth banks: the stadium was shaped like a hair-pin, one end curved and the other—the starting point—either open as at Athens and Delphi or squared as at Olympia, where a tunnelled entrance survives. In the Roman period, stone seating was normal. Occasionally, as at Nicopolis, a Roman stadium was rounded at both ends. The standard length was 600 feet which gave a straight course for the sprint race of about 200 yards: in the 400-yard race, the runners had to round a post at the far end of the course. The two-grooved starting line is seen at Corinth (in the Agora), Delphi and Olympia; post-holes indicate a separation of the runners at the start. It appears to have been a standing-start, at the drop of a horizontal signal arm at the top of the post.

STEATITE: a stone with a soapy feel and look about it, from the Greek word for tallow: sometimes used in Minoan art for ornamental vases, and covered with gold foil.

STELE: a stone slab set up in a public place, with an inscription recording a victory, treaty or a decree: also a grave-stone. Many beautiful funeral stelai, sculptured in relief, are to be seen in the National Museum, Athens.

STIRRUP-JAR: a pottery vase of strange shape, characteristic of the Mycenaean period: the vase is spheroidal with a narrow foot, but gets its name from the double handle. This is somewhat in the shape of a stirrup and rises on either side of a false, narrow, central spout which is, in fact, a support for the horizontal top of the handle. The actual spout is also narrow and is set forward of the flat-arched handle.

STYLOBATE: the top surface of the stepped platform on which the line of columns stands in a Greek building.

TALENT: In Pericles' time at Athens, we know that the talent was equivalent in value to 6,000 drachmae, and that a normal wage for a week's work was three and a half drachmae.

TELESTERION: a hall of initiation to the Mysteries, for example, at Eleusis (the largest roofed building in Greece).

TEMENOS: the enclosed area in which stood a temple.

TEMPLUM-IN-ANTIS: the simplest form of temple in which 'the house of the god' is the same in plan as the ordinary house: a rectangular room, with the long side walls extended to form the walls of a porch, and with two columns between the antae (or wall endings) to support the porch roof and make a fine entry to the temple. cf. the so-called Treasury of the Athenians at Delphi.

Glossary of Technical Terms

THEATRE: an essential building in every city, to the Greek mind. But drama had its origins not in a theatre but on the village threshing-floor, after the grain was stored and the wine pressed, in the joyful, thanksgiving song and dance in honour of Dionysus, god of fertility and of the vine, in the presence of watching villagers. A dialogue between the leaders of this chorus, or dance, is the germ of Greek drama. Later, close to a temple of Dionysus at Athens a permanent, levelled circular space for the dance, with the god's altar in the centre, was prepared where, in the hollow southern slope of the Acropolis, the citizens could sit on the hillside to watch. There is no stage; but a hut on the edge of the circle, where suitable clothes and ritual gear for the dance could be stored, provided a background on which some painted scene could be set up. Wooden seats were provided for the citizens.

The next step was taken when the actors separated themselves from the chorus and moved to the roof of the 'shed' which thus became a stage. It is not yet certain at what date this move was made. A new and permanent background building was set up with a façade with three doorways in it—the scene-building. As the particular play required, an actor would come on through the centre doorway which might represent the palace of a king, or from a side door to indicate, perhaps, arrival from the country; or entry might be made by one of the parodoi. The cavea was rather more than a semicircle in plan, the curve of the circle near the stage being struck from a centre different from that of the greater part of the semicircle, so as slightly to straighten the wings of the semicircle as they neared the stage. The seating in the cavea was in plan divided into wedge-shaped sections by gangways as radii stretching up and out to the topmost rows. There were thirteen such radial gangways at Epidaurus, doubled in number above a wide, horizontal passage (diazoma—girdle) which ran all round the semicircle, dividing the upper twenty-one tiers from the lower thirty-three. At the top, a high wall enfolded the cavea and no doubt helped acoustically. The front row of seats was reserved at Athens for the priests of the various temples, with the high-priest of Dionysus in the centre. To deal with the quantity of rain-water in this large stone-surfaced catchment, a deep drain was constructed round the orchestra. At Delos this leads to a fine cistern, with its top supported on a long row of arches. The largest theatres in the Greek world were those of Syracuse and Ephesus which held some 20,000 spectators. The theatre at Epidaurus, however, is the best preserved and most beautiful of all: it seated 16,000 people.

THERMAE: the Spartans are believed to have invented the heated sweat-room as a method of removing dirt from the skin, a strigil being used to scrape away the sweat which carried the dust with it out of the pores of the skin. This process was followed by a cold plunge. Cicero refers to this kind of bath as 'Laconicum'. But the Greeks did not go so far as to provide great public buildings for this purpose, merely attaching limited bathing facilities to their gymnasia. The Thermae are a development of the Imperial Roman period, and very large, beautiful and elaborate public bathing centres were built in Rome and in all the major cities of the Empire, and small ones even in some villages. In Ephesus three large Thermae have already been excavated.

The Thermae of Caracalla at Rome cover an area (27 acres) greater than that of the Houses of Parliament. But there were very many others too in Rome in the latest period. In Carcopino's fascinating *Daily Life in Ancient Rome*, he says 'in building the thermae the emperors put personal hygiene on the daily agenda of Rome and within reach of the humblest; and the fabulous decoration lavished on the baths made the care and exercise of the body a pleasure for all, a refreshment accessible even to the very poor'. For, in addition to the actual baths (sweat rooms, hot wash-rooms, cooling-off rooms and cold plunge baths), there were facilities for swimming sports and spectators, gymnastics and sports and games in the modern sense, massage, libraries, gardens, rest-rooms, fountains, sculpture, exhibitions, with shops and refreshments available nearby in the colonnades on the outside of the vast building. The afternoons of Roman citizens were often spent in the Thermae. Mixed bathing was not forbidden till the time of Hadrian. First, games and exercise; then the series of baths; then the relaxation in beautiful surroundings.

THOLOS: a circular building, such as that at Epidaurus, where the circular maze-like foundations can be seen, or at Delphi,

Glossary of Technical Terms

where a Doric tholos has had several fallen columns re-erected: also of the numerous underground beehive tombs of the Mycenaean period, of which the wrongly-styled 'Treasury of Atreus' at Mycenae is the best preserved and finest.

TREASURY: the word used for the well-built, often marble, small buildings, put up by leading city-states at such Pan-hellenic centres as Delphi or Olympia; an Athenian citizen, going to Delphi, for instance, would find an Athenian official on duty in his Treasury to advise him: doubtless festival robes and sacred vessels, etc., for use by representatives would be stored there.

TRIGLYPH: a feature in the frieze of a building in the Doric Order, the three-grooved slab which alternated in the frieze with the metope: originally when buildings were wooden, a terracotta slab to protect rafter-ends from the weather. In the Classical period there was a triglyph over each column and another in each intercolumniation (space between columns). In the Propylaea the architect first dared a span wide enough for two triglyphs in the intercolumniation. This is only usual in Hellenistic times.

TRILOGY: when Greeks went to the theatre to see a tragedy played, they were prepared to sit all day: for the great themes were divided into three plays which were put on in succession, e.g. the drama of Orestes in the plays *Agamemnon*, *Choephoroi*, and *Eumenides*: and the trilogy was concluded, for the relief of tension, with a satyric play.

TRIPOD: Homer writes of bronze tripods—large, three-footed vessels like cauldrons as prizes; Linear B tablets from Knossos show a careful count of these valued objects: in Classical times we hear of their use, beautifully decorated, sometimes even made of gold, as gifts devoted to a god: on the plaster or beaten earth floor of a Mycenaean room, a three-legged vessel (or stand for a large amphora) would find stability more readily. But granted this advantage to a tripod, and the possible explanation of its use as a means of storing wealth in bronze or other metals in negotiable form, the attraction of it to the Greek mind remains a mystery.

TRIREME: the standard warship of the fifth and fourth centuries B.C. which displaced the old penteconter with twenty-five oarsmen a side. The trireme was about 120 feet long overall, with a beam of perhaps twenty feet and a shallow draught. It was of light construction, liable to hog or sag at the extremities and so likely to leak in a seaway that permanent undergirding cables were fitted (if one can judge from the carved relief of the stern quarters of a trireme on the rock-face at Lindos in Rhodes). The bow was fitted with a bronze ram, and a heavy transverse beam projected close to the bow to port and starboard as a fender to protect the 'oar-box' or outrigger which was built out well above the waterline. Steering was by a heavy pivoted steering oar on the overhang of the stern. The vessel was decked only at the bow and stern and, apart from a central catwalk, open amidships. Auxiliary sail was carried, but mast and gear were either put ashore or lowered and stowed on the centre line, for action. Propulsion in battle at least was by trained oarsmen. Speed and power of quick manœuvre so as to turn unexpectedly and break off an enemy's oars, or to ram, was a prime aim. If it might be physically possible to arrange for three tiers of oars in a trireme, or even conceivably four tiers in a quadrireme introduced by the Carthaginians, it is ludicrous to read, as one can, of ships with 'ten banks . . . sixteen banks . . . and even thirty banks of oars.' We do not know how the Greeks managed even the oars of a trireme (the word cannot mean 'with three banks of oars'.) The 'bank' idea is now abandoned. It is thought that perhaps the oarsmen's benches were not transverse, but in plan like a series of sergeants' stripes, making a chevron pattern. Three oarsmen could then sit on each arm of each 'chevron' bench and row through their three small ports. The suggestion made that all three used a single port is not tenable. It is much to be hoped that a sunken trireme may be found, by the new aqua-lung technique, buried in sand. Meanwhile . . . quot homines tot sententiae, i.e. all have ideas, probably all wrong.

VOLUTE: the spiral-patterned element in the capital of the Ionic, Corinthian and composite Orders: derived from the voluted ram's horns, or of Geometrical origin, or perhaps suggested by the perfect natural spiral of the seed-box of one of the commonest Greek clovers.

VOTIVE: the offering to a deity of a terracotta model, often of an animal, seems to have been a device in Mycenaean times to make the donor's prayer more likely to be remembered by the deity: 'my prayer will be effective if it has my name on it'— though never literally. When thanksgiving for a favour from heaven and not petition is the motive, a man, a city, or a general might dedicate a statue or a golden tripod or some valuable object, so that a collection of *objets d'art* was gathered round the temple. In Tinos today there is a picture gallery in which oil-paintings and choice furniture are evidence to the valuable gifts made to God by men. This is fully in line with ancient practice. Little plaques of silver embossed with a leg, eye, ear, heart, arm, etc., are today often attached to an ikon on the iconastasis of a church, and are either thanks-givings or petitions for the recovery of the limb or organ so devoted. A collection of many plaques will ultimately be melted down and will help to cover the whole ikon, the face excluded, with embossed silver.

XOANON: a primitive wooden image, so unlike marble sculpture that it was supposed to have fallen from heaven and was accordingly deeply revered. Such an image (of Athena) was housed in the Erechtheum and dressed in a new robe (peplos) at her great Panathenaic festival every fourth year.

CRETE	CYCLADES

6100–2500 B.C. Numerous settlements in islets off Crete and in Crete, some in caves, but chief settlement at Knossos, deep under Minoan palace levels: here earliest evidence is a camp-site of 6100 B.C. [by 'carbon 14' test of burnt grain].

Settlements, especially at Melos w◦ obsidian as a cutting tool is sourc◦ wealth by export: 'Harpist' sculptur◦

BRONZE A◦

MINOAN CIVILIZATION IN CRETE

2500–2000 B.C. *Early Minoan:* settlement of Minoan peoples from Asia Minor over Crete, especially E. coast and Messara plain. No palaces yet built.

Phylakopi, in Melos, continues flourish as only source of durable cut◦ tools till knowledge of metal smel◦ advances.

2000–1700 B.C. *Middle Minoan I and II: Old Palace period:* great palaces built at Knossos, Phaestos and Mallia: Kamares polychrome pottery, 'light on dark'. All three palaces destroyed by earthquake *c.* 1700 B.C.

1700 B.C. *Middle Minoan III: New Palace period:* the great days of Minoan civilization begin: palace buildings of new architectural style and plan constructed at Knossos, Phaestos and Mallia (substantially those we see); use of colonnades, light-wells and pillared entrance-halls. Knossos is supreme. Houses of Nobility built close round the palace. Linear A Script: faience work. Severe earthquake damage.

Melos now has a Minoan settlem◦ Kamares style pottery from Crete fo◦ in Melos, but Melos develops own s◦ of vases too.
Traces of Linear A script in Melos.

c. 1575 B.C. *Late Minoan I:* much building activity in Crete: palaces repaired. Early frescoes: fine vases with floral and tendril pattern decoration: later marine motives common. Decoration now 'dark on light'. The horse first appears in Crete as also on the mainland: also 'figure of eight' shields, so large and heavy as to suggest use in chariot fighting.

c. 1500 B.C. Earthquake and tidal waves, probably from eruption at Thera, devastate coastal regions, including Mallia, which was abandoned. Knossos damaged but repaired: Phaestos suffered and was not repaired.

1300 B.C. Mycenaeans supplant Min◦ traders in Melos. In the Melian 'Fish◦ men Vase' figures of men make perh◦ first appearance on vase painting (N◦ Mus.).
Delos a Mycenaean centre: car◦ ivories (Delos museum).

c. 1450 B.C. Throne room now built at Knossos: Linear B script, a form of Greek, now in use at Knossos, but not elsewhere in Crete. Rest of Crete at standstill. This is the *Late Minoan II* period (1475–1400 B.C.), of 'Palace style' pottery peculiar to Knossos, and similar to pottery at this period in use in Mycenaean Greek centres on the mainland and elsewhere. It would seem that Mycenaean Greeks are in control at Knossos.

c. 1400 B.C. Sudden destruction of Knossos by fire and probably by sword. The enemy is unknown.

c. 1400–1100 B.C. *Late Minoan III:* palace ruins deserted: gradual fading out of Minoan civilization. At time of Trojan War (*c.* 1250 B.C.) rulers of Crete are Achaeans (Mycenaean Greeks).

Note i: The periodic divisions are chiefly those of pottery styles, and of architectural differences.

Note ii: No Minoan dating scheme is yet acceptable to all scholars. A minority—the Palmer School—reject a Greek ascendancy in the fifteenth century, and place it only in the thirteenth.

THE DORIAN INVASION OF GREECE: IRO◦

1100–900 B.C. A period of chaos and movement o◦ peoples in Greece and the Aegean area◦ the art of writing is lost: wandering◦ bards keep alive the memory of the grea◦ Mycenaean days, ended by the Doria◦ Invasion.
FIRST PHASE OF COLONIZATION

900–700 B.C. GEOMETRI◦
Emergence of aristocratic government◦ in Greece in place of kings: soon to giv◦ way to rule of Tyrants. Simultaneously◦ dissatisfaction grows among the people◦

. TO 2500 B.C.

MAINLAND GREECE	TROY
the plains of Thessaly and Boeotia: numerous sites: also to North,	3000–2500 B.C. First small 'city' of
it to the West of Pindus Range: later, walled villages at Sesklo and	Troy; fortification walls
mini.	protect palace area:
	clear foundations of a
	megaron. Destroyed by
	fire.

500–1100 B.C.

(Neolithic period in Thessaly continues to about 2000 B.C.)	2500–2100 B.C. *Troy II:* fortified acro-
0–1580 B.C. *Middle Helladic period:* First immigration of Greek-speaking peoples from North. Megaron-type houses: Minyan pottery: Mycenae an important centre.	polis: ramp to gateway. Schliemann's gold treasure came from this
0–1100 B.C. *MYCENAEAN (ACHAEAN) CIVILIZATION IN GREECE AND AEGEAN. Late Helladic period:*	city. *Troy III and IV:* mere
Mycenaean I (1580–1500 B.C.). At Mycenae, a powerful dynasty: shaft graves with abundant treasure (Schliemann's excavation) and second grave-circle (B) outside	villages, but with fortifications.
walls *c.* 1600–1550 B.C.	*c.* 1800 B.C. *Troy V.*
Mycenaean II (1500–1425 B.C.): Many Mycenaean citadels established, especially in Peloponnese (Mycenae,	1800–1275 B.C. *Troy VI:* a new people build a fine fortified
Tiryns, Pylos, etc.): king's throne in megaron of palace: art forms based on Minoan style.	city, and trade with Mycenaean Greece.
5–1100 B.C. *Mycenaean III:* Acropolis at Mycenae and at Tiryns fortified with Cyclopean walls: fresco painting in palaces: 'Palace' style pottery develops towards a stylized decoration and shape: important trade with all Eastern Mediterranean, and Sicily and Egypt: Mycenae has own trading ports in Rhodes, Cyprus and elsewhere. *The great age of Mycenaean power.* 'Treasury of Atreus' (tholos tomb) *c.,* 1300. 'Tomb of Clytemnestra' later in period.	
c. 1250 B.C. Additional fortifications at Mycenae and Tiryns suggest danger imminent: at Mycenae, Lion Gate, Postern gates, South Cyclopean wall (enclosing grave-circle A): later, underground cistern enclosed. Agamemnon king and leader of all Achaeans.	1275 B.C. Troy VI severely damaged by earthquake: walls rebuilt and acropolis crowded with troops and stores in tightly-packed small houses. This is
c. 1250 B.C. Siege and capture of Troy by Mycenaeans (Achaeans).	*c.* 1250 B.C. *Troy VIIA,* sacked by
0–1100 B.C. During this period, destruction of all Mycenaean citadels throughout Greece, e.g. Orchomenos (Boeotia) Tiryns, Pylos and Mycenae. Only Athens survived this Dorian Invasion.	Agamemnon.

E BEGINS 1100 B.C.   THE 'DARK AGES'

ian, Ionian and Dorian colonies ded in the Aegean islands and on ern Asia Minor coast, in the nern, central, and southern sectors ectively. Of twelve Ionian cities, os, Ephesus and Miletus present.	*Troy VIIB:* temporary brief occupation by ex-Danubian folk.

RIOD

he Laws are not yet written down: the powerful know them, and it is who administer them.	700 B.C. *Troy VIII:* the Greek city: marble Doric temple (*c.* 350 B.C.). [Roman period: *Troy IX*]

SECOND PHASE OF COLONIZATION

780–550 B.C. 180 Greek cities founded in large-scale colonization of Mediterranean seaboard and Black Sea, e.g.:

Sixty cities of Sicily and S. Italy and West Mediterranean, e.g.:

Syracuse (733 B.C.), Sybaris (720 B.C.), Paestum (Poseidonia) (700 B.C.), Gela (688 B.C.), Selinus (628 B.C.); also Corcyra (734 B.C.).

Fifty colonies on coasts of Dardanelles, Marmara and Black Sea, e.g. Byzantium. Also in N. Aegean, e.g. Thasos; and N. Africa coast, e.g. Cyrene: also many in Asia Minor coastal fringe, south as well as west: and on Adriatic coast. Massilia (Marseilles) founded 600 B.C.

Great influence of Delphi in colonization.

Early attempts to codify Law in many places.

776 B.C. FIRST OLYMPIAD.

No major building survives; but cotta models of temples 750 B.C. at Perachora and Argos show h plan, i.e. long walls, apsidal at or and porch supported by pillars at high pitched roof, probably thatch

Corinth, richest of all trading cities in Greece: her pottery widely exported: she has a strong fleet.

c. 655 B.C. Tyrants in Corinth: Cypselus, followed by his son, Periander (625 B.C.) who built *diolchos* across Isthmus.

Sparta, the great military power.

621 B.C. *Athens*: Draco drew up a Code of Laws.

594 B.C. Solon's democratic reforms begin a century of swift rise by Athens: law-courts established.

582 B.C. First Pythian Games at Delphi.

560 B.C. Croesus, king of Lydia.

Peisistratus, tyrant in Athens: text of Homer written down at Athens.

546 B.C. Cyrus, king of Persia, begins advance towards West by capture of Lydia.

526 B.C. Polycrates, tyrant of Samos: builds vast temple of Hera.

514 B.C. *Athens*: Harmodius and Aristogeiton hailed as tyramicides.

508 B.C. Democratic reforms of Cleisthenes.

500 B.C. Ionian cities of Asia Minor in revolt against Persia, leading to Persian War and invasion of Greece.

494 B.C. Siege and capture of Miletus by Persia.

493 B.C. *Athens*: Themistocles begins fortification of Piraeus.

492 B.C. Aegina in conflict with Athens: receives Persian envoys, but later submits to Athens.

First Persian expedition wrecked off Mt. Athos.

490 B.C. Battle of Marathon: Athenians drive Persians into the sea.

485 B.C. Death of Darius: Xerxes, king of Persia.

483 B.C. Themistocles' plan to build 200 triremes from profit of Attic mines.

480 B.C. Battle of Thermopylae: Spartans die to a man, resisting Persian host.

Citadel of Athens destroyed by Persians.

Battle of Salamis: victory of Greek fleet over Persians.

479 B.C. Battle of Plataea: 31 Greek city-states contributed contingents to victorious Greek army.

Doric wooden temple of Hera at Ol: Ionic order evolving in Aeolia and

e.g. Temple of Hera at Samos.

Temple of Artemis at Eph

c. 600 B.C. Temple of Artemis Or Sparta.

Of seventeen known sixth-century temples, eleven are in Italy and at Paestum, Metapontum, Syr Acragas, Selinus.

c. 550 B.C. Doric Temple of Apc Corinth.

c. 510 B.C. Athena Pronaia at Del

SCULPTURE	VASES	LITERATURE

SCULPTURE

cotta votive figures especially
imals.
votives at Sparta.
ze figurines in great numbers
ariety in eighth century and
rds.
ture in stone rare and crude.
den figures are roughly carved,
on thick plank-like blocks,
s on rounded timber, i.e.
on of a tree-trunk.

VASES

900–700 B.C. Finest products
of art are the Geometric
vases, e.g. the sepulchral
Dipylon vases: this style was
carried throughout the
Aegean by emigration.

LITERATURE

HOMER, the father of poetry, composes the *Iliad*
from traditional heroic ballads, in Chios about
730 B.C.
HESIOD, perhaps 700 B.C.
The *Odyssey*, composed about 660 B.C.

ze figurines numbered in
sands: bronze griffin heads,
aps from Anatolia, from
ath and sixth centuries.
elopment of the Kouroi and
i figures, i.e. nude male,
ed female, standing (left foot
ard) sculptured marble figures:
figures have hair rendered
gyptian 'wig' style:
590 B.C. Kouros fr. Sunium
    (Nat. Mus.).
    Cleobis and Biton
    (Delphi).
570 B.C. Moscophorus (Acr.
    Mus. Athens).
560 B.C. Tall, thin, exciting
    Melos Kouros (Nat.
    Mus. Athens).
520 B.C. Splendid 'Kroisos'
    from Anavyssos
    (Nat. Mus. Athens).
-500 B.C. The lovely Korai
    (Acr. Mus. Athens).
525 B.C. Frieze relief of
    Siphnian Treasury,
    Delphi.
er Kouroi in museums at Delos,
sos, Samos.
ool of Sculpture in Aegina,
ous for its bronzes.

725–550 B.C. Corinthian
pottery of distinctive orien-
talizing (textile pattern)
designs: widely exported:
Rhodian Wild Goat pottery
somewhat similar and widely
spread in E. Greek cities.
570–450 B.C.
Attic Black-figure Vases
Excellence of Athenian
pottery ousts Corinthian
c. 550 B.C from almost all
markets. Eminent vase
painters: Amasis, Exekias,
Nikosthenes.

The change to red figures
on black background begins
slowly about 525 B.C.; Andocides and Euphronios emi-
nent.

c. 676 B.C. Terpander of Lesbos, lyric poet.
c. 670 B.C. Archilochos of Paros, elegiac poet: led
    party of colonists to Thasos.
c. 650 B.C. Earlier Homeric Hymns composed; e.g.
    Hymn to Delian Apollo, Hymn to
    Demeter.
c. 640 B.C. Tyrtaeus, elegiac poet, wrote battle songs
    for Spartans during Messenian War.
    Alcman first to compose choral lyric.
c. 600 B.C. Alcaeus and Sappho, lyric poets of Lesbos.
c. 580 B.C. Ionian school of philosophy:
        624–546 Thales of Miletus.
        c. 560 Anaximander of Miletus.
        c. 540 Anaximenes of Miletus.
    inquire into the nature of the universe.
c. 560 B.C. Pythagoras of Samos fl.: mathematical
    and physical philosopher.
534 B.C. Thespis, at Dionysia festival, takes a step
    forward in development of drama by
    introduction of dialogue.
c. 530 B.C. Xenophanes in Sicily, philosopher-theo-
    logian, rejects the Homeric deities:
    argues the probability of one supreme
    deity sustaining all things by his thought.
504 B.C. Heraclitus of Ephesus, the last of Ionian
    physical philosophers.
499 B.C. Aeschylus' first plays produced at Athens.
    Pindar (518–446 B.C.), lyric poet, especi-
    ally famed for his Odes in honour of
    victors at the panhellenic Games.
490 B.C. Simonides of Cos wrote epigram on
    Marathon: later, on Thermopylae,
    Salamis and Plataea.

ARCHITECTURE

Fortification of Athens.

477 B.C. Confederacy of Delos (against renewed Persian attack) formed under the lead of Athens.

458 B.C. Building of the Long Walls between Athens and Piraeus.

457 B.C. Athens conquers Aegina: forces her into the Confederacy which is becoming in fact the Athenian Empire.

454 B.C. Treasury of the Confederacy transferred from Delos to Athens under Pericles.

449 B.C. Peace signed with Persia.
Pericles' policy to help Athens become the 'School of Hellas' by making it the most beautiful city of Greece with its superlative quality of marble building.
The great days of democratic Athens: all the arts at their zenith: but Athens is ruthless in forcing members of the Confederacy to stay in it and pay tribute to her.

431–404 B.C. The Peloponnesian War between the rival leaders of Greece: Athens, strong at sea, against Sparta the renowned military power. Five invasions of Attica by Sparta in seven years.

430 B.C. Plague at Athens where the rural population of Attica was crowded inside the fortified city and the Long Walls.

429 B.C. Death of Pericles.

425 B.C. Surrender of Spartan force on Sphacteria to Athenians.

416 B.C. Murderous attack on Melos by Athens because she was not a member of the Confederacy and refused to join.

415–413 B.C. Expedition by Athens against Syracuse to win wealth and territory in Sicily. The brilliant and erratic Alcibiades, one of the three Athenian commanders, deserts to join Sparta. Total loss of fleet and army of the expedition.

411 B.C. Oligarchy seizes power in Athens—the rule of 'Four Hundred'.

407 B.C. Cyrus of Persia takes steps to negotiate alliance with Sparta.

405 B.C. Naval defeat of Athens at Aegospotami by Spartan fleet under command of Lysander.

404 B.C. Surrender of Athens to Sparta: Spartan troops demolish the Long Walls: Spartan garrison on the Acropolis.
The beginning of the end of the brightest pages in Greek history.

479 B.C. Temple of Athena Aphaia in Aegina.

465– Temple of Zeus at Olympia:

457 B.C. Libon architect.
(Polygnotus painted murals for Stoa Poikile in Agora at Athens: and Lesche at Delphi.)

450 B.C. Temple of Apollo at Bassae.

449 B.C. Temple of Hephaestus—'the Theseum'—at Athens.

447 B.C. Building of Parthenon begun. Ictinus architect.

444 B.C. Temple of Poseidon at Sunium.

440 B.C. Temple of Ares near Athens.

437 B.C. Propylaea at Athens begun: Mnesicles architect.

435 B.C. Parthenon completed.
Under Pericles, Theatre of Dionysus rebuilt (only traces of scene-building remain): Hall of Initiation at Eleusis takes final form.

425 B.C. Temple of Wingless Victory at Athens.

421– Erechtheum at Athens.

407 B.C.

416 B.C. Stoa of Temple of Artemis at Brauron.

The exhaustion of a long war, material and spiritual, slowed down artistic achievement. Failure to complete the Propylaea at Athens is symptomatic of decline.

THE FOURTH CENTURY

In this period Athens made some recovery: built a fleet and rebuilt the dismantled Walls, in revolt against Sparta. But Thebes, under Epaminondas, was the decisively rising power:

371 B.C. Epaminondas defeated the Spartan army at Leuctra: even invaded Sparta itself. Sparta is finished.
Rise of Macedon under Philip II, determined to unite all

338 B.C. Greece. His victory at Chaeronea over the rest of Greece. The day of the city-state, in decline since 404 B.C., is now ended.

336 B.C. Alexander the Great of Macedon succeeds: crosses the

334 B.C. Hellespont and sets out to conquer Persia and then the world.
After extraordinary success which took him as far as the

323 B.C. Indus valley, he died at the age of 33.

353 B.C. Monumental tomb of Mausolus satrap of Caria: one of Seven Wonders of the World.

350 B.C. The most beautiful of Greek theatres at Epidaurus designed by Polyclitus the Younger, also the Tholos of the Asclepieion.

Pella, capital of a forcibly united Greece (now under excavation).

SCULPTURE

Myron puts movement and action into sculpture in the round.

Bronze Charioteer at Delphi. Bronze Zeus hurling his thunderbolt (Nat. Mus. Athens).

Olympia: sculpture of E. and W. pediments (Olympia Museum).

Pheidias makes chryselephantine statue of Athena for Parthenon: designs pediment sculpture: and supervises sculpture of metopes and frieze.

Pheidias makes chryselephantine statue of Zeus—one of 'The Seven Wonders of the World'.

Polyclitus of Argos develops the sculpture of the athlete: lays down a canon of proportions: worked in bronze (marble copies survive).

Winged Victory of Paeonius at Olympia.

Relief of 'Victory tying her sandal' from Temple of Victory (Acr. Mus.).

Caryatids of Erechtheum (one in British Museum)

Sculpture from Brauron (Nat. Mus. Athens).

s a pause before the next great
e emerges.

Praxiteles floruit.

Scopas working on Mausoleum at Halicarnassus.

Lysippus floruit: made new canon of proportions: Greek portrait sculpture begins with Lysippus. (For his work, see 'Agias' at Delphi.)

VASES

With the introduction of the Red-figure style, vase-painters show human form in variety of new poses and movement. Drawing is fine and expressive: detail of figure and drapery important: scenes tend to greater dignity.

Vases of this period provide valuable evidence of Athenian domestic life, customs, entertainment, music, sport, furniture, clothing, etc.

Some fifth-century vase painters reflect the dignity of classical sculpture, e.g. the ACHILLES painter whose white-ground lekythoi with quiet figures finely drawn and painted in several colours are the best.

Others try to adapt to vase decoration the great themes of mural painting by Polygnotus, etc, and experiment with perspective and arrangement in depth: less care is given to matching design to shape of vase. Style develops towards florid overcrowded decoration, sometimes with gilded relief ornament.

At the beginning of the Classical period DOURIS and BRYGOS are great names: at the end MEIDIAS, with his fine drawing but over-elaborate scenes.

Decline in Attic vase painting continues in fourth century despite some attempt to return to the Classical style: majority of vases cluttered with crowded scenes where perspective is attempted and fails: white paint and gold adds to over-elaborate decoration. Aphrodite and winged Eros favourite figures.

By 320 B.C. Attic R.F. style is ended. Vases are now plain or moulded, and painted in lustrous black.

LITERATURE

Tragedians
  525–456 B.C. Aeschylus
  496–406 B.C. Sophocles
  485–406 B.C. Euripides

Writer of Old Comedy
  450–385 B.C. Aristophanes

Historians
  c. 484–425 B.C. Herodotus
  c. 460–400 B.C. Thucydides

Philosophers
  469–399 B.C. Socrates
  384–322 B.C. Aristotle
  500–428 B.C. Anaxagoras: first scientist to come to Athens.

Asclepiad
  Hippocrates of Cos.

Orators
  c. 495–429 B.C. Pericles
  436–338 B.C. Isocrates
  c. 390–330 B.C. Aeschines
  384–322 B.C. Demosthenes

399 B.C. Socrates executed.
  Xenophon-soldier and writer.
  Aristophanes still producing plays.
386 B.C. Plato teaching in Academy.
367 B.C. Aristotle in Athens.
349 B.C. Death of Plato.
335 B.C. Aristotle teaches in the Lyceum.
321 B.C. Menander, writer of New
–292 Comedy floruit.
306 B.C. Epicurus opens school of philosophy in Athens.

ARCHITECTURE

After the death of Alexander (323 B.C.), his generals—'the Successors'—take power each in his own area, and all that was unified is soon subdivided into warring dynasties: Ptolemies in Egypt, Seleucids at Antioch, Attalids at Pergamum; in Macedon Lysimachus succeeded, but was killed in battle at the age of 79 and his kingdom was broken up.
THE ENTRY OF ROME FIRST INTO MACEDON AND LATER INTO ALL GREECE AND ASIA MINOR IS THE CENTRAL FACT OF THIS PERIOD. GREECE BECOMES A ROMAN PROVINCE. Intelligent Romans admire her people's intellectual and artistic gifts, and all Romans carry off as much of her artistic treasures as they can.

Technical skill now high. Building
many parts of Greece and Asia Mino

- c. 314–166 B.C. Delos becomes a commercial centre of high importance.
- 168 B.C. Aemilius Paullus, consul, completely defeats Macedonia: sacks Epirus. Rome soon dominates all Greece.
- 146 B.C. Mummius totally destroyed Corinth.
- 133 B.C. Attalus III bequeaths Pergamum to Rome.
- 88 B.C. Delos destroyed by Mithradates.
- 86 B.C. Sulla reduces Athens by siege.
- 42 B.C. Battle of Philippi: Antony defeats Brutus and Cassius.
- 31 B.C. Battle of Actium: Antony is defeated by Octavian.

Pergamum: acropolis magnifice
adorned with buildings.
Ephesus: large-scale building in new
sited city.
c. 150 B.C. Stoa of Attalus built on E
side of Agora in Athens. (Rebuilt
American School of Classical Studies

IMPERIAL ROMA
31 B.C.

- A.D. 49–54 St. Paul at Perge, Miletus, Ephesus, Troas, Philippi, Salonica, Athens, Corinth and perhaps Nicopolis. Nero performs in the Games at Olympia.
- A.D. 67 Nero cuts the first sod of the Corinth Canal. Nero 'beautifies' the Parthenon, putting his brazen name and titles upon its architrave!
- c. A.D. 90 St. John Theologos writes the Revelation in the cave at Patmos, as tradition believes.
- A.D. 125 Hadrian tours Greece.
- A.D. 150 Pausanias writes his Guide to the Ancient Sites and legends.
- A.D. 267 Barbarian Goths and Herulian Gauls ravaging Greece: they capture Athens.

A.D. 125 Hadrian, philhellene, orders
extension of city of Athe
builds Arch of Hadrian: cc
pletes the great temple of Z
at Athens.
A.D. 161 Herodes Atticus builds Ode
at Athens.
Under Antoninus Pius (A.D. 86–16
Asclepieion at Pergamum enlarged a
gains international repute.

SCULPTURE

uge output of technically fine
ture in this period.

'8 B.C. Rhodes has school of sculpture: bronze Colossos of
Rhodes.
Winged Victory of Samo-
thrace. (Louvre.)

0 B.C. Boy Jockey (Nat. Mus.
Athens).

3–174 Pergamene school of sculp-
.C. ture: Altar of Zeus: 'dying
Gaul'.

5 Aphrodite of Melos.

VASES

New methods of decorating vases are
adopted: the Red-figure style is
finished.
The majority of vases now imitate
metal ware: the most popular are
'Megarian' bowls decorated on the
outside in relief by means of moulds
and fired black: made in many Greek
cities besides Megara. Other vases
have applied decoration in medallions,
etc. Sicily and S. Italy provide local
variations.
In Greek cities of Asia Minor, plain
vases are fired to a red colour: some,
i.e. plates, etc., have impressed decoration: this East Greek style is called
'Pergamene'.

LITERATURE

c. 294 B.C. Zeno, founder of Stoic
School, floruit.
c. 310–250 Theocritus of Sicily, pas-
B.C. toral poet.
c. 235 B.C. Great Library at Alexandria.
c. 203–120 Polybius, historian.
B.C. Library at Pergamum.
c. 50 B.C. Andronicus of Rhodes
published first complete
edition of Aristotle.

RIOD
. 330

c. A.D. 50– Plutarch, philosopher,
120 wrote biographies.
A.D. 50–62 Paul writes letters to
the Churches.
A.D. 70–80 Luke, a Greek physician, writes the Acts.

A.D. 112 Pliny, governor of Bi-
thynia, writes to Trajan
seeking instruction on
treatment of Christians.
c. A.D. 200 Galen of Pergamum
died: great anatomist:
court physician to Mar-
cus Aurelius.

y Roman marble copies of Greek
ze originals, and much Roman
pture done in the Greek manner.

BYZANTINE PERIOD
A.D. 330—1453

A.D. 330 Byzantium renamed New Rome as capital of the Empire by Constantine. The City soon adopts the Emperor's own name. Christianity now the official religion: Sundays to be public holidays.

c. A.D. 390 Christian Emperor Theodosius closes down pagan sanctuaries and dismantles many temples, e.g. of Zeus at Olympia (393); of Apollo at Delphi (390).

A.D. 396 Alaric at the walls of Athens, sees the statue of Athena Promachos on the Acropolis and decides to withdraw.

A.D. 431 Council of Ephesus (243 Bishops) in Twin Churches of St. Mary declare Mary to be 'the Bearer of God'.
Church of the Holy Spirit at Salonika, earliest basilica existing in Greece.

A.D. 535 Emperor Justinian builds Santa Sophia, and converts to churches some surviving temples, e.g. Parthenon and 'Theseum' at Athens.
Fine churches built at Philippi and in Paros.

A.D. 565 By end of Justinian's reign, Byzantine empire at its greatest extent: from western limits of Mediterranean, through Italy, Balkans, Asia Minor to East coast of Black Sea; Syria, Palestine, Egypt and North coast of Africa.
Justinian Code of Law introduced: Byzantine style of mosaics first developed, later to excel all others.

A.D. 726–843 Iconoclasts in power: non-representational art alone allowed in churches: mosaics and paintings of earlier times obliterated.

A.D. 800 Charlemagne becomes Emperor of the West. In the East, Byzantine Empire continues.
Under the Macedonian dynasty (867–1056) and the Comnene (1081–1185) Byzantine art is at its most brilliant: palaces and churches richly decorated with superb mosaics: delicate ivory carving: gold and silver work: enamels: beautiful woven materials and embroidery.

A.D. 904 Saracens capture Salonika: for a hundred years their pirates had been ravaging and depopulating the smaller islands of the Aegean.
Political importance of Athens fades for some centuries.

A.D. 1019 Emperor Basil, the Bulgar-slayer, visits Parthenon for thanksgiving service after re-establishing Byzantine rule in Balkans. Many monasteries and churches at Athens, Daphni, Osios Loukas, Mistra, Salonika, etc. (mosaics at Osios Loukas 1000–1025: Daphni c. 1100).
After Basil's death (1025), Seljuk Turks begin advance into Asia Minor. Independent Republic of St. Mark set up in Venice: Norman kingdom in Sicily.

A.D. 1040 Normans storm the Piraeus.

A.D. 1147 Athens captured by Roger of Sicily.

A.D. 1187 Saladin captures Jerusalem.

A.D. 1204 Fourth Crusade: the Latins sack Byzantium, including Santa Sophia, and install Latin Bishops in place of Byzantine Greeks.

A.D. 1261–1453 Palaeologue dynasty in Constantinople: Empire reduced by pressure on every side, especially from East where Ottoman Turks supplant Seljuks.

A.D. 1309 Knights of St. John make Rhodes the new advanced post of Christianity.

A.D. 1349 Byzantines recover most of Peloponnese (the Morea) from the West—the Franks, and build up in Mistra a strong centre of Byzantine culture, religion, fresco-painting, and philosophy. Last Byzantine Emperor crowned at Mistra in the Metropole Cathedral: . . . 'on the eve of her definite ruin all Hellas was reassembling her intellectual energy to throw a last splendid glow'. (Lavisse and Rambaud.)

A.D. 1453 Turks capture Constantinople: and bring down Byzantine Empire (including therefore Greece).

PERIOD OF TURKISH RULE

A.D. 1466   Parthenon becomes a mosque: all Greece falls into Turkish hands but despite nearly 400 years of Moslem domination the Greeks continue both to be a people endowed with a burning national spirit and to be a Christian people.

A.D. 1522   Capture of the Knights' fortress of Rhodes by the Turks.

A.D. 1571   Sea battle of Lepanto: the Christian West under Don Juan (aged 23) defeats the Turkish fleet.

A.D. 1687   Venetians at war with Turks: Turks use Parthenon as powder-magazine with disastrous result.

MODERN PERIOD

A.D. 1821–1834   The War of Independence against the Turks: the Greeks valiantly recover South and Central Greece, but not Epirus or Macedonia. For Epirus they waited until 1881, and for part of Macedonia until they won their victories in the Balkan War in 1913.

A.D. 1827   Battle of Navarino Bay: the 'accidental' battle which gave Greece her freedom.

A.D. 1912   Italians at war with Turks, seize Rhodes then under Turkish rule, also Dodecanese Islands.

A.D. 1915   Unsuccessful British attempt to force Dardanelles (a) by naval bombardment; (b) by landings in great force in Gallipoli by British, Anzac and French forces.

A.D. 1941–1944   Temporary German occupation of Greece.

A.D. 1948   Greeks recover Rhodes.

Short Index

Achaeans; *see* Mycenaean Greeks
Acheron, R., 162
Achilles, 148–9
Actium, battle of, 158–161, 167, 226
Aegeus, king of Athens, 32
Aegina, 27, 35, 194–7, 281; coinage of, 196; temple of Athena Aphaia at, 194–6
Aemilius Paulus, 99, 165
Aeschines, 46, 50
Aeschylus, 41, 55, 68, 163
Agamemnon, 63, 95, 130–4, 139
Agrippa, Odeum of, 49
Alcibiades, 55
Alcinous, king of the Phaeacians, 151–3, 157
Alexander the Great, 48, 74, 221–4, 230, 244
Alpheus, R., 93, 104
Altis; *see* Olympia
Amazons, battle of Greeks and, 37, 188
Ambracian Gulf, 158, 159
Amnisos, 109
Anatolia, 106; goddess of fertility, 229
Antoninus Pius, Emperor, 56, 149
Antony, 158–161, 225–6
Apelles, painter, 168, 222
Aphrodite of Cnidos, 285; of Melos, 202, 287; temple of Aphrodite, at Corinth, 171; at Kythera, 198
Apollo, 71–82, 83–92, 174, 276–277; at Amyclae, 278; at Athens (Patroos), 46; at

Sparta (Carneius), 183; Homeric Hymns to, 75, 85; in art, 79, 104–5, 276–7; Oracle of; *see* Delphi; temples at Bassae, 186–9; Corinth, 172; Delos, 88, 89, 90; Delphi, 72, 76, 77–78; Thasos, 218, 220
Aqueduct, 237, 254
Arachova, 73
Archaeological excavation, 18; American, 44–5, 141–3, 145–150, 215–6, 256; Austrian, 228, 230; British, 82, 108, 114, 156, 182, 231; Danish, 246; French, 72, 88, 108, 128, 219–20; German, 58, 93, 98, 101, 104, 145, 210; Greek, 63–9, 108, 128, 164–5, 221, 227; Italian, 108, 126; Swedish, 193, 197
Archilaus of Macedon, 222–3
Archilochus of Paros, 200–1, 217
Architecture, 270–5; *see* also under Doric, Ionic, Corinthian Orders; also *see* Glossary of technical terms
Areopagus; *see* Athens
Ares, 95; temple of, 47–8
Argos, 131, 139, 193; gulf of, 192; plain of, 18, 137
Ariadne, 108
Aristides the Just, 51, 85
Aristogeiton (Tyrannicide), 48
Aristophanes, 41
Aristotle, 22, 80, 163, 223, 278
Artemis, 63–6, 84, 154, 182–3, 229; temple at Brauron, 65–

Index

Index

Index

Index

Index

Index

Index